WORLD ATLAS OF CONTEMPORARY HOUSES
WELTATLAS ZEITGENÖSSISCHER WOHNHÄUSER

INTERNATIONAL
HOUSES ATLAS

Casey C.M. Mathewson

FEIERABEND
UNIQUE BOOKS

© 2007 Feierabend Unique Books
Judenpfad 61, D-50996 Cologne
info@feierabend-unique-books.de

Editor, author of English and German texts,
layout, and typesetting:
mab - Casey C.M. Mathewson, Berlin
        www.ma-b.net
Assistance layout: mab - Anna Borgman
Artdirection and Production: artwork-factory.com
Cover photo: Benny Chan / Fotoworks, p. 382

photographer: p. 162, Alessandro Ciamp; p. 307, Peter Hyatt and Tony Mille

Idea and Concept: Peter Feierabend, Casey C.M. Mathewson

Printed in China

ISBN 978-3-939998-05-1

FOREWORD / VORWORT

Slope House - Hintersdorf, Austria - Lichtblau.Wagner Architekten - Photographer Bruno Klomfar

138

Haus Lutz, Bregenz, Austria
Philip Lutz Architektur - 2003
Photo: Oliver Heissner

Foreword

One of the most essential commonalities uniting all mankind is the necessity for shelter. In spite of all the differences that age-old differing cultural and societal traditions have wrought across the globe, the archetypal need for housing as a "place of home" remains unchanged as one of the most pressing demands facing humanity. In the face of an ever-tighter woven world the traditional cultural and regional chasms that once generated vastly different residential solutions within individual regions, countries, and continents are invariably being dissolved. As an expression of the common desire for humans everywhere to live in dignity, the houses portrayed here document an ever-increasing commonality in residential architecture worldwide wherein a triumphant renaissance of the ideals of Modernist architecture serves as a common denominator in the creation of exuberant new house solutions.

Single family residences were chosen as the clear focus for this book since they offer architects and their clients the most creative platform for experimenting with individual spatial compositions and new building materials. Most of the homes presented serve as proving grounds for young architects and they therefore are especially indicative of new trends being explored by not-yet established, innovative firms. The architectural language that the new generation of architects is currently developing on these residential commissions will form the foundation for their body of work and the principles defined here will be applied to larger, more significant projects in the years to come. Therefore this book documents not only the broad range of current solutions for single-family residences worldwide. It also provides insight into the architectural trends that will most certainly determine the best architecture of the next decades.

Analysis of the projects presented here shows that - although attention to local, regional, and national traditions continues to play a central role in the creation of memorable, meaningful homes - a common set of basic concerns and goals unites all of the works. These include such diverse unifying aspects as the attainment of a sense of appropriate representation, the attention to the interrelationship between the home and its surroundings, the inquiring search for solutions adequate to answer to climatic conditions of the given site, the accommodation of the special needs of each individual client, building within given budget limits, and the concern for sustainable design to protect natural resources and save energy. Spanning the breadth of six continents this book documents the impressive residential solutions that can be achieved when these central design themes are appropriately addressed.

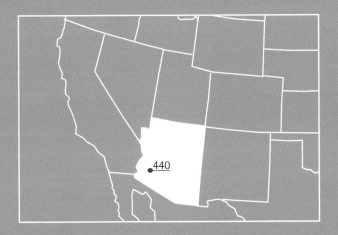

Zeros Residence, Phoenix, AR, USA
blank studio inc. – 2005
Photo: Bill Timmermann

Vorwort

Eine der universellen Gemeinsamkeiten der
Menschheit besteht in dem essentiellen
Bedürfnis nach Obdach. Trotz aller kulturellen
und gesellschaftlichen Unterschiede, welche die
Weltkulturen voneinander trennen, besteht doch
das Bedürfnis aller Menschen nach einem Zuhause
als „Ort des Behaustseins" überall gleichermaßen.
Angesichts einer immer enger erscheinenden
Welt lösen sich zahlreiche einst gravierende
kulturelle und regionale Unterschiede innerhalb
der einzelnen Regionen, Länder und Kontinente
auf. Als Ausdruck des gemeinsamen Wunsches
aller Menschen, in Sicherheit und Würde zu leben,
dokumentieren die hier vorgestellten Häuser die
wachsende Gemeinsamkeit der Wohnarchitektur(en)
weltweit, wobei die Projekte zugleich die
triumphale Wiederkehr der Ideale der Moderne
als den gemeinsamen Nenner bei der Schaffung
innovativer Wohnlösungen auf internationaler Ebene
verdeutlichen.
Einfamilienhäuser wurden als Fokus dieses Buches
ausgewählt, da sie Architekten und ihren Bauherren
die kreativste Plattform zum Experimentieren
mit individuellen räumlichen Kompositionen und
neuen Baumaterialien bieten. Die meisten der hier
vorgestellten Häuser dienen als Meisterstücke der
jungen Architekten und geben gleichzeitig Einblick in
die aktuellen Architekturtrends, welche gegenwärtig
von noch unetablierten, innovativen Architekturbüros
erprobt werden. Die hier entwickelte Entwurfssprache
der jungen Büros wird in Zukunft auch bei größeren
Projekten Anwendung finden. Somit dokumentiert
dieses Buch nicht nur das breite Spektrum der
heutigen Lösungsansätze für Einfamilienhäuser,
sondern bietet auch Einsicht in die Architekturtrends,
welche in den nächsten Jahrzehnten die weltweite
Architekturszene bestimmen werden.
Die Analyse der hier dargestellten Projekte zeigt,
dass es obwohl lokale, regionale und nationale
Traditionen weiterhin eine zentrale Rolle bei der
Schaffung einprägsamer Häuser spielen, dennoch
einen gemeinsamen Satz grundlegender Aspekte
und Ziele gibt, welcher sämtliche Arbeiten verbindet.
Hierzu gehört die Funktion eines Hauses als
Repräsentationsobjekt, die Beziehung zwischen
Haus und Umgebung, die Suche nach Lösungen, die
den klimatischen Bedingungen des Grundstückes
entsprechen, die Berücksichtigung von besonderen
Nutzerwünschen und des finanziellen Rahmens
sowie die Entwicklung nachhaltiger Entwurfsansätze,
die Ressourcen schonen und Energie sparen. Alle
sechs Weltkontinente umspannend dokumentiert
dieses Buch die beeindruckenden Lösungen, welche
erreicht werden können, wenn diese zentralen
Entwurfsthemen umfassend berücksichtigt werden.

Europe

Recent years have seen the long-envisioned political unification of the continent become reality. Whereas politicians continue to debate the appropriate extent of this development, architects have long since begun to span the national borders and engage in a fruitful dialogue with colleagues across Europe. The increasing importance of the countries of Eastern Europe that are struggling to define new identities has also found expression in the new residential architecture of the refreshing and uncompromising projects documented extensively in this book.
The former "developing" regions of Southern Europe have made up much lost ground: an increased standard of living in Spain and Portugal, generated by the influx of international citizens moving to the sunny coasts, has resulted in significant new residential work. Whereas Britain, not yet a member of the political union, profits from its special role, the Benelux countries have developed into a flourishing economy as is evidenced in the refreshingly creative new work emerging there. Scandinavia continues to provide some of the best residential architecture worldwide: the traditional Scandinavian concern for natural, organic forms in tune with nature has been perfected and refined in the new works that also include inexpensive, pre-fabricated wooden starter homes.
Germany and Austria, at the very centre of Europe, demonstrate differing developments over the past years. Germany, struggling with the costly transformation and economic hardship necessitated by German Reunification, has produced contemplative residential work often exemplified by the implementation of sustainable building technology. The new work emerging in Austria is an expression of the healthy economy of Germany's smaller, more flexible neighbour. Here, a new generation of impressively creative architects has realised the perhaps most notable European residential architecture since 2000. This work shows special concern for new building technologies, including inexpensive pre-fabricated houses and innovative approaches to the utilisation of solar energy.

Europa

In den vergangenen Jahren ist die lang angestrebte politische Vereinigung Europas weiter fortgeschritten. Während die Politiker noch über das angemessene Tempo dieser Entwicklung debattieren, haben sich die Architekten schon lange bemüht, nationale Grenzen zu überwinden und einen fruchtbaren Dialog mit Kollegen quer durch Europa zu führen. Die zunehmende Bedeutung der nach neuen Identitäten strebenden Länder Osteuropas findet inzwischen auch ihren Ausdruck in einer neuen Wohnarchitektur mit erfrischenden und konsequenten Projekten, die in diesem Buch ausführlich dokumentiert werden.
Die ehemaligen „Entwicklungsregionen" Südeuropas hingegen haben deutlich aufgeholt: der verbesserte Wohnstandard in Spanien und Portugal profitiert auch von der Zuwanderung zahlloser sonnenhungriger Neubewohner in den Küstengebiete und hat bemerkenswerte neue Wohnhäuser entstehen lassen. Großbritannien, noch kein Mitglied in der EU, profitiert von dieser Sonderrolle, während die gesunde Wirtschaft der Beneluxländer zu kreativen neuen Architekturbeispielen geführt hat. In Skandinavien werden weiterhin manche der besten Wohnbeispiele weltweit gebaut: die traditionell skandinavische Betonung natürlicher, organischer Formen, welche im Einklang mit der Natur stehen, wird weiter perfektioniert, wobei neue Aspekte - wie kostengünstige Holzhäuser aus vorgefertigten Elementen - die Diskussion dort zusätzlich beleben.
Deutschland und Österreich, in der Mitte des Kontinents gelegen, zeigen in den letzten Jahren unterschiedliche Entwicklungen auf. Deutschland hat, die Last der Kosten der Wiedervereinigung tragend, eher kontemplative Wohnhäuser hervorgebracht, welche sich durch die Entwicklung nachhaltiger Bauweisen auszeichnen. Die neue österreichische Architektur ist Ausdruck der florierenden Wirtschaft von Deutschlands kleinem, jedoch flexiblerem Nachbarn. Hier hat die neue Architektengeneration seit 2000 die vielleicht bemerkenswerteste Wohnarchitektur Europas realisiert. Diese zeichnet sich durch den Umgang mit neuen Bautechnologien aus wie z.B. durch vorfabrizierte Fertighäuser oder die Integration von Solarenergie.

Africa

The fact that Africa could find relatively little exposure in this book is indicative of the situation of this grand continent in general. Restrictive political societal models in the majority of her nations generate respective architectural results that are characterised by an extreme chasm between the affluent and poor inhabitants. Additionally, the border-transcending freedom of speech and information presented by the internet has yet to be fully attained here, making it difficult for Africans to make their achievements known elsewhere. It is indicative that the African country that has most actively pushed democratisation and betterment of human rights over the past years – South Africa – is producing the most exciting residential solutions. The architects are influenced by the differing culture they are confronted with: they derive architecture from their distant European roots, from the internationally prevalent principles of Modernism, and from their own African culture wherein bush buildings in the South African outback blend into and complement the broad landscapes.

The most exciting new South African work demonstrates a commitment to the furthering of Modernism, oftentimes poetically reduced to an abstract minimalist approach. The Beau Constance Winery complex shows that this approach can be applied to a rural, hillside landscape whereas the Pearl Bay and St. Leon residences provide exemplary proof that beach houses can be sculpted to perfection and brought into balanced alignment with the pristine natural surroundings. The Steenkamp House achieves its own impressive merge with the bush landscape whilst pursuing a more earthbound, natural synthesis with its surroundings. The challenge facing Africa will be to continue the societal transformation begun in South Africa in the other, struggling nations over the coming decades. If this development concretises this continent has the potential for creation of important, social solutions that will address the alarming problems facing the continent.

Afrika

Die Tatsache, dass Afrika in diesem Buch relativ wenig Vertiefung erfährt spiegelt die Situation dieses Kontinents wider. Restriktive politische und gesellschaftliche Modelle in der Mehrheit der Länder hat zu einem extremen Gefälle zwischen armen und reichen Bewohnern geführt. Zudem hat sich die Grenzen überwindende Informationsfreiheit, die das Internet bieten kann, hier noch nicht überall durchsetzen können, was es den Afrikanern erschwert, tatsächlich erzielte Fortschritte anderswo bekannt zu machen. Es ist bezeichnend, dass das afrikanische Land, das am aktivsten die Demokratisierung und Wahrung der Menschenrechte vorangetrieben hat – Südafrika – die aufregendsten neuen Wohnbeispiele hervorgebracht hat. Die Architekten dort reagieren auf die verschiedenen Kulturen mit denen sie konfrontiert werden: sie schaffen Architektur, die den Grundlagen der Moderne verbunden ist und integrieren zudem ihre eigene afrikanische Kultur etwa in neuen Landhäusern weitab der Städte im südafrikanischen Hinterland.

Die besten neuen Arbeiten weisen einen konsequenten Bezug zur Moderne auf, wobei hier oftmals poetisch reduzierte Werke von abstraktem Minimalismus entstehen. Das Beau Constance Weingut verdeutlicht, wie sich diese Herangehensweise in hügligen, ländlichen Lagen bewährt, während die Pearl Bay und St. Leon Häuser den Beweis liefern, dass skulpturenähnliche Strandhäuser in Einklang mit dem unberührten Naturraum gebracht werden können. Das Steenkamp Haus hingegen versucht eine ganz eigene Vereinigung mit der Steppenlandschaft und erreicht dadurch eine eher erdgebundene, natürliche Synthese mit seiner Umgebung. Die Herausforderung der kommenden Jahre besteht für Afrika darin, die Anfänge der gesellschaftlichen Transformation Südafrikas auch in anderen Ländern fortzusetzen. Sollte dies gelingen, birgt die Region das Potential zur Erprobung sozialer und innovativer Wohnlösungen, welche die alarmierenden Probleme des Kontinents effektiv angehen.

Asia

Asia has long been a source of inspiration for architects everywhere. The residential designs of Japanese traditional architecture inspired countless architects to integrate its tenets into the incubus of Modernism. Even seemingly incompatible architectural icons such as Frank Lloyd Wright and Mies van der Rohe sought inspiration in the seamless interconnection between built and natural spaces and in the clarity of construction exemplified in traditional Asian residential architecture. The further development of these same qualities continues to make the work being explored in Japan engaging and exemplary. In addition, the extreme urban density within which most of the projects are developed generates especially creative solutions for small, cost-efficient houses that display an impressive use of minimalist spatial composition. These often abstract, poetic solutions continue to be especially characterised by the dramatic marriage of interior and exterior space typical in Japanese tradition. Whereas workhorse Japan remains the most exciting focus for contemporary Asian residential work, China and India are rapidly emerging with innovative new solutions tailored to the special cultural backgrounds found there. The new generation of Chinese architects is seemingly concerned with importing Western architectural approaches, especially the tradition of Modernism, to their locale. The exponential economic growth presently occurring here gives architects virtually unlimited possibilities to realise their visions. Wang Yun, for example, the Chinese architect featured in this chapter, studied in Tokyo and works within the finest tradition of the Modern icon, Le Corbusier.
It remains to be seen whether the present focus on Western architectural role models may someday give way to a more indigenous Chinese approach to residential architecture, especially with regard to the pressing need to create new residences for the ever-growing Chinese population.

Asien

Asien hat schon Generationen von Architekten weltweit begeistert. Die Wohnbauten der traditionellen japanischen Architektur inspirierten zahllose Architekten, japanische Grundsätze in die Formulierung einer modernen Architektursprache einfließen zu lassen. Selbst Ikonen der Moderne wie Frank Lloyd Wright und Mies van der Rohe ließen sich anregen von nahtlos fließenden Innen- und Außenräumen und der einfachen Klarheit der asiatischen Baukonstruktion. Die Weiterentwicklung eben dieser Aspekte in der heutigen japanischen Architektur verschafft dieser eine exemplarische Qualität. Hinzu kommt die Auseinandersetzung mit äußerst dicht bebauten Grundstücken, die besonders kreative Lösungen fordern für kleine, kosteneffiziente Häuser, die minimalistische Raumkompositionen auf beeindruckende Weise umsetzen. Diese oftmals abstrakten, poetisch anmutenden Lösungen zeichnen sich zudem durch die dramatische Verschmelzung von Innen- und Außenraum aus und stellen damit einen direkten Bezug zur japanischen Tradition her. Auch wenn das Zugpferd Japan weiterhin das aufregendste Zentrum der zeitgenössischen Wohnarchitektur Asiens bleibt, streben inzwischen auch andere asiatische Länder wie China und Indien ihre eigenen Rollen an. Eine neue Generation chinesischer Architekten scheint sich hauptsächlich für den Import westlicher Architekturansätze insbesondere der Moderne zu interessieren. Das exponentielle Wirtschaftswachstum Chinas bietet Architekten schier unbegrenzte Möglichkeiten zur Verwirklichung ihrer Visionen. Wang Yun zum Beispiel, der chinesische Architekt dessen Arbeit hier vertieft präsentiert wird, studierte in Tokio und arbeitet im Stile der Ikone der Moderne, Le Corbusier.
Es bleibt noch offen, ob der aktuelle Fokus auf westliche Vorbilder eines Tages durch eine eher eigene chinesische Herangehensweise zur Wohnarchitektur ersetzt bzw. ergänzt wird, insbesondere um adäquaten neuen Wohnraum für die unaufhaltsam wachsende Bevölkerung Chinas zu schaffen.

Oceania

As the name suggests, this region is characterised by its island nations that radiate a sense of innovation and lightness that reminds of the pioneer times when immigrants settled here only decades ago. Given this, and the fact that their populations continue to expand and their economies are sound, Australia and New Zealand have long since developed into innovative centres at the forefront of the international discussion on new residential architectural solutions. Profiting from the near equal proximity to both North America and Japan, the influences of both regions merge here to create new modern, yet indigenous homes.

The Australian metropolises Melbourne and Sydney have spawned exciting new residential work, some of the best of which is located within the ever-denser city limits, such as the Cohen Residence by Ian Moore that converts a former industrial site to residential use on a very confined, urban site.

But the unparalleled natural settings of the Australian and New Zealand landscapes continue to offer the architects operating in this region with the most challenging and exciting scenarios within which they skilfully integrate their work. While strikingly modern and often abstract, this work is also often imbued with a sense of warm, relaxed naturalness that easily intermarries with the broad landscape of the building sites.

At the same time, the architects in this region demonstrate a convincing command of "high-tech" architecture due to the established industrial infrastructure in place for prefabrication of building elements, the friendly climate that allows light, informal architectural detailing, and the cultural attitude that accepts shorter building lifespans. Their mutually abstract, yet welcoming quality makes the projects at once contemporary and at the same time steadfastly anchored within the recent pioneer tradition of these young societies that will certainly continue to provide new impetus over the coming decades.

Ozeanien

Schon der Name suggeriert eine Region von Inselstaaten, die Innovation und Leichtigkeit ausstrahlen und an gar nicht so lange zurückliegende Pionierzeiten erinnern, als Auswanderer sich dort ansiedelten. Dank dieser Qualität und der Tatsache, dass die dortigen Bevölkerungszahlen konstant zunehmen und die Wirtschaft sich in einer gesunden Lage befindet, sind Australien und Neuseeland schon längst in den Vordergrund der internationalen Auseinandersetzung um neue Wohnarchitektur gerückt. Die nahezu gleiche Entfernung zu Nordamerika und Japan legt es nahe, Einflüsse aus beiden Regionen gleichermaßen aufzunehmen, um neue ortgebundene Wohnhäuser zu schaffen.

In den australischen Metropolen Sydney und Melbourne findet sich besonders bemerkenswerte neue Wohnarchitektur. Manche der besten Beispiele entstehen innerhalb der immer dichter werdenden Stadtgebiete, wie z.B. das Cohen Haus von Ian Moore, das eine ehemals industrielle, eingeengte Parzelle einer Wohnnutzung zuführt.

Doch die unübertroffenen Naturlagen der australischen und neuseeländischen Landschaft bieten den Architekten der Region noch immer die wichtigsten herausfordernden Szenarien für die Verwirklichung ihres Werkes. Obwohl konsequent modern und oftmals abstrakt, strahlen diese Arbeiten eine warme, entspannte Natürlichkeit aus, die der weiten Landschaft entspricht.

Zugleich beweisen diese Architekten eine beeindruckende Beherrschung der „high tech" Architektur. Dies geht auf das Vorhandensein einer industriellen Infrastruktur zur Fertigung der Bauteile zurück. Das freundliche Klima, das leichte, eher informelle Architekturdetails erlaubt, und die gemäßigte Erwartungshaltung der Australier an die Lebensdauer ihrer Bauten tragen ebenfalls dazu bei. Die zugleich abstrakte und einladende Qualität lässt diese Häuser sowohl zeitgenössisch als auch fest in der Pioneertradition dieser jungen Gesellschaften verwurzelt wirken. Diese Region wird in den kommenden Jahren sicherlich reichlich neue Impulse für die internationale Wohnarchitektur liefern.

North America

The regions of this manifold continent are open and easily accessible. Research via the internet revealed an exciting spectrum of residential solutions being explored in the various regions. The work documented here from Canada and the American Northwest often displays a special concern for integration with the existing, pristine natural environment. The Seattle region, with one of the healthiest economies in the US, has generated countless striking examples over the past 10 years. The precisely detailed wood-frame construction perfected by James Cutler in the 1980's been further refined by the new generation of Seattle architects. Los Angeles, however, is currently the most creative centre for new residential architecture in the US. This development has been powered by the healthy economy and Southern California's continued population growth. With real estate prices rising to unbelievable levels, architects are faced with the challenge of creating homes on sites that were previously considered unsuited for building, such as extremely steep hillsides or locations adjacent to sensitive ecological preserves. The current generation of Los Angeles architects, most of whom studied at the Southern California Institute of Architecture or UCLA, have risen to this challenge and realised innovative works that capture the special, informally relaxed quality of traditional Southern California living models, that range from the archetypical ranch house to the Modern incubus Case Study houses built in 1950's Los Angeles. The desert Southwest - especially the Phoenix region - where the influx of sun-hungry retirees continues to multiply the population, has developed into another of the vibrant architectural nodes on the American scene. The architects here pursue an uncompromising stance on Modernism that seems especially suited to the abstract starkness of the breathtaking desert landscape.
Typological residential models developed in North America are currently being adapted to locales in Middle America such as Mexico, where the architects show their own, Latin brand of creativity that incorporates local traditions and responds to the hot, humid climate.

Nordamerika

Die vielfältigen Regionen Nordamerikas sind offen zugänglich und gut erschlossen, und sie bieten ein weites Spektrum von Wohnsituationen in den diversen Regionen. Die Beispiele aus Kanada und dem Nordwesten der USA weisen einen besonders sensiblen Umgang mit dem oftmals unberührten Naturraum der Bauplätze auf. Die Gegend um Seattle, eine der stärksten Volkswirtschaften des Landes, hat in den letzten 10 Jahren bemerkenswerte Beispiele hervorgebracht. Die präzis formulierte Holzbauweise eines James Cutler in den 80er Jahren wird durch die neue Generation weitergeführt.
Los Angeles ist jedoch momentan das kreativste Zentrum für neue Wohnarchitektur in den USA, befördert von einer starken wirtschaftlichen Entwicklung und einem stetigen Bevölkerungswachstum. Dadurch erreichten die Immobilienpreise ein derart hohes Niveau, dass die Architekten sich nunmehr der Herausforderung stellen mussten, Lösungen für bisher als unbebaubar geltende Grundstücke - wie extreme Hanglagen oder Parzellen in unmittelbarer Nähe zu Naturschutzgebieten - zu entwickeln. Die heutige Architektengeneration hat diese Herausforderung angenommen und dabei innovative Werke geschaffen, welche der besonderen informellen Qualität traditioneller südkalifornischer Wohnmodelle wie der archetypischen „ranch houses" oder der legendären „case study houses" der 50er Jahre keineswegs nachstehen.
Der wüstengeprägte Südwesten - besonders die Region um Phoenix - wo sonnenhungrige Pensionäre weiterhin die Bevölkerungszahl ansteigen lassen, hat sich ebenfalls zu einer der lebendigsten Zentren der neuen Wohnarchitektur entwickelt. Die Architekten zeigen dort eine kompromisslose Haltung zur Moderne, welcher der abstrakten Schlichtheit der Wüste auf beeindruckender Weise entspricht. Wohnhaustypologien Nordamerikas begegnet man inzwischen auch in Mittelamerika, z.B. in Mexiko, wo die dortigen Architekten ihre eigene Kreativität entwickeln, die lokale Traditionen einfließen lässt und das heiße, schwüle Klima gebührend berücksichtigt.

South America

Reputed after WWII as the world's premier architectural laboratory for Modernism – as exemplified by the uncompromising work of Brazilian legends such as Oscar Niemeyer or Lúcio Costa – this often underestimated continent has once again emerged as one of the most exciting sources for impetus in world residential architecture. It is indicative that the relatively stable societies in Chile, Peru and Brazil have generated the most notable recent work. Even given the serious social problems facing these regions, the architects continue to respond with an exciting creativity that defiantly transcends the often adverse circumstances within which they operate.

The long coastlines of Peru and Chile offer spectacular locations where the architects virtually stage their striking architectural compositions. Seemingly simple forms built of locally available materials that are often left in their natural, unhandled state, characterise this work. At second glance, the works, such as the in-situ concrete cube of the Poli House on the Southern Chilean coast, demonstrate a refined spatial complexity inside that contrasts the austerity of the formal language evident on the exterior.

But Brazil, with its contrasting metropolises Rio de Janeiro and São Paulo, remains the most vibrant centre for new residential architecture in South America. São Paulo, the world's third largest urban conglomeration, is renowned for the macabre contrast between its boundless ugliness and pulsating liveliness. The city, as the current centre of the Brazilian avant-garde, provides the visual and societal grit necessary to generate innovation. The best work here formulates a fresh redefinition of Modernism that explores the potentials of this architectural philosophy and avoids the pitfalls of relentless monotony that some ill-fated modern works displayed. The creation of a striking balance between cool abstractness and natural warmth remains the most convincing achievement of the new Brazilian work and serves as an example for both South American architects and colleagues all around the globe.

Südamerika

Bekannt geworden nach dem zweiten Weltkrieg als das größte Labor der Moderne – und in den kompromisslosen Werken von Oscar Niemeyer und Lúcio Costa noch heute bewundert – zeigt sich dieser oftmals unterschätzte Kontinent heute erneut an der Vorderfront der gegenwärtigen internationalen Wohnarchitektur. Es ist kennzeichnend, dass sich die besten neuen Beispiele in den relativ stabilen Ländern Peru, Chile und Brasilien befinden. Trotz der ernsthaften sozialen Herausforderungen dieser Regionen antworten die Architekten noch immer mit einer bemerkenswerten Kreativität, welche geradezu kämpferisch die teils widrigen Umstände zu überwinden sucht.

Die langen Küstenstrecken von Peru und Chile bieten den Architekten spektakuläre Bauplätze für gekonnte architektonische Kompositionen. Scheinbar einfache Formen, aus lokal verfügbaren Materialien erbaut, werden oftmals in ihrem natürlichen, unbehandelten Zustand belassen. Erst auf den zweiten Blick, wie z.B. beim Sichtbetonkubus des an der südchilenischen Küste gelegenen Poli Hauses, zeigt sich die Komplexität und Vielfalt der Innenräume als Komplettierung der schlichten äußeren Formen.

Doch Brasilien mit den sich ergänzenden Metropolen Rio de Janeiro und São Paulo bleibt das lebendigste Zentrum der südamerikanischen Architekturszene. São Paulo, die drittgrößte Städteversammlung der Erde, ist für eine maßlose Hässlichkeit bei gleichzeitig pulsierender Vitalität bekannt. Mit dieser Kombination aus visueller und gesellschaftlicher Spannung hat sich die Stadt gegenwärtig zum Sammelbecken der brasilianischen Avantgarde entwickelt. Die besten Arbeiten versuchen eine frische Neuinterpretation der Moderne, welche deren philosophischen Potentiale erforscht, ohne jemals monoton oder unterkühlt zu wirken. Eben dieser Balanceakt zwischen der Schaffung einer kühlen Abstraktheit bei gleichzeitigem Entstehen einer natürlichen Wärme ist die überzeugendste Errungenschaft der neuen brasilianischen Werke, die als Beispiel – nicht nur für südamerikanische Architekten – dienen.

556

BR House, Araras, Rio de Janeiro, BR
Marcio Kogan - 2004
Photo: Nelson Kon

Outlook

In an interdependent world characterized by ever-tighter interrelationships made both possible by advances in communication technology and necessary due to the increased prevalence of challenges that affect the entire planet, such as dwindling energy resources, climate change, population explosion, poverty, and regional societal conflicts, the architects portrayed in this book are actively exploring the potentials inherent in a global culture, and at the same time seeking solutions for the problems facing them at their specific locations.

The residential solutions shown here serve as vehicles for experimentation, and are therefore laboratories for exploring ways of improving the quality of life for their inhabitants. The lessons made here could be applied to future houses that effectively deal with local challenges and better the standard of living within more difficult contexts far removed from the affluence and luxury of these select works. By placing the needs and wishes of their clients in the foreground the architects here show that attention to human experience of space is the premier concern of any architectural work. The sensitive reaction to the given context of any project provides another example that can be applied to future residential work in other contexts. The focus on integrating the design into natural surroundings and merging interior with exterior spaces is a central aspect that unifies all the projects documented here and can

be applied to other design challenges, such as social or low-income housing. The integration of progressive building technologies, such as pre-fabrication, into the design is another hallmark notion that will certainly be increasingly explored in future residential house designs. The concern for sustainable design with efficient implementation of building material, reduction of the use of natural resources, and energy efficiency that almost all of these projects demonstrate has become a common denominator for architects operating everywhere around the world, especially in the face of increasing climate change. This is another aspect that will play an increasingly important role in the design of future residential projects.

These common principles need always to be put into the local, regional perspective within which each architect operates. The goal for today's architects is therefore to implement the potentials that our global community provides us with to effectively create solutions that address the specific demands presented by each design scenario and location. The projects documented here show that a myriad of possibilities exist to reach this goal. Our sincere thanks go out to the publisher, the creative architects, the house owners, and the gifted photographers who have actively made this book possible.

Casey C.M. Mathewson
Berlin, April 2007

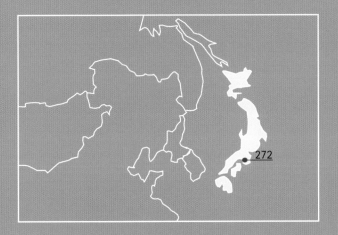

House in Oono, Hiroshima, JP
Tanijiri Makoto - 2004
Photo: Yano Yukinori

Ausblick

Wir leben in einer Weltgemeinschaft der immer enger werdenden Bindungen und Abhängigkeiten, die auch durch Fortschritte der Kommunikationstechnologie ermöglicht werden. Eben diese Mittel können zur Lösung der dringlichen Probleme des Planeten – wie verschwindende Energieressourcen, Klimawandel, Bevölkerungsexplosion, Armut und regionale Konflikte – auch förderlich sein. Die Architekten, die in diesem Buch präsentiert werden, sind aktiv dabei, die Potentiale einer globalen Kultur zu erforschen und sich gleichzeitig mit den Problemen auseinander zu setzen, die sie an ihren jeweiligen Standorten konfrontieren. Die hier dokumentierten Wohnlösungen dienen als Experimentierflächen, als Labore zur Erforschung der Möglichkeiten, bessere Wohnstandards zu erreichen. Die Lehren, die hieraus gezogen werden, könnten auch hilfreich sein beim Entwickeln künftiger Häuser in schwierigeren Kontexten, die sich weitab des Wohlstands und Luxus dieser auserwählten Beispiele befinden. Indem sie die Bedürfnisse und Wünsche der jeweiligen Bauherrschaft in den Vordergrund stellen beweisen die Architekten, dass das menschliche Erleben von Raum die primäre Ausgangsbasis einer ganzheitlichen Architektur bildet. Das sensible Eingehen auf die Besonderheiten eines jeden Bauortes verdeutlicht ein weiteres Prinzip, das auch bei künftigen Wohnprojekten einfacherer Art beherzigt werden kann. Das Bestreben, ein Bauwerk in den ihn umgebenden Naturraum einzubetten und hierbei Innen- und Außenräume miteinander zu verschmelzen ist ein weiterer zentraler Aspekt der hier präsentierten Arbeiten. Auch andere Bauaufgaben, wie z.B. soziale oder kostengünstige Wohnbauten, könnten davon profitieren. Die Beschäftigung mit fortschrittlichen Bautechnologien – etwa bei komplett vorgefertigten Bauwerken - ist ein zentrales Thema dieses Buches, das zunehmend an Bedeutung gewinnt. Nachhaltiges Bauen entwickelt sich zunehmend zum unbedingten Standard. Diese gemeinsamen Prinzipien sind immer im Rahmen der lokalen, regionalen Perspektive jedes Architekten neu zu bewerten. Das Ziel der heutigen Architekten ist daher, die Potentiale der globalen Gemeinschaft kreativ einzusetzen, um auf die spezifischen Herausforderungen jedes Entwurfsszenarios adäquat zu reagieren. Die hier präsentierten Projekte weisen nach, dass es unzählige Möglichkeiten gibt, dieses Ziel zu erreichen. Unser Dank gilt an dieser Stelle dem Verleger, den kreativen Architekten, den engagierten Hauseigentümern und den begabten Photographen, die mit ihrer resoluten Unterstützung dieses Buchprojekt ermöglicht haben.
Casey C.M. Mathewson
Berlin, April 2007

Villa Pszczolka - Beroun, Czech Republic - HŠH Architekti - Photographer Ester Havlova

EUROPE / EUROPA

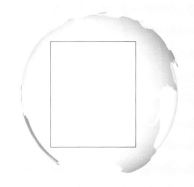

HOUSE MOBY DICK
JYRKI TASA

This house – conceived by the architects as a "biomorphic" residence - is entered via a stone stair and a steel bridge that lead up to the main entrance where one moves through the organically curved, white shell of the outer wall to enter the light-filled interior. Inside, the levels are connected by an open stair and a two-storey-high winter-garden.

Dieses von den Architekten als biomorph konzipiertes Haus wird über eine steinerne Treppe und eine Stahlbrücke erschlossen. Am Haupteingang durchschreitet man die organisch gekrümmte weiße Schale der Außenwand, um zum Lichtdurchfluteten Inneren zu gelangen. Die verschiedenen Ebenen werden über eine offene Treppe und einen zweigeschossigen Wintergarten miteinander verbunden.

Three translucent glass-steel bridges additionally interconnect the interior spaces. The stair that forms the core of the spatial composition is lit by a large skylight that directs natural light into the interior spaces from above. All interior walls are laid out orthogonally to form an especially dynamic contrast to the freely curving forms of the outer shell.

Drei Glasbrücken schaffen weitere Verbindungen zwischen den Raumzonen. Die zentrale Treppe, die den Kern der räumlichen Komposition bildet, erhält natürliches Licht über ein großes Oberlicht. Die Innenwände wurden im rechten Winkel angelegt, um einen dynamischen Kontrast zu den freien Formen der äußeren Schale zu schaffen.

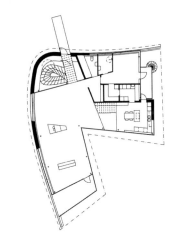

+1

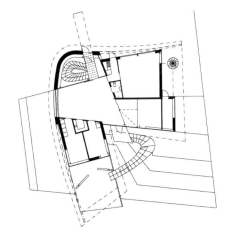

+0

COUNTRY / LAND	FINLAND / FINNLAND	HOUSE NAME / BEZEICHNUNG DES HAUSES	HOUSE MOBY DICK
LOCATION (CITY/REGION) / LAGE (STADT/REGION)			ESPOO
ARCHITECT / ARCHITEKT		JYRKI TASA YEAR OF COMPLETION / BAUJAHR	2003
PHOTOGRAPHER / FOTOGRAF		JUSSI TIAINEN, JYRKA TASA SQUARE FEET / QUADRAT METER	5165 / 480
CITY AND COUNTRY ARCHITECT / STADT UND LAND ARCHITEKT			HELSINKI, SUOMI
WEBSITE ARCHITECT / HOMEPAGE ARCHITEKT			WWW.N-R-T.FI

24

The cabin is located in a wood between open meadows and a lake. The buildings are sited along a pathway that winds through birch trees. This path begins on the edge of the meadow and leads through the villa, to the sauna and lakeshore. The black stain finish of the timber buildings reinterprets the dark tone of the pine forest. The building opens towards the lake and is almost totally closed toward the meadow. The site was left in its natural state. The heat-storing fireplace and bathrooms are organised about the central masonry wall.

Die pavillonartige Hausanlage liegt im Wald zwischen offenen Weiden und einem See. Die Bauten sind entlang eines Pfades angelegt, der am Weidenrand beginnt und durch das Haus, zur Sauna und weiter zum Seeufer führt. Die schwarz gebeizte Holzschalung greift den dunklen Ton des Kieferwalds auf. Der Bau öffnet sich zum See hin und verschließt sich zu den Weiden auf der Rückseite. Der Bauplatz wurde im natürlichen Zustand belassen. Ein Kamin und die Badezimmer wurden um eine zentrale Massivmauer gruppiert.

VILLA LINNANMÄKI
HUTTUNEN & LIPASTI
ARCHITECTS

COUNTRY / LAND	FINLAND / FINNLAND	HOUSE NAME / BEZEICHNUNG DES HAUSES	VILLA LINNANMÄKI
LOCATION (CITY/REGION) / LAGE (STADT/REGION)			SOMERNIEMI
ARCHITECT / ARCHITEKT	HUTTUNEN & LIPASTI ARCHITECTS	YEAR OF COMPLETION / BAUJAHR	2002
PHOTOGRAPHER / FOTOGRAF	MARKO HUTTUNEN	SQUARE FEET / QUADRAT METER	1291 / 120
CITY AND COUNTRY ARCHITECT / STADT UND LAND ARCHITEKT			HELSINKI, SUOMI
WEBSITE ARCHITECT / HOMEPAGE ARCHITEKT			WWW.HUTTUNEN-LIPASTI.FI

VILLA NINA
KIMMÖ KÖPILÄ
TOPI LAAKSONEN

The gently sloping site dominated by coniferous trees borders on Seksmiilari Bay where it connects with the open Baltic Sea. The floor plan creates diverse protected outdoor spaces such as a sheltered atrium, a roofed outdoor dining area, and a terrace that can be used in even the harsh Nordic winters. The family enjoys spending time in the kitchen, but their favourite place is around the dining table. These spaces form the heart of the home. The living areas are organized to face the sunset, while the bedrooms are located in a separate wing oriented toward the morning sun.

Das zum Meer hin abfallende Waldgrundstück liegt direkt am Seksmiilari Ufer mit Blick zur offenen Ostsee. Der U-förmige Grundriss definiert geschützte Außenbereiche wie ein Atriumhof, ein überdachter Essplatz und eine Terrasse, die auch im harschen nordischen Winter benutzt werden. Die Familie hält sich gerne in der Küche auf, aber der Eßplatz daneben ist ihr Lieblingsort. Dieser Bereich bildet das Herz des Hauses. Die Wohnbereiche orientieren sich nach Westen, die Schlafbereiche befinden sich in einem separaten Flügel mit Orientierung zur Morgensonne hin.

COUNTRY / LAND	FINLAND / FINNLAND	HOUSE NAME / BEZEICHNUNG DES HAUSES	VILLA NINA
LOCATION (CITY/REGION) / LAGE (STADT/REGION)			KUSTAVI / BALTIC COAST
ARCHITECT / ARCHITEKT	KIMMÖ KÖPILÄ, TOPI LAAKSONEN	YEAR OF COMPLETION / BAUJAHR	2005
PHOTOGRAPHER / FOTOGRAF	TOMMI GRÖNLUNG, HANS KOISTINEN	SQUARE FEET / QUADRAT METER	1022 / 95
CITY AND COUNTRY ARCHITECT / STADT UND LAND ARCHITEKT			TURKU, SUOMI
WEBSITE ARCHITECT / HOMEPAGE ARCHITEKT			xxx

VILLA OLSEN
ONV ARCHITECTS

+0   +1

Prefabricated houses enjoy growing popularity. Here, the Danish architects conceived a simple, rectangular form ideally suited for transportation by truck. The house was completely assembled in a factory and then transported to the site in Sweden. In spite of the industrial fabrication methods used, the house's light, informal ambience created is especially conducive to living in direct interconnection with the natural surroundings of the seaside site.

Vorgefertigte Häuser erfreuen sich zunehmender Beliebtheit. Hier konzipierten die dänischen Architekten eine einfache Form, die sich ideal für den Transport mit LKW eignet. Das in einer Fabrik komplett vorgefertigte Haus wurde dann zur Endmontage nach Schweden gefahren. Trotz der verwendeten industriellen Fertigungsmethoden wirkt das Haus hell und nahtlos mit dem umgebenden Naturraum des in Meernähe gelegenen Grundstückes verbunden.

COUNTRY / LAND	SWEDEN / SCHWEDEN	HOUSE NAME / BEZEICHNUNG DES HAUSES	VILLA OLSEN
LOCATION (CITY/REGION) / LAGE (STADT/REGION)			BÅSTAD
ARCHITECT / ARCHITEKT		ONV ARCHITECTS YEAR OF COMPLETION / BAUJAHR	2002
PHOTOGRAPHER / FOTOGRAF		STATION 1, PER JOHANSEN SQUARE FEET / QUADRAT METER	2260 / 210
CITY AND COUNTRY ARCHITECT / STADT UND LAND ARCHITEKT			VANLØSE, DANMARK
WEBSITE ARCHITECT / HOMEPAGE ARCHITEKT			WWW.ONV.DK

This house was consciously stretched across the site to create a clear spatial wall fronting the garden. The cantilevered concrete slab of the covered entrance is the only visible element of the main construction that is made of in-situ concrete.

Dieses Haus wurde über die Breite des Grundstücks gestreckt, um eine räumliche Front zum Garten hin auszubilden. Die auskragende Betonscheibe des Vordaches ist das einzige sichtbare Element der aus Ortbeton gegossenen Hauptkonstruktion.

HOUSE K
THAM & VIDEGÅRD HANSSON

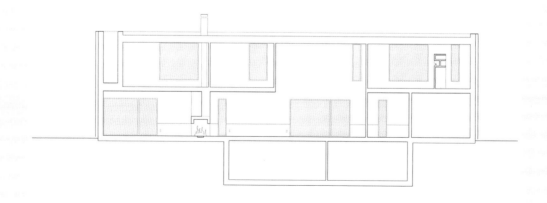

32

Thermal insulation slabs were used as forms for the poured concrete walls to achieve savings and kept the costs of this unique home comparable to conventional construction costs. The exterior is clad in dark-stained sheathing that gives way to bright spaces inside. The clear floor plan employs two-storey spatial volumes that create a sense of generosity and spaciousness that underscores the minimalist vocabulary used throughout.

Um Kosten zu sparen wurden Wärmedämmplatten verwendet, um die massiven Betonwände einzuschalen. Dadurch wurde das Haus nicht teuerer als in herkömmlicher Bauweise erbauten Vergleichshäuser. Die Außenhülle wurde mit dunkel gebeizten Schuppen versehen, die Innenräume hingegen wurden hell gehalten. Zweigeschossige Räume betonen den minimalistischen Ansatz und lassen den Grundriss klar erkennen.

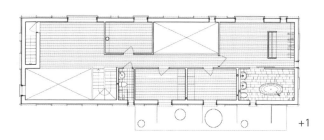

+1

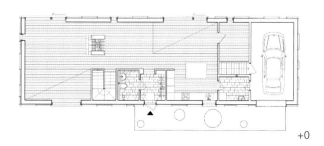

+0

COUNTRY / LAND	SWEDEN / SCHWEDEN	HOUSE NAME / BEZEICHNUNG DES HAUSES	HOUSE K
LOCATION (CITY/REGION) / LAGE (STADT/REGION)			STOCKSUND, STOCKHOLM
ARCHITECT / ARCHITEKT	THAM & VIDEGÅRD HANSSON ARKITEKTER	YEAR OF COMPLETION / BAUJAHR	2004
PHOTOGRAPHER / FOTOGRAF	ÅKE E:SON LINDMAN	SQUARE FEET / QUADRAT METER	3067 / 285
CITY AND COUNTRY ARCHITECT / STADT UND LAND ARCHITEKT			STOCKHOLM, SVERIGE
WEBSITE ARCHITECT / HOMEPAGE ARCHITEKT			WWW.TVH.SE

34

The architects used traditional Swedish rural architecture as a point of departure when they designed this low-budget home for a couple in their early 60's. The red wood sheathing and simple form echo the materials and forms of nearby barns and interconnect the modern house with local tradition. The skilful, cost-effective reduction of forms was countered by innovative integration of new design elements such as skylights and window shading louvers that make the house comfortable, informal, and welcoming for their owners and their guests.

Die ländliche Architektur der Umgebung diente als Inspiration beim Entwurf dieses kostengünstigen Hauses für ein älteres Ehepaar. Die rote Holzschalung und die einfachen Formen interpretieren die Materialien und Formen nahe gelegener Schuppen auf moderne Weise und schaffen somit eine gestalterische Verbindung zur lokalen Tradition. Die gekonnte, kosten sparende Reduktion der Formen wird durch neue Designelemente wie Oberlichter und Fensterklappen, die dem Haus eine angenehme Lockerheit verleihen, relativiert.

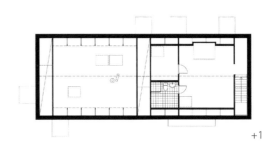

+1

HOUSE KARLSSON
<u>THAM & VIDEGÅRD</u>
<u>HANSSON ARKITEKTER</u>

COUNTRY / LAND	SWEDEN / SCHWEDEN	HOUSE NAME / BEZEICHNUNG DES HAUSES	HOUSE KARLSSON
LOCATION (CITY/REGION) / LAGE (STADT/REGION)			TIDÖ-LINDO, VÄSTERÅS
ARCHITECT / ARCHITEKT	THAM & VIDEGÅRD HANSSON ARKITEKTER	YEAR OF COMPLETION / BAUJAHR	2002
PHOTOGRAPHER / FOTOGRAF	ÅKE E:SON LINDMAN	SQUARE FEET / QUADRAT METER	2152 / 200
CITY AND COUNTRY ARCHITECT / STADT UND LAND ARCHITEKT			STOCKHOLM, SVERIGE
WEBSITE ARCHITECT / HOMEPAGE ARCHITEKT			WWW.TVH.SE

Faced with the challenge of creating a duplex house on a tight site north of Stockholm, the architects responded with a creative solution far from the dreary boredom of typical European duplexes. Although the floor plans are basically mirrored each half of the house has its own unique character. The house form was unified to form a harmonious whole rendered in blue-black plaster and modulated by the Oak windows that protrude out from the wall surfaces.

Konfrontiert mit der Herausforderung, ein Doppelhaus auf einem engen Grundstück nördlich von Stockholm zu entwerfen, antworteten die Architekten mit einer kreativen Lösung weitab der Langweiligkeit typischer Doppelhäuser. Obwohl die Grundrisse weitgehend gespiegelt wurden hat jede Haushälfte einen eigenen Charakter. Die Gesamtform des Hauses wurde jedoch als ein harmonisches Ganzes gestaltet: Fenster aus Eiche treten aus den Fassadenflächen aus blau-schwarzen Putz.

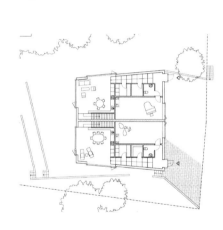

+0

TWO FAMILY HOUSE KANOTEN
THAM & VIDEGÅRD HANSSON

COUNTRY / LAND	SWEDEN / SCHWEDEN	HOUSE NAME / BEZEICHNUNG DES HAUSES	TWO FAMILY HOUSE KANOTEN
LOCATION (CITY/REGION) / LAGE (STADT/REGION)			LIDINGÖ
ARCHITECT / ARCHITEKT	THAM & VIDEGÅRD HANSSON ARKITEKTER	YEAR OF COMPLETION / BAUJAHR	2005
PHOTOGRAPHER / FOTOGRAF	ÅKE E:SON LINDMAN, THAM & VIDEGÅRD HANSSON	SQUARE FEET / QUADRAT METER	2152 / 200
CITY AND COUNTRY ARCHITECT / STADT UND LAND ARCHITEKT			STOCKHOLM, SVERIGE
WEBSITE ARCHITECT / HOMEPAGE ARCHITEKT			WWW.TVH.SE

THE MILLHOUSE
GERT & KARIN WINGÅRDH

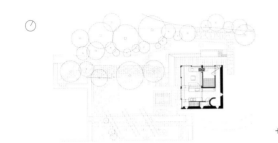

+0

This annex extends an existing complex of rural buildings that were converted to residential use. It contains a sauna and accompanying spaces and can also be used as a guest cottage. Designed as a manifestation of the Swedish ritual of sauna and bathing, the annex is crafted with the precision of fine cabinetry and the craftsmanship and the materials used – oak and limestone – infuse it with an atmosphere of warmth and interconnection to nature.

Dieser Anbau erweitert eine bestehende Anlage aus ehemals landwirtschaftlich genutzten Bauten, die zu Wohnzwecken umgebaut wurden. Er enthält eine Sauna und Begleiträume und kann auch als Gästebereich benutzt werden. Als Manifestation der schwedischen Tradition der Sauna und des Badens wurde der Bau aus edlen Materialien wie Eiche und Sandstein mit äußerster Präzision erbaut. So wurde ein wohltuendes Ambiente von Wärme und Naturnähe erzeugt.

COUNTRY / LAND	SWEDEN / SCHWEDEN	HOUSE NAME / BEZEICHNUNG DES HAUSES	THE MILLHOUSE
LOCATION (CITY/REGION) / LAGE (STADT/REGION)			VÄSTRA KARUP
ARCHITECT / ARCHITEKT	GERT & KARIN WINGÅRDH	YEAR OF COMPLETION / BAUJAHR	2000
PHOTOGRAPHER / FOTOGRAF	ÅKE E:SON LINDMAN, JAMES SILVERMAN	SQUARE FEET / QUADRAT METER	990 / 92
CITY AND COUNTRY ARCHITECT / STADT UND LAND ARCHITEKT			GÖTEBORG, SVERIGE
WEBSITE ARCHITECT / HOMEPAGE ARCHITEKT			WWW.WINGARDHS.SE

To create a sense of exclusivity and privacy the architect opted for placing the house at the very back of its site nestled at the forest's edge. At the same time, the entire western-facing elevation was completely glazed to open out to the view of the nearby seashore. The floor plan is an exercise in restrained clarity.

Um das Gefühl der Exklusivität zu erhöhen entschied sich der Architekt, den Bau möglichst weit an den Waldrand an die hintere Grundstücksgrenze zu rücken. Gleichzeitig wurde die komplette Westansicht verglast und damit der Blick auf das Meer eröffnet. Der Grundriß ist gekennzeichnet durch zurückhaltende Klarheit.

VILLANN
GERT WINGÅRDH

Comprised of three rooms – the living room with adjoining kitchen on the ground floor and two bedrooms on the upper level – it succinctly defines all of the spaces necessary for living at one with nature and the elements. To respond to the rough, seaside site clear forms were utilized. The carefully chosen palette of materials - glass, in-situ concrete, and stone flooring - emanates a sense of refinement that forms an impressive counterpart to the rough natural surroundings.

Das Haus besteht aus lediglich drei Haupträumen – Wohnzimmer und Küche im Erdgeschoss und zwei Schlafzimmer im Obergeschoss – und definiert eine klare Komposition, die im engen Bezug zum umliegenden Naturraum stehen. Als Reaktion auf die Naturbelassenheit der Lage wurden klare Formen verwendet. Die vorsichtig ausgewählte Materialienpalette aus Glas, Ortbeton und Stein setzt gestalterische Präzision gegen die rohen Formen der Natur.

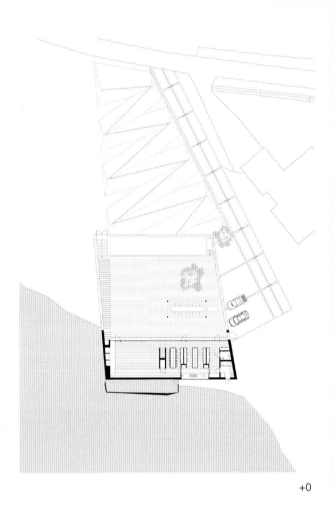

+0

COUNTRY / LAND	SWEDEN / SCHWEDEN	HOUSE NAME / BEZEICHNUNG DES HAUSES	VILLANN
LOCATION (CITY/REGION) / LAGE (STADT/REGION)			GÖTEBORG
ARCHITECT / ARCHITEKT	GERT WINGÅRDH	YEAR OF COMPLETION / BAUJAHR	2005
PHOTOGRAPHER / FOTOGRAF	JAMES SILVERMAN	SQUARE FEET / QUADRAT METER	3723 / 346
CITY AND COUNTRY ARCHITECT / STADT UND LAND ARCHITEKT			GÖTEBORG, SVERIGE
WEBSITE ARCHITECT / HOMEPAGE ARCHITEKT			WWW.WINGARDHS.SE

VILLA ASTRID
GERT & KARIN WINGÅRDH

Instead of placing the house above the rocky hillside site it was decided to integrate both the building mass into the site and the site into the building. This merging of house and site is seen immediately from outside. The building forms slope down to express the hillside topography and the exterior materials chosen translate colours and textures of the natural materials found on the site.

Anstatt die Baumasse oberhalb des felsigen Hangs zu platzieren wurde entschieden, sowohl die Baumasse in die Landschaft als auch die Landschaft in das Hausinnere zu integrieren. Die Verschmelzung von Haus und Landschaft ist von außen klar wahrnehmbar. Die Dachformen übertragen die abfallende Linie der Topografie in die Architektur, die Materialien und Texturen nehmen Bezug zur Umgebung.

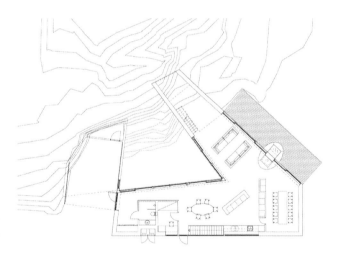

+0

The design strategy was consequently pursued inside the house as well. The natural slope was left exposed and integrated into the living room and diagonal views through the spaces interconnect the various spaces - that also include a three-storey atrium – with the surrounding natural landscape and views out to the nearby sea.

Dieser Entwurfsansatz wurde im Inneren konsequent weiterverfolgt. Der Felshang wurde in den Wohnraum integriert und Durchblicke verbinden die Raumzonen, die um ein dreigeschossiges Atrium angeordnet werden, untereinander mit den Ausblicken auf das nah gelegene Meer.

COUNTRY / LAND	SWEDEN / SCHWEDEN	HOUSE NAME / BEZEICHNUNG DES HAUSES	VILLA ASTRID
LOCATION (CITY/REGION) / LAGE (STADT/REGION)			GÖTEBORG
ARCHITECT / ARCHITEKT	GERT & KARIN WINGÅRDH	YEAR OF COMPLETION / BAUJAHR	2005
PHOTOGRAPHER / FOTOGRAF	JAMES SILVERMAN	SQUARE FEET / QUADRAT METER	4304 / 400
CITY AND COUNTRY ARCHITECT / STADT UND LAND ARCHITEKT			GÖTEBORG, SVERIGE
WEBSITE ARCHITECT / HOMEPAGE ARCHITEKT			WWW.WINGARDHS.SE

THE RED HOUSE
<u>JARMUND / VIGSNÆS ARKITEKTER</u>

The program called for creation of a new house on the site of an existing house
– without impeding its view of the adjacent forest. This motivated the architects
to compactly organise the spaces in a long rectangular volume oriented parallel to
the sloping site. Wood-frame construction was implemented for all major structural
elements including the exterior and interior walls, the floors, and the roof.

Das Programm für ein neues Gebäude hatte zur Bedingung, den Ausblick eines
bereits auf dem Grundstück befindlichen Hauses in den umliegenden Wald nicht
zu beeinträchtigen. So ordneten die Architekten die Räume in einen kompakten
länglichen Baukörper an, der quer zum steil abfallenden Gefälle platziert wurde.

This resulted in reduced building time and lower costs. The sense of leisurely easiness achieved hereby makes the home comfortable and pleasant. The major spaces – living room and kitchen -- are located together with a bedroom on the upper level with views out to the surrounding forest landscape. The building volume extends here to enclose a generous loggia. Additional bedrooms are located on the lower level that embeds into the hillside. The bright red creates a cheery accent in winter and forms a pleasant contrast to the greenery in summer.

Alle Hauptbauelemente - die Innen- und Außenwände, die Decken und die Dachkonstruktion – wurden kosten- und zeitsparend in Holzbauweise errichtet. Hierdurch wirkt das Haus locker und angenehm. Die Haupträume – Wohnzimmer und Küche – befinden sich auf der oberen Ebene, weitere Schlafzimmer wurden im Geschoss darunter, untergebracht , das in den Hang eingebaut ist. Das helle rot der Fassaden wirkt im grauen Winter fröhlich und bildet eine Kontrast zum grün der Bäume im Sommer.

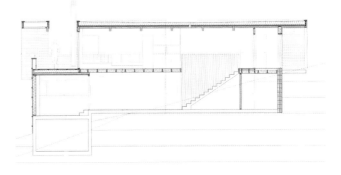

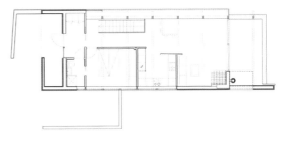

+0

COUNTRY / LAND	NORWAY / NORWEGEN	HOUSE NAME / BEZEICHNUNG DES HAUSES	THE RED HOUSE
LOCATION (CITY/REGION) / LAGE (STADT/REGION)			OSLO
ARCHITECT / ARCHITEKT	JARMUND / VIGSNÆS ARKITEKTER	YEAR OF COMPLETION / BAUJAHR	2002
PHOTOGRAPHER / FOTOGRAF	NILS PETTER DALE	SQUARE FEET / QUADRAT METER	1829 / 170
CITY AND COUNTRY ARCHITECT / STADT UND LAND ARCHITEKT			OSLO, NORGE
WEBSITE ARCHITECT / HOMEPAGE ARCHITEKT			WWW.JVA.NO

VILLA ONV-A3
ONV ARCHITECTS

This house documents two major tendencies that are currently being explored in Denmark – the use of wood and prefabrication technology to create cost-effective and attractive new homes. The simple rectangular form of the prefabricated house seems to hover above the ground plane and is modulated by the generous porch that serves both as the main entry and as a covered terrace.

Diese Haus dokumentiert zwei Haupttendenzen der gegenwärtigen dänischen Architektur – das Bauen mit Holz und den Einsatz von vorgefertigten Bauteilen zur Schaffung von kosten sparenden, jedoch zugleich sehr wohnlichen Häusern. Das Rechteck des Baukörpers scheint über dem Erdniveau zu schweben und wird durch die ausgehöhlte Terrasse gegliedert, die zugleich als überdachter Eingangsbereich dient.

COUNTRY / LAND	DENMARK / DÄNEMARK	HOUSE NAME / BEZEICHNUNG DES HAUSES	VILLA ONV-A3
LOCATION (CITY/REGION) / LAGE (STADT/REGION)			GILLELEJE
ARCHITECT / ARCHITEKT		ONV ARCHITECTS YEAR OF COMPLETION / BAUJAHR	2004
PHOTOGRAPHER / FOTOGRAF		STATION 1, PER JOHANSEN SQUARE FEET / QUADRAT METER	1442 / 134
CITY AND COUNTRY ARCHITECT / STADT UND LAND ARCHITEKT			VANLØSE, DANMARK
WEBSITE ARCHITECT / HOMEPAGE ARCHITEKT			WWW.ONV.DK

Two building volumes accommodate the varied spaces of this house – a cottage with separate guest quarters and the main house with a generous two-storey living/dining room as its main focus. A stair with a perforated wall leads from the dining space up to the living room located on the upper gallery level.

Zwei Baukörper beherbergen die diversen Raumzonen dieses Hauses- ein Gästehaus und das Haupthaus mit dem zweigeschoßigen Wohn- und Essraum als Schwerpunkt. Eine Treppe mit einer perforiert wirkenden Wand führt hinauf auf die Galerieebene, wo sich der Wohnbereich befindet.

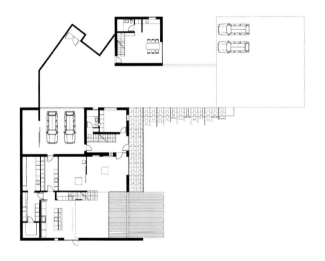

LOOP HOUSE
CEBRA

COUNTRY / LAND	DENMARK / DÄNEMARK	HOUSE NAME / BEZEICHNUNG DES HAUSES	LOOP HOUSE
LOCATION (CITY/REGION) / LAGE (STADT/REGION)			ÅRHUS
ARCHITECT / ARCHITEKT		CEBRA YEAR OF COMPLETION / BAUJAHR	2004
PHOTOGRAPHER / FOTOGRAF	MIKKEL FROST, MORTEN FAUERBY	SQUARE FEET / QUADRAT METER	5649 / 525
CITY AND COUNTRY ARCHITECT / STADT UND LAND ARCHITEKT			ÅRHUS, DANMARK
WEBSITE ARCHITECT / HOMEPAGE ARCHITEKT			WWW.CEBRA.INFO

The normal typology of suburban houses was reversed here: part of the living room and the entire kitchen are located on the upper level with a good overview of the garden. The bedrooms - that can also serve as offices with direct public access - are located on the ground floor with direct garden access. The central living room space on the ground floor interconnects spatially via a gallery to the light-filled living/dining space under the pitched roof above.

Hier wird die herkömmliche Typologie eines Vorstadthauses mal umgekehrt angeordnet: ein Teil des Wohnzimmers inklusive der Küche wurde im Obergeschoss angeordnet, um einen großzügigen Überblick auf den Garten zu erhalten. Dafür befinden sich die Schlafzimmer, die auch als Heimbüros genutzt werden können, im Erdgeschoss mit direkter Anbindung an den Garten. Der zentrale Wohnbereich vor den Schlafzimmern wird über eine Galerie mit der Wohnküche darüber räumlich verbunden.

+0

VILLA UP-DOWN
<u>CEBRA</u>

COUNTRY / LAND	DENMARK / DÄNEMARK	HOUSE NAME / BEZEICHNUNG DES HAUSES	VILLA UP-DOWN
LOCATION (CITY/REGION) / LAGE (STADT/REGION)			SILKEBORG
ARCHITECT / ARCHITEKT		CEBRA YEAR OF COMPLETION / BAUJAHR	2002
PHOTOGRAPHER / FOTOGRAF	HASSE TRABERG-ANDERSEN	SQUARE FEET / QUADRAT METER	2529 / 235
CITY AND COUNTRY ARCHITECT / STADT UND LAND ARCHITEKT			ÅRHUS, DANMARK
WEBSITE ARCHITECT / HOMEPAGE ARCHITEKT			WWW.CEBRA.INFO

The urban site dictated that all spaces be oriented internally as no translucent street-facing windows were possible or wished by the client. The architects met this challenge by creating two interconnected building volumes about a reflecting pool. The main living spaces are contained in the street-side wing and the back wing houses an atelier. Diverse minor spaces, including bedrooms and bathrooms, are contained in the connecting wing.

Das innerstädtische Grundstück diktierte eine interne Ausrichtung aller Räume, da keine von außen einsehbaren Fenster von den Bauherren gewünscht wurden. Die Architekten reagierten auf diese Herausforderung durch Anordnung der Räume um einen internen Wasserhof. Der straßenseitige Baukörper nimmt die Hauptwohnräume auf, ein Atelier befindet sich im rückwärtigen Gebäudeteil. Ein schlanker Seitenflügel, der Nebenräume beherbergt dient als Verbindung.

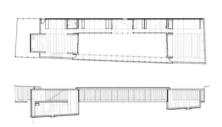

HOUSE 1A
TONKIN LIU

57

COUNTRY / LAND	ENGLAND	HOUSE NAME / BEZEICHNUNG DES HAUSES		HOUSE 1A
LOCATION (CITY/REGION) / LAGE (STADT/REGION)				LONDON
ARCHITECT / ARCHITEKT		TONKIN LIU	YEAR OF COMPLETION / BAUJAHR	2000
PHOTOGRAPHER / FOTOGRAF		MIKE TONKIN	SQUARE FEET / QUADRAT METER	1184 / 110
CITY AND COUNTRY ARCHITECT / STADT UND LAND ARCHITEKT				LONDON, UK
WEBSITE ARCHITECT / HOMEPAGE ARCHITEKT				WWW.TONKINLIU.CO.UK

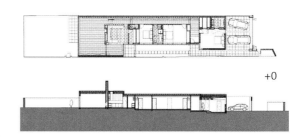

+0

The challenge of a narrow lot within an older housing complex led to an innovative floor plan. A long hall serves as a connector between the front living/dining space and the garage. Bedrooms are accessed off this hall that additionally follows the lightly falling topography of the site. Brick was used for both wall and roof surfaces to heighten the sculptural effect of this urban house.

Eine schlanke Parzelle führte zur Entwicklung eines innovativen Grundrisses. Ein Korridor verbindet den Wohn- /und Essraum mit der Garage. Schlafzimmer gliedern sich seitlich an den Gang, der zudem der leicht abfallenden Topografie folgt. Um die kubische Wirkung der Baukörper zu betonen. wurde Backstein für Wand- und Dachflächen verwendet.

BRICK HOUSE
FKL ARCHITECTS

COUNTRY / LAND	IRELAND / IRLAND	HOUSE NAME / BEZEICHNUNG DES HAUSES		BRICK HOUSE
LOCATION (CITY/REGION) / LAGE (STADT/REGION)				DUBLIN
ARCHITECT / ARCHITEKT		FKL ARCHITECTS	YEAR OF COMPLETION / BAUJAHR	2003
PHOTOGRAPHER / FOTOGRAF		PAUL TIERNEY	SQUARE FEET / QUADRAT METER	1991 / 185
CITY AND COUNTRY ARCHITECT / STADT UND LAND ARCHITEKT				DUBLIN, IRELAND
WEBSITE ARCHITECT / HOMEPAGE ARCHITEKT				WWW.FKLARCHITECTS.COM

OP DEN BERG
JACO D. DE VISSER

+0

Due to local building regulations it was possible to array the spaces of this house on four levels. The main tower-like volume contains the underground garage, the kitchen/dining room, and bedrooms. The living room forms a one-storey wing with direct garden access at the base of the tower. Metal sheathing, glass and wood were successfully employed to create a variegated sculptural composition.

Die örtlichen Bauvorschriften erlaubten es, die Räume dieses Hauses auf vier Ebenen anzuordnen. Der Turmbaukörper nimmt die Garage, den Koch- und Essbereich sowie Schlafzimmer auf. Das eingeschossige Wohnzimmer zu Füßen des Turmes verfügt über einen direkten Gartenzugang. Metallverkleidung, Glas und Holz wurden virtuos eingesetzt, um diese vielfältige Bauskulptur zu gliedern.

59

COUNTRY / LAND	THE NETHERLANDS / NIEDERLANDE	HOUSE NAME / BEZEICHNUNG DES HAUSES	OP DEN BERG
LOCATION (CITY/REGION) / LAGE (STADT/REGION)			AMERSFOORT
ARCHITECT / ARCHITEKT		JACO D. DE VISSER YEAR OF COMPLETION / BAUJAHR	2002
PHOTOGRAPHER / FOTOGRAF		CHRISTIAN RICHTERS SQUARE FEET / QUADRAT METER	2152 / 200
CITY AND COUNTRY ARCHITECT / STADT UND LAND ARCHITEKT			VREESWIJK, NEDERLAND
WEBSITE ARCHITECT / HOMEPAGE ARCHITEKT			WWW.DEVISSERBV.NL

The challenge met here was to optimize density without resorting to conventional drab suburban forms. The split-levels of this hovering wedge-shaped house are accessed by a sky-lit central stair. It leads from the basement level with bicycle parking via the kitchen/dining level to the living room and bedrooms above. Zinc-plated metal was used to sheath the sculptural form and merge with the often-grey Dutch sky.

Die Herausforderung bestand hier darin, die Baudichte zu optimieren – ohne auf konventionelle Bauformen zurück zu greifen. Die halbgeschossig versetzten Ebenen werden über eine von oben belichtete Treppe erschlossen, die von den Fahrradstellplätzen im Untergeschoss zum Wohnbereich und zu den Schlafzimmern hinauf führt. Die Metallverkleidung stellt eine Verbindung zum oft grauen niederländischen Himmel her.

HARMELEN HOUSE
JACO D. DE VISSER

61

COUNTRY / LAND	THE NETHERLANDS / NIEDERLANDE	HOUSE NAME / BEZEICHNUNG DES HAUSES	HARMELEN HOUSE
LOCATION (CITY/REGION) / LAGE (STADT/REGION)			HARMELEN
ARCHITECT / ARCHITEKT		JACO D. DE VISSER	YEAR OF COMPLETION / BAUJAHR	2003
PHOTOGRAPHER / FOTOGRAF		ROOS ALDERSHOFF	SQUARE FEET / QUADRAT METER	3400 / 316
CITY AND COUNTRY ARCHITECT / STADT UND LAND ARCHITEKT			VREESWIJK, NEDERLAND
WEBSITE ARCHITECT / HOMEPAGE ARCHITEKT			WWW.DEVISSERBV.NL

In response to the dense urban site a patio house typology was implemented for this group of three houses. The houses orient to private patio courtyards enclosed by high garden walls. In spite of the limited space available a generous two storey living room space was foreseen. The facade surfaces of the cube-like forms alternate between carefully oriented closed and glazed surfaces that meet the simultaneous needs for both privacy and openness.

Die hohe Dichte bei dieser aus drei Häusern bestehenden Anlage führte zu der Entscheidung für eine Hofhaus-Typologie. Die Häuser orientieren sich zu privaten, uneinsehbaren Höfen. Trotz der Enge des zur Verfügung stehenden Raums wurden zweigeschossige Wohnhallen vorgesehen. Die Fassadeflächen wechseln sich zwischen geschlossen und offenen Flächen ab, die so platziert wurden, dass gleichzeitig Privatsphäre und Offenheit trotz hoher Dichte ermöglicht werden.

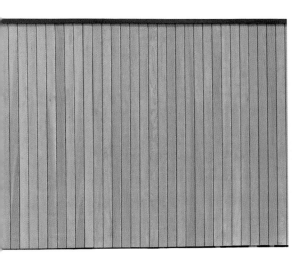

FOLDING WALLS
CASANOVA + HERNÁNDEZ ARCHITECTS

COUNTRY / LAND   **THE NETHERLANDS / NIEDERLANDE**   HOUSE NAME / BEZEICHNUNG DES HAUSES   **FOLDING WALLS**

LOCATION (CITY/REGION) / LAGE (STADT/REGION)   **GRONINGEN**

ARCHITECT / ARCHITEKT   **CASANOVA + HERNÁNDEZ ARCHITECTS**   YEAR OF COMPLETION / BAUJAHR   **2005**

PHOTOGRAPHER / FOTOGRAF   **JOHN MARSHALL, VAN DER VLUGT**   SQUARE FEET / QUADRAT METER   **6585 / 612**

CITY AND COUNTRY ARCHITECT / STADT UND LAND ARCHITEKT   **ROTTERDAM, NEDERLAND**

WEBSITE ARCHITECT / HOMEPAGE ARCHITEKT   **WWW.CASANOVA-HERNANDEZ.COM**

LAMINATA HOUSE
KRUUNENBERG VAN DER ERVE ARCHITECTEN

As a monument to glass, this house totally redefines its use as a building material. At the same time, despite its most unconventional application of glass it is not merely an experimental structure, but a functional residence. The Miesian quality of lightness and transparency so sought after by modernist architects has given way to a solidity and materiality seldom associated with the use of glass. The internal and external walls are constructed of 13,000 laminated glass sheets that vary in thickness from 10 to 170 centimeters.

Beim Bau dieses Hauses wurden neue Möglichkeiten für die Verwendung von Glas als Baustoff erprobt. Dennoch ist es nicht nur eine experimentelle Bauhülle, sondern dient als bewohntes Haus. Hier wird Glas verwendet, um eine Solidität und eine Stofflichkeit zu erzielen, die zeigen, das Glas mehr ermöglichen kann, als nur Leichtigkeit und Transparenz. Die Innen- und Außenwände wurden aus 13.000 laminierten Glasscheiben in Dicken von 10 bis 170 cm erbaut.

COUNTRY / LAND	THE NETHERLANDS / NIEDERLANDE	HOUSE NAME / BEZEICHNUNG DES HAUSES LAMINATA HOUSE
LOCATION (CITY/REGION) / LAGE (STADT/REGION)		LEERDAM
ARCHITECT / ARCHITEKT	KRUUNENBERG VAN DER ERVE ARCHITECTEN	YEAR OF COMPLETION / BAUJAHR XXX
PHOTOGRAPHER / FOTOGRAF	L.F. KRAMER	SQUARE FEET / QUADRAT METER XXX
CITY AND COUNTRY ARCHITECT / STADT UND LAND ARCHITEKT		AMSTERDAM, NEDERLAND
WEBSITE ARCHITECT / HOMEPAGE ARCHITEKT		WWW.KVDE.NL

The architects used this design to explore modern prefabrication methods to create archetypal forms that answer to present-day needs and at the same time achieve a sense of timelessness. To reduce the impact on the site and to emphasize lightness the house was designed to hover above the ground plane on point foundations. Wood was used throughout – the exterior shell is clad with larch shingles and exposed plywood was used on the interior walls.

Die Architekten begriffen diesen Entwurf als eine Herausforderung, die Potentiale moderner Vorfertigungstechnologie einzusetzen, um gleichzeitig eine möglichst zeitlose archetypische Form zu schaffen. Der scheinbar schwebende Baukörper wurde ganz in Holz erbaut – Lärchenschindeln wurden für die Außenhülle, OSB-Platten für die Innenwände verwendet.

POB 62
BERTRAND COUNSON ARCHITECTE

67

COUNTRY / LAND	BELGIUM / BELGIEN	HOUSE NAME / BEZEICHNUNG DES HAUSES	POB 62
LOCATION (CITY/REGION) / LAGE (STADT/REGION)			LES TAILLES
ARCHITECT / ARCHITEKT	BERTRAND COUNSON ARCHITECTE	YEAR OF COMPLETION / BAUJAHR	2003
PHOTOGRAPHER / FOTOGRAF	LAURENT BRANDAJS	SQUARE FEET / QUADRAT METER	667 / 62
CITY AND COUNTRY ARCHITECT / STADT UND LAND ARCHITEKT			VIELSALM, BELGIUM
WEBSITE ARCHITECT / HOMEPAGE ARCHITEKT			WWW.COUNSON-ARCHITECTE.NET

The horizontal strip of this home's mass culminates in the light-filled two-story living room. The interconnection with the natural surroundings is heightened by the use of continuous glazing ribbons and natural textures and materials, such as brick, exposed concrete, and wood.

Der horizontal lagernde Baukörper findet seinen Abschluss im zweigeschossigen Wohnsaal. Die Verbindung mit der Umgebung wurde durch den Einsatz von durchgehenden Fensterbändern und natürlichen Materialien und Texturen, wie Klinker, Sichtbeton und Holz verstärkt.

+0

RESIDENCE CARTUYVELS
META
ARCHITECTUURBUREAU

COUNTRY / LAND	BELGIUM / BELGIEN	HOUSE NAME / BEZEICHNUNG DES HAUSES	RESIDENCE CARTUYVELS
LOCATION (CITY/REGION) / LAGE (STADT/REGION)			HEUSDEN-ZOLDER
ARCHITECT / ARCHITEKT	META ARCHITECTUURBUREAU	YEAR OF COMPLETION / BAUJAHR	2000
PHOTOGRAPHER / FOTOGRAF	TOON GROBET	SQUARE FEET / QUADRAT METER	2851 / 265
CITY AND COUNTRY ARCHITECT / STADT UND LAND ARCHITEKT			ANTWERP, BELGIUM
WEBSITE ARCHITECT / HOMEPAGE ARCHITEKT			WWW.META-ARCHITECTUUR.BE

This addition to an existing house creates a generous living room that alleviates the cramped spatial situation with simple, inexpensive means. Two completely glazed walls that allow unimpeded views out to the gardens are countered by a "thick" wall into which cabinets with matte glass doors were integrated. Wood and glass in various textures and formats were used throughout.

Dieser Anbau eines bestehenden Hauses schafft ein großzügiges Wohnzimmer, das die beengte Raumsituation mit einfachen, kostengünstigen Mitteln auflöst. Zwei komplett verglaste Fronten, die ungehinderten Ausblick in den Garten ermöglichen, werden durch eine massive geschlossene Wand, in die Glasvitrinen eingebaut wurden, gestalterisch komplettiert.

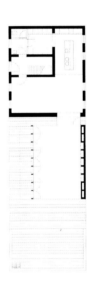

+0

RESIDENCE KINT-VERBEECK
<u>META ARCHITECTUURBUREAU</u>

COUNTRY / LAND	BELGIUM / BELGIEN	HOUSE NAME / BEZEICHNUNG DES HAUSES	RESIDENCE KINT-VERBEECK
LOCATION (CITY/REGION) / LAGE (STADT/REGION)			HEVERLEE
ARCHITECT / ARCHITEKT	META ARCHITECTUURBUREAU	YEAR OF COMPLETION / BAUJAHR	2004
PHOTOGRAPHER / FOTOGRAF	TOON GROBET	SQUARE FEET / QUADRAT METER	2862 / 266
CITY AND COUNTRY ARCHITECT / STADT UND LAND ARCHITEKT			ANTWERP, BELGIUM
WEBSITE ARCHITECT / HOMEPAGE ARCHITEKT			WWW.META-ARCHITECTUUR.BE

RESIDENCE DE VIJLDER 2
<u>META ARCHITECTUURBUREAU</u>

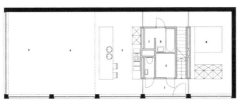

+0

The minimalist language employed here lives from strong contrasts. Closed wall surfaces are played off against completely glazed walls and the coolness stark of the box-like mass is countered with the warmth of the bricks used on both exterior and interior surfaces.

Die minimalistische Sprache, die hier eingesetzt wurde, lebt von starken Kontrasten. Geschlossene Wände werden gegen komplett geöffnete gesetzt und die Kühle der kistenartigen Baumasse wird durch die Wärme des im Innen- und Außenbereich verwendeten Klinkers relativiert.

COUNTRY / LAND	BELGIUM / BELGIEN	HOUSE NAME / BEZEICHNUNG DES HAUSES	RESIDENCE DE VIJLDER 2
LOCATION (CITY/REGION) / LAGE (STADT/REGION)			HERENTALS
ARCHITECT / ARCHITEKT	META ARCHITECTUURBUREAU	YEAR OF COMPLETION / BAUJAHR	2000
PHOTOGRAPHER / FOTOGRAF	TOON GROBET	SQUARE FEET / QUADRAT METER	1861 / 173
CITY AND COUNTRY ARCHITECT / STADT UND LAND ARCHITEKT			ANTWERP, BELGIUM
WEBSITE ARCHITECT / HOMEPAGE ARCHITEKT			WWW.META-ARCHITECTUUR.BE

A classic L floor plan with two wings containing the living/ kitchen space and the bedrooms was creatively modified to form a semi-private terrace contained by a brick-clad exterior wall. The material mix of red brick, natural wood surfaces, and large glass window elements creates a leisurely sense of informality and openness.

Der klassische L-Grundriss mit zwei Flügeln, die den Wohn-Kochbereich und die Schlafräume beherbergen, wurde gekonnt durch eine Gartenmauer modifiziert, um eine halbprivate Terrasse zu schaffen. Die Materialienpalette aus rotem Klinker, Holz und großen Glaselementen schafft ein privates, offenes Ambiente.

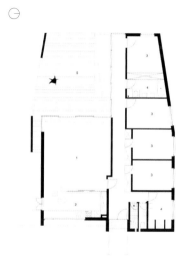

+0

HOUSE CLUYTENS-PUTSEYS
BOB 361 ARCHITECTS

73

COUNTRY / LAND	BELGIUM / BELGIEN	HOUSE NAME / BEZEICHNUNG DES HAUSES	HOUSE CLUYTENS-PUTSEYS
LOCATION (CITY/REGION) / LAGE (STADT/REGION)			LINDEN
ARCHITECT / ARCHITEKT		BOB 361 ARCHITECTS YEAR OF COMPLETION / BAUJAHR	2001
PHOTOGRAPHER / FOTOGRAF		ANDRÈ NULLENS SQUARE FEET / QUADRAT METER	1937 / 180
CITY AND COUNTRY ARCHITECT / STADT UND LAND ARCHITEKT			BRUSSELS, BELGIUM
WEBSITE ARCHITECT / HOMEPAGE ARCHITEKT			WWW.BOB361.COM

The massiveness and conventionality of an existing neo-Tudor home were augmented by radically new glass forms that transform the entrance hall and create a garden pavilion. To minimise structural elements and increase transparency, the glass façade panels were dimensioned to bear the roof loads and make columns unnecessary.

Der Massivität und Konventionalität eines bestehenden, im Neo-Tudorstil erbauten Hauses wurden radikal neue Glasformen entgegengesetzt, die das Foyer transformieren und einen Gartenpavillon ausbilden. Um den Kontrast zwischen alt und neu zu erhöhen wurden die Glasscheiben selbst tragend – ohne Stützen - ausgebildet.

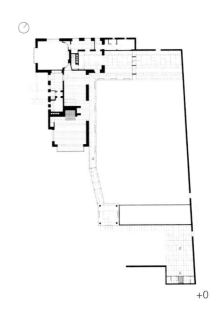

+0

PROJECT L
WIM GOES ARCHITECTUUR

COUNTRY / LAND	BELGIUM / BELGIEN	HOUSE NAME / BEZEICHNUNG DES HAUSES		PROJECT L
LOCATION (CITY/REGION) / LAGE (STADT/REGION)				KORTRIJK
ARCHITECT / ARCHITEKT		WIM GOES ARCHITECTUUR	YEAR OF COMPLETION / BAUJAHR	2003
PHOTOGRAPHER / FOTOGRAF		KRISTIEN DAEM	SQUARE FEET / QUADRAT METER	3282 / 305
CITY AND COUNTRY ARCHITECT / STADT UND LAND ARCHITEKT				GENT, BELGIUM
WEBSITE ARCHITECT / HOMEPAGE ARCHITEKT				WWW.BELGIUM-ARCHITECTS.COM/WIMGOES

FONTAINE-KRANTZ HOUSE
<u>PIERRE HEBBELINCK</u>

Sensitively embedded into the light slope of its site, this home creates a sleek, high-tech counterpart to the surrounding neighbourhood. The roof forms rise up toward the end walls to create dynamic spaces inside the pavilion-like structure. The completely glazed living room walls are contrasted by the closed, metal-clad facades of the bedrooms.

Sensibel in die leicht abfallende Lage eingebettet, schafft dieses Haus einen schlichten, „High-Tech" Gegenpol zur umliegenden Nachbarschaft. Die Dachformen steigen zu den Stirnwänden an, um dynamische Innenräume zu schaffen. Die verglasten Wohnzimmerfronten stehen in bewusstem Kontrast zu dem in Metall verkleideten Schlafzimmertrakt.

COUNTRY / LAND	BELGIUM / BELGIEN	HOUSE NAME / BEZEICHNUNG DES HAUSES	FONTAINE-KRANTZ HOUSE
LOCATION (CITY/REGION) / LAGE (STADT/REGION)			UCCLE
ARCHITECT / ARCHITEKT	ATELIER D'ARCHITECTURE PIERRE HEBBELINCK	YEAR OF COMPLETION / BAUJAHR	2005
PHOTOGRAPHER / FOTOGRAF	MARIE-FRANCOISE PLISSART	SQUARE FEET / QUADRAT METER	3874 / 360
CITY AND COUNTRY ARCHITECT / STADT UND LAND ARCHITEKT			LIEGE, BELGIUM
WEBSITE ARCHITECT / HOMEPAGE ARCHITEKT			WWW.PIERREHEBBELINCK.NET

An old, memory-filled, 1930's summer house on the site was replaced with a new home that effectively transcends the ever present associations of the old. Room sizes and distribution of uses echo those of the razed predecessor. The wood structure extends to form a pergola that integrates the house with its lakeside surroundings. Red cedar was used for wood sheathing on the exterior.

Ein mit Erinnerungen behaftetes Haus aus den 1930er Jahren wird durch hier ein neues Haus ersetzt, das diese Erinnerungen überwindet. Um eine Baugenehmigung zu erhalten mußten die Dimensionen und die Disposition der Räume des abgebrochenen Hauses weitgehend erhalten werden. Die Holzkonstruktion setzt sich im Freien in einer Pergola fort. Die Außenhülle besteht aus Zedernholz, die Oberflächen im Innern aus weiß lasiertem Ahorn, Leder und farbig lackierten Oberflächen.

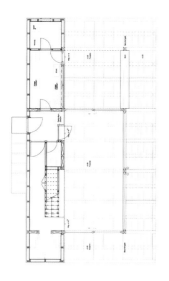

SCHWANENWERDER HOUSE
NÄGELI ARCHITEKTEN

COUNTRY / LAND	GERMANY / DEUTSCHLAND	HOUSE NAME / BEZEICHNUNG DES HAUSES		LAKESIDE HOUSE
LOCATION (CITY/REGION) / LAGE (STADT/REGION)				BERLIN
ARCHITECT / ARCHITEKT		NÄGELI ARCHITEKTEN	YEAR OF COMPLETION / BAUJAHR	2004
PHOTOGRAPHER / FOTOGRAF		ULRICH SCHWARZ	SQUARE FEET / QUADRAT METER	1033 / 96
CITY AND COUNTRY ARCHITECT / STADT UND LAND ARCHITEKT				BERLIN, DEUTSCHLAND
WEBSITE ARCHITECT / HOMEPAGE ARCHITEKT				WWW.NAEGELIARCHITEKTEN.DE

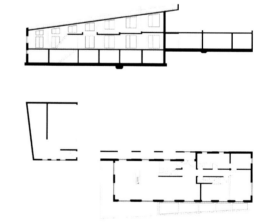

The hillside slope above Eichstätt is echoed in the enigmatic roof form of this residence. A plaza-like exterior space forms an entrance court where recessed façade openings mark the main entrance. Inside, the connecting stair rises up with the topography to adjoin the various spaces.

Der steil abfallende Hang wird in der markanten Dachform dieses Hauses aufgenommen. Vom platzartigen Vorhof aus wird der Eingang über in die Fassade eingelassenen Öffnungen betreten. Die Haupttreppe im Inneren steigt mit der Topografie an und läßt die Hanglage im Inneren des Hauses sichtbar werden.

HOUSE FROEHLE
HILD UND K ARCHITEKTEN

COUNTRY / LAND	GERMANY / DEUTSCHLAND	HOUSE NAME / BEZEICHNUNG DES HAUSES	HOUSE FROEHLE
LOCATION (CITY/REGION) / LAGE (STADT/REGION)			EICHSTÄTT
ARCHITECT / ARCHITEKT	HILD UND K ARCHITEKTEN	YEAR OF COMPLETION / BAUJAHR	2002
PHOTOGRAPHER / FOTOGRAF	MICHAEL HEINRICH	SQUARE FEET / QUADRAT METER	5219 / 485
CITY AND COUNTRY ARCHITECT / STADT UND LAND ARCHITEKT			MÜNCHEN, DEUTSCHLAND
WEBSITE ARCHITECT / HOMEPAGE ARCHITEKT			WWW.HILDUNDK.DE

HOUSE IN AGGSTALL
HILD UND K
ARCHITEKTEN

This country home translates the simple forms of nearby barns into a new residential composition. Diagonally laid brickwork seeks to pleasantly modulate the surfaces of the end facades without diluting the clear, crisp forms or resorting to superficial decoration.

Dieses Landhaus übersetzt die Bauformen nahe gelegener Scheunen in eine neue Wohnkomposition. Das diagonal verlegte Verblendermauerwerk der Stirnfassaden schafft hier eine angenehme Maßstäblichkeit, ohne auf oberflächliche Dekoration zurückzugreifen.

COUNTRY / LAND	GERMANY / DEUTSCHLAND	HOUSE NAME / BEZEICHNUNG DES HAUSES	HOUSE IN AGGSTALL
LOCATION (CITY/REGION) / LAGE (STADT/REGION)			AGGSTALL
ARCHITECT / ARCHITEKT	HILD UND K ARCHITEKTEN	YEAR OF COMPLETION / BAUJAHR	2000
PHOTOGRAPHER / FOTOGRAF	MICHAEL HEINRICH	SQUARE FEET / QUADRAT METER	4842 / 450
CITY AND COUNTRY ARCHITECT / STADT UND LAND ARCHITEKT			MÜNCHEN, DEUTSCHLAND
WEBSITE ARCHITECT / HOMEPAGE ARCHITEKT			WWW.HILDUNDK.DE

HAUS WOLLENWEBER
TERRAIN: LOENHART & MAYER

Built in memory of the owner's grandmother's house on the same site that was demolished to make room for the new home, the challenge here was to build within the financial limitations of a catalogue house. Wood-frame construction was therefore implemented. The dark-stained wood cladding and the large garden window both echo the former house and create a dynamic juxtaposition between new and old.

Erbaut in Erinnerung an das ehemals hier befindliche Haus der Großmutter, bestand die Herausforderung beim Bau dieses Hauses darin, den Preis eines Fertighauses nicht zu übersteigen. Deshalb erfolgte die Entscheidung für die Holzbauweise. Das dunkel gebeizte Holz der Fassaden und das große Blumenfenster sind Elemente aus dem Vorgängerbau, die hier gekonnt auf neue Weise interpretiert wurden.

COUNTRY / LAND	GERMANY / DEUTSCHLAND	HOUSE NAME / BEZEICHNUNG DES HAUSES	HAUS WOLLENWEBER
LOCATION (CITY/REGION) / LAGE (STADT/REGION)			STOCKDORF, MÜNCHEN
ARCHITECT / ARCHITEKT	TERRAIN: LOENHART & MAYER	YEAR OF COMPLETION / BAUJAHR	2004
PHOTOGRAPHER / FOTOGRAF	EDWARD BEIERLE, TERRAIN	SQUARE FEET / QUADRAT METER	1539 / 143
CITY AND COUNTRY ARCHITECT / STADT UND LAND ARCHITEKT			MÜNCHEN, DEUTSCHLAND
WEBSITE ARCHITECT / HOMEPAGE ARCHITEKT			WWW.TERRAIN.DE

The compact form of this house opens up to reveal a surprisingly generous, two story living/dining space inside. From here an open stair leads to the upper level, where two bedrooms are nestled under the steeply sloping roof surfaces.

Die kompakte Form dieses Hauses umhüllt einen überraschend großzügigen, zweigeschossigen Wohn-/Essraum im Inneren. Von hier aus führt eine offene Treppe auf die obere Ebene, wo sich unter den Dachschrägen zwei Schlafzimmer befinden.

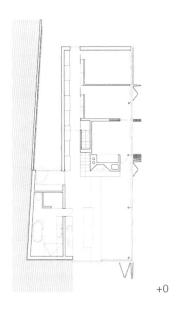

+0

WOHNHAUS DAUM / MAYR
TERRAIN: LOENHART & MAYER

COUNTRY / LAND	GERMANY / DEUTSCHLAND	HOUSE NAME / BEZEICHNUNG DES HAUSES	WOHNHAUS DAUM / MAYR
LOCATION (CITY/REGION) / LAGE (STADT/REGION)			WEßLING, OBERPFAFFENHOFEN
ARCHITECT / ARCHITEKT		TERRAIN: LOENHART & MAYER	YEAR OF COMPLETION / BAUJAHR 2006
PHOTOGRAPHER / FOTOGRAF		EDWARD BEIERLE, TERRAIN	SQUARE FEET / QUADRAT METER 1722 / 160
CITY AND COUNTRY ARCHITECT / STADT UND LAND ARCHITEKT			MÜNCHEN, DEUTSCHLAND
WEBSITE ARCHITECT / HOMEPAGE ARCHITEKT			WWW.TERRAIN.DE

Towards the neighbouring suburban site this house presents itself with an interesting feature - the unorthodox covered entrance that doubles as a carport. Creative organisation of the U-shaped floor plan resulted in a protected inner courtyard onto which the major rooms orient.

Zur Vorstadtumgebung hin präsentiert sich dieses Haus mit einer unorthodoxen Geste – die ungewöhnliche überdachte Eingangsvorzone, die zugleich als Carport dient. Die kreative Organisation des U-förmigen Grundrisses schafft einen geschützten inneren Hof zu dem sich die Haupträume orientieren.

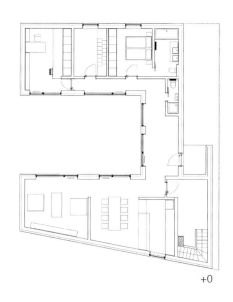

+0

HAUS GÖPPNER
BAYER I UHRIG ARCHITEKTEN

COUNTRY / LAND	GERMANY / DEUTSCHLAND	HOUSE NAME / BEZEICHNUNG DES HAUSES	HAUS GÖPPNER
LOCATION (CITY/REGION) / LAGE (STADT/REGION)			RAMSTEIN
ARCHITECT / ARCHITEKT	BAYER I UHRIG ARCHITEKTEN	YEAR OF COMPLETION / BAUJAHR	2003
PHOTOGRAPHER / FOTOGRAF	MICHAEL HEINRICH	SQUARE FEET / QUADRAT METER	1991 / 185
CITY AND COUNTRY ARCHITECT / STADT UND LAND ARCHITEKT			KAISERSLAUTERN, DEUTSCHLAND
WEBSITE ARCHITECT / HOMEPAGE ARCHITEKT			WWW.BAYER-UHRIG.DE

The street is like countless others, lined by "normal" houses concerned with little more than maintaining normalcy. In response to this context the building, constructed of massive wood planks, is conceived as a sculptural object. The resultant play of lightness and sheer mass shifts the house's scale and strikes up an engaging dialogue with the neighbours. Inside, ground floor and mezzanine levels create a zone of flowing spaces.

Eine Straße wie tausend andere, gesäumt von „normalen" Häusern - alle scheinbar bemüht, keinesfalls aufzufallen. Um in dieser Umgebung bestehen zu können, wird der Bau aus massiven Holzbohlen als skulpturales Objekt aufgefasst. Im Zusammenspiel aus Leichtigkeit und Schwere heben Maßstab und Erscheinungsform den Bau von seiner Umgebung ab. Im Inneren ist das Erd- und Galeriegeschoss als fließendes Raumgefüge über zwei Ebenen gestaltet.

EBELING HOUSE
ARCHIFACTORY.DE

COUNTRY / LAND	GERMANY / DEUTSCHLAND	HOUSE NAME / BEZEICHNUNG DES HAUSES		EBELING HOUSE
LOCATION (CITY/REGION) / LAGE (STADT/REGION)				DORTMUND
ARCHITECT / ARCHITEKT		ARCHIFACTORY.DE	YEAR OF COMPLETION / BAUJAHR	2000
PHOTOGRAPHER / FOTOGRAF		GERNOT MAUL	SQUARE FEET / QUADRAT METER	1248 / 116
CITY AND COUNTRY ARCHITECT / STADT UND LAND ARCHITEKT				BOCHUM, DEUTSCHLAND
WEBSITE ARCHITECT / HOMEPAGE ARCHITEKT				WWW.ARCHIFACTORY.DE

The compact building envelope optimises solar gain. Translucent polycarbonate façade panels capture the sun's warmth and store it in the massive walls behind. In spite of the limited space available, the kitchen/dining area was foreseen as a double-height space. Large window openings on both of its sides allow morning and afternoon light to traverse the house.

Die kompakte Gebäudehülle optimiert den Gewinn von Solarwärme. Durchsichtige Fassadenpaneele fangen die Wärme ein, die in den massiven Wänden dahinter gespeichert wird. Trotz des engen zur Verfügung stehenden Raumes wurde die Küche als zweigeschossige Halle vorgesehen. Große Fensteröffnungen zu beiden Seiten führen sowohl Morgen-, als auch Abendlicht in das Hausinnere.

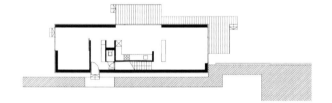

HAUS SUNOKO
SOHO ARCHITEKTUR

COUNTRY / LAND	GERMANY / DEUTSCHLAND	HOUSE NAME / BEZEICHNUNG DES HAUSES	HAUS SUNOKO
LOCATION (CITY/REGION) / LAGE (STADT/REGION)			MEMMINGEN
ARCHITECT / ARCHITEKT		SOHO ARCHITEKTUR YEAR OF COMPLETION / BAUJAHR	2002
PHOTOGRAPHER / FOTOGRAF		RETZLAFF RAINER, WALTENHOFEN SQUARE FEET / QUADRAT METER	1130 / 105
CITY AND COUNTRY ARCHITECT / STADT UND LAND ARCHITEKT			AUGSBURG, DEUTSCHLAND
WEBSITE ARCHITECT / HOMEPAGE ARCHITEKT			WWW.SOHO-ARCHITEKTUR.DE

The archetypical pitched-roof house so often found in banal suburbs was abstracted to its very essence here. By eliminating roof eaves and cladding the clear form in the same wood as that used for the surrounding deck the house merges with its surroundings without repeating the dreary monotony of the neighbouring tract homes.

Das archetypische Satteldachhaus, das das banale Gesicht zahlloser Vorstädte prägt, wurde hier auf seine Essenz abstrahiert. Durch Weglassung von Dachüberständen und Verkleidung des Baukörpers und der umliegenden Terrasse im selben Holz verschmilzt das Haus mit der Umgebung, ohne jedoch die einfältige Monotonie der umliegenden Vorstadthäuser fortzusetzen.

HAUS N.I.H
SOHO ARCHITEKTUR

COUNTRY / LAND	GERMANY / DEUTSCHLAND	HOUSE NAME / BEZEICHNUNG DES HAUSES	HAUS N.I.H
LOCATION (CITY/REGION) / LAGE (STADT/REGION)			AITRACH
ARCHITECT / ARCHITEKT		SOHO ARCHITEKTUR	YEAR OF COMPLETION / BAUJAHR 2003
PHOTOGRAPHER / FOTOGRAF		RETZLAFF RAINER, WALTENHOFEN	SQUARE FEET / QUADRAT METER 1399 / 130
CITY AND COUNTRY ARCHITECT / STADT UND LAND ARCHITEKT			AUGSBURG, DEUTSCHLAND
WEBSITE ARCHITECT / HOMEPAGE ARCHITEKT			WWW.SOHO-ARCHITEKTUR.DE

The various uses of this house are dispersed on three levels. Additionally, a separate studio was foreseen to the major spaces such as the living/dining area and the bedrooms on their respective levels. Recessing the windows deep into the façade emphasizes the sculptural quality of the building masses with the characteristic falling slope of the roof above as a transition to the realm of the sky above.

Die diversen Funktionen dieses Hauses sind auf drei Ebenen verteilt. Ein autarkes Studio wurde zusätzlich zu den Hauptwohnräumen vorgesehen. Das Wohnzimmer und die Schlafzimmer sind übereinander angeordnet. Die Fenster sind mit tiefen Leibungen versehen, um die skulpturale Wirkung der Baukörper zu erhöhen, die durch die abfallende Dachlinie charakterisiert werden.

HOUSE WITH STUDIO
GOETZ UND HOOTZ ARCHITEKTEN

COUNTRY / LAND	GERMANY / DEUTSCHLAND	HOUSE NAME / BEZEICHNUNG DES HAUSES	HOUSE WITH STUDIO
LOCATION (CITY/REGION) / LAGE (STADT/REGION)			WESSLING, BAYERN
ARCHITECT / ARCHITEKT	GOETZ UND HOOTZ ARCHITEKTEN	YEAR OF COMPLETION / BAUJAHR	2004
PHOTOGRAPHER / FOTOGRAF	TOM VACK, MICHAEL HEINRICH	SQUARE FEET / QUADRAT METER	3228 / 300
CITY AND COUNTRY ARCHITECT / STADT UND LAND ARCHITEKT			MÜNCHEN, DEUTSCHLAND
WEBSITE ARCHITECT / HOMEPAGE ARCHITEKT			WWW.GOETZUNDHOOTZ.DE

The various spaces of this house are organized within a concrete hull that is much more than a simple box, although the home's austerity seems at first reduced to a minimalist essence. The four exterior walls spatially contain a rich diversity of residential spaces.

Die unterschiedlichen Räume dieses Hauses wurden innerhalb einer Hülle aus Beton angeordnet. Sie ist alles andere als eine einfache Kiste, auch wenn die Schlichtheit des Hauses beim ersten Blick auf eine minimalistische Essenz reduziert zu sein scheint.

HOUSE VOSS
LÉON WOHLHAGE
WERNIK ARCHITEKTEN

The two-story dining space unites the lower with the upper level and orients toward the exterior garden to the south. The generously dimensioned living room space views on to a patio courtyard that is enclosed by the same austere in-situ concrete walls that were left exposed on both the interior and exterior of this residence.

Der zweigeschossige Essraum verbindet die Ebenen und orientiert sich zum Außengarten im Süden. Das großzügige Wohnzimmer ist mit Ausblick auf einen Innenhof angelegt. Dessen Wände sind aus Ortbeton, wobei die glatten Oberflächen sowohl außen und innen sichtbar bleiben.

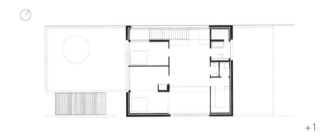

+1

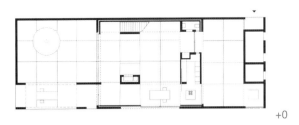

+0

COUNTRY / LAND   GERMANY / DEUTSCHLAND   HOUSE NAME / BEZEICHNUNG DES HAUSES   HOUSE VOSS

LOCATION (CITY/REGION) / LAGE (STADT/REGION)   MUNSTERLAND REGION

ARCHITECT / ARCHITEKT   LÉON WOHLHAGE WERNIK ARCHITEKTEN   YEAR OF COMPLETION / BAUJAHR   2000

PHOTOGRAPHER / FOTOGRAF   CHRISTIAN RICHTERS   SQUARE FEET / QUADRAT METER   3228 / 300

CITY AND COUNTRY ARCHITECT / STADT UND LAND ARCHITEKT   BERLIN, DEUTSCHLAND

WEBSITE ARCHITECT / HOMEPAGE ARCHITEKT   WWW.LEONWOHLHAGEWERNIK.DE

This house on Estonia's Baltic Coast demonstrates the emergence of a new generation of architects operating in Eastern Europe. Three volumes are arranged to create a lively composition. A one-storey central living space with fully glazed walls connects the two major wings that are clad in orange-stained wood panels that translate the colours and materials of the surrounding dune landscape in the architecture.

Dieses Haus an der Ostseeküste Estlands dokumentiert das Erscheinen einer neuen Generation von Architekten in Osteuropa. Drei Baukörper wurden intelligent angelegt, um eine lebendige Komposition zu schaffen. Der zentrale, eingeschossige Raum verbindet die beiden Hauptflügel, die mit orange gebeizten Holzpanellen verkleidet wurden. Diese greifen die Farben und Materialien des umgrenzenden Dünenwalds in der Architektur auf.

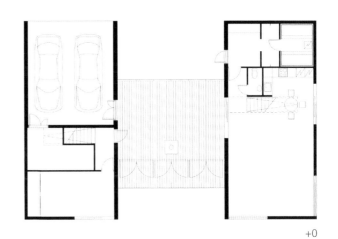

+0

SUMMER HOUSE
KOKO ARCHITECTS

COUNTRY / LAND	ESTONIA / ESTLAND	HOUSE NAME / BEZEICHNUNG DES HAUSES	SUMMER HOUSE
LOCATION (CITY/REGION) / LAGE (STADT/REGION)			LAULASMAA
ARCHITECT / ARCHITEKT		KOKO ARCHITECTS YEAR OF COMPLETION / BAUJAHR	2003
PHOTOGRAPHER / FOTOGRAF		KAIDO HAAGEN SQUARE FEET / QUADRAT METER	2152 / 200
CITY AND COUNTRY ARCHITECT / STADT UND LAND ARCHITEKT			TALINN, ESTLAND
WEBSITE ARCHITECT / HOMEPAGE ARCHITEKT			WWW.KOKO.EE

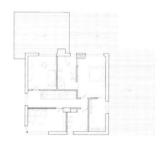

+1

The cube-like volume of this residence serves as an especially
economical form that nonetheless is skilfully varied. Bold orange
surfaces alternate with window ribbons on the street-side façade.
Inside, precisely designed details such as the cantilevered kitchen
island and the hovering aquarium demonstrate the special care
lavished on the details on both interior and exterior surfaces.

Die kubische Form dieses Hauses dient als eine besonders
wirtschaftliche Grundform, die dennoch gekonnt variiert wird.
Die Straßenfassade wird belebt durch orangefarbene Ebenen und
alternierenden Fensterstreifen. Im Inneren zeugen durchdachte
Details von einer kreativen gestalterischen Sorgfalt wie die
auskragende Kücheninsel oder ein schwebendes Aquarium.

DWELLING SUKILELIU
TRAINAUSKAS,
VARNAUSKAS

COUNTRY / LAND	LITHUANIA / LITHAUEN	HOUSE NAME / BEZEICHNUNG DES HAUSES	DWELLING SUKILELIU
LOCATION (CITY/REGION) / LAGE (STADT/REGION)			KAUNAS
ARCHITECT / ARCHITEKT		TRAINAUSKAS, VARNAUSKAS YEAR OF COMPLETION / BAUJAHR	2003
PHOTOGRAPHER / FOTOGRAF		TOMAS LOPATA SQUARE FEET / QUADRAT METER	2260 / 210
CITY AND COUNTRY ARCHITECT / STADT UND LAND ARCHITEKT			VILNIUS, LITHUANIA
WEBSITE ARCHITECT / HOMEPAGE ARCHITEKT			WWW.4PLIUS.LT

LAJSTA HOUSE
<u>MEDUSA GROUP</u>

+0

The building site called for a strip-like floor plan. The spaces stretch out along the backbone formed by the connecting hallway that opens onto various intermediary spaces including the living-dining space and two courtyards that form protected inside-outside spaces and increase the spaciousness of the adjoining interior rooms. Wood was used to clad the exterior surfaces and also on the ceiling strip of the connecting hall axis to emphasize its dramatic length.

Der Zuschnitt des Grundstücks erzeugte einen streifenartigen Grundriss. Die Räume erstrecken sich entlang des verbindenden Ganges, der sich zu verschiedenen Zwischenstationen, wie dem Wohn-Esszimmer und zwei Höfen hin öffnet. Die Höfe lassen die Innenräume größer wirken. Holz wurde sowohl als Außenverkleidung als auch im Inneren als Deckenmaterial des Verbindungsgangs verwendet, um dessen dramatische Länge zu betonen.

COUNTRY / LAND	POLAND / POLEN	HOUSE NAME / BEZEICHNUNG DES HAUSES	LAJSTA HOUSE
LOCATION (CITY/REGION) / LAGE (STADT/REGION)			ZERNICA, SILESIAN DISTRICT
ARCHITECT / ARCHITEKT		MEDUSA GROUP YEAR OF COMPLETION / BAUJAHR	2004
PHOTOGRAPHER / FOTOGRAF		JULIUSZ SOKOLOWSKI SQUARE FEET / QUADRAT METER	2862 / 266
CITY AND COUNTRY ARCHITECT / STADT UND LAND ARCHITEKT			GLIWICE, POLSKA
WEBSITE ARCHITECT / HOMEPAGE ARCHITEKT			WWW.MEDUSAGROUP.PL

HOUSE WITH A CAPSULE
ROBERT KONIECZNY –
KWK PROMES ARCHITEKCI

The rectangular plan of this home consciously contrasts with the landscape and at the same time unites architecture and nature. The edges of the square building volume are perforated to create the covered entry/patio space that is accentuated by the curving wooden surfaces of the central capsule that contains the kitchen, dining, and bathroom spaces. Wood for the fireplace is stacked in a special façade opening that allows the building to change appearance through the seasons -depending on the amount of wood currently stored.

Die Rechteckform dieses Hauses steht in bewusstem Kontrast zur Landschaft und schafft zugleich eine Synthese von Architektur und Natur. Die Ränder des Baukörpers wurden geöffnet um eine überdachte Eingangs- und Hofzone zu schaffen. Diese wird akzentuiert durch die runden Formen des zentralen Kerns. Er beherbergt Küche, Essplatz und Badezimmer Brennholz für den Kamin wird in einer besonderen Fassadenöffnung aufbewahrt, so dass die Fassade sich ständig je nach Jahreszeit und Menge des aufbewahrten Holzes wandelt.

COUNTRY / LAND	POLAND / POLEN	HOUSE NAME / BEZEICHNUNG DES HAUSES	HOUSE WITH A CAPSULE
LOCATION (CITY/REGION) / LAGE (STADT/REGION)			RUDA SLASKA, HALEMBA
ARCHITECT / ARCHITEKT	ROBERT KONIECZNY - KWK PROMES ARCHITEKCI	YEAR OF COMPLETION / BAUJAHR	2004
PHOTOGRAPHER / FOTOGRAF	JULIUSZ SOKOLOWSKI	SQUARE FEET / QUADRAT METER	1377 / 128
CITY AND COUNTRY ARCHITECT / STADT UND LAND ARCHITEKT			KATOWICE, POLSKA
WEBSITE ARCHITECT / HOMEPAGE ARCHITEKT			WWW.KWK-ARCH.PL

The rectangular building envelope was inserted into the light slope to both integrate and create an orthogonal contrast to the surrounding landscape. Inside, the major spaces on the ground floor step down to mirror the hillside slope outside. The bedrooms are contained in the wood-clad volume of the upper level that hovers above the glass façades of the light ground floor plinth.

Die kubische Baumasse wurde in den Hang eingebettet um einen rechtwinkligen Kontrast zur Landschaft zu schaffen und diese zugleich zu integrieren. Die Bodenhöhen der Haupträume im Erdgeschoss folgen der leichten Neigung des Hangs. Darüber schwebt der holzverkleidete Schlafzimmertrakt über den leichten Glasfassaden des Erdgeschosses.

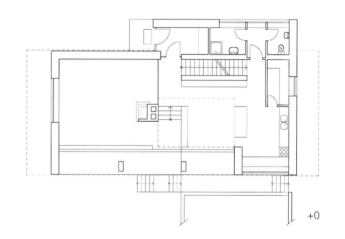

+0

VILLA IN CERCANY
VYSEHRAD ATELIER

COUNTRY / LAND	CZECH REPUBLIC / CZECHIEN	HOUSE NAME / BEZEICHNUNG DES HAUSES	VILLA IN CERCANY
LOCATION (CITY/REGION) / LAGE (STADT/REGION)			CERCANY
ARCHITECT / ARCHITEKT		VYSEHRAD ATELIER YEAR OF COMPLETION / BAUJAHR	2000
PHOTOGRAPHER / FOTOGRAF		FILIP ŠLAPAL SQUARE FEET / QUADRAT METER	2798 / 260
CITY AND COUNTRY ARCHITECT / STADT UND LAND ARCHITEKT			PRAHA, CZECH REPUBLIC
WEBSITE ARCHITECT / HOMEPAGE ARCHITEKT			WWW.VYSEHRAD-ATELIER.CZ

The steel frame structure is comprised of 24 cubes within which the various spaces of the house were skilfully placed. The strict grid of the floor plan was also applied to the façades of the long, rectangular building mass. The grid is varied to create dynamic spatial combinations inside and lively façade rhythms outside. The main living/dining space occupies six spatial modules on the ground floor. By limiting the materials used to concrete, steel, and glass the architects created a non-compromising, poetic statement that is at the same time light-filled and spacious - in spite of the strict grid of the basic structural frame.

Das räumliche Gerüst dieses Hauses besteht aus 24 Kuben, in denen die verschiedenen Räume gekonnt angeordnet wurden. Das strikte Raster des Grundrisses wurde auch auf die Fassaden des langen, rechteckigen Hauses übertragen. Dennoch wird das Raster variiert, um innen spannende Raumkompositionen und außen dynamische Fassaden zu schaffen. Der Wohn-Kochbereich nimmt sechs Module im Erdgeschoss ein. Durch Reduktion der Materialien auf Beton, Stahl und Glas formulieren die Architekten ein kompromißloses Raumgefüge, das dennoch hell und großzügig wirkt – trotz der Rigidität des Haupttragwerks.

VILLA PSZCZOLKA
HŠH ARCHITEKTI

The concrete screeding of the floors, the in-situ concrete wall slabs, and the prefabricated concrete ceiling slabs were all left exposed.
These light grey surfaces were inserted into the black-painted steel framework to emphasise the grid of the main structure. The grid proves surprisingly flexible: the diverse rooms such as bathrooms, bedrooms, stairwell, and foyer were are integrated into it with gracious ease.

Der Betonestrich der Fußböden, der Ortbeton der Wandscheiben und die vorgefertigten Deckenelemente aus Beton wurden allesamt sichtbar gelassen.
Diese hellgrauen Ebenen wurden in das schwarz gestrichene Tragwerk eingefügt, um das Hauptraster zu betonen. Dieses Raster erweist sich als überraschend flexibel: die diversen Räume wie Badezimmer, Schlafzimmer, Treppenhaus und Foyer wurden mit spielender Leichtigkeit eingefügt.

+1

+0

COUNTRY / LAND	CZECH REPUBLIC / CZECHIEN	HOUSE NAME / BEZEICHNUNG DES HAUSES	VILLA PSZCZOLKA
LOCATION (CITY/REGION) / LAGE (STADT/REGION)			BEROUN
ARCHITECT / ARCHITEKT		HŠH ARCHITEKTI	YEAR OF COMPLETION / BAUJAHR	2004
PHOTOGRAPHER / FOTOGRAF		ESTER HAVLOVA	SQUARE FEET / QUADRAT METER	XXX
CITY AND COUNTRY ARCHITECT / STADT UND LAND ARCHITEKT			PRAHA, CZECH REPUBLIC
WEBSITE ARCHITECT / HOMEPAGE ARCHITEKT			WWW.HSHARCHITEKTI.CZ

The proximity to a nearby protected landscape led the architects to develop a creative solution. By embedding the house in the light slope of the hillside they were able to obtain planning permission for a site that was previously considered unfit for building. The flat roofs were foreseen with green planting and slanting skylight shafts that direct light inside.

Die Nähe zu einem Landschaftsschutzgebiet inspirierte die Architekten, einen besonders kreativen Entwurfsansatz zu entwickeln. Dank der Einbettung des Hauses in das leicht abfallende Gelände erhielten sie eine Baugenehmigung für das als unbebaubar geltende Grundstück.. Die flachen Dächer sind begrünt und schräge Oberlichtschächte führen Licht nach innen.

SLOPE HOUSE HINTERSDORF
LICHTBLAU.WAGNER ARCHITEKTEN

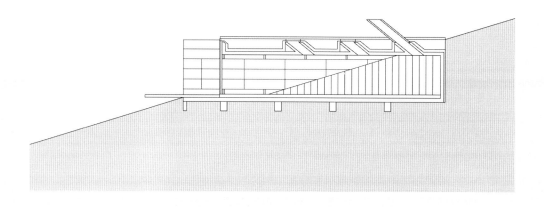

The side walls express the slanting slope with triangular window openings that grow ever larger toward the entirely glazed southern façade with its view into the adjacent forest. White walls and ceilings, and wood plank flooring create a welcoming, light-filled ambience inside.

Die dreieckigen Glasflächen der Seitenwände folgen der Bodenneigung und werden zur Front hin größer – sie ermöglichen einen freien Blick auf den umliegenden Wald. Weiße Wände und Decken in Kombination mit Fußbodendielen aus Naturholz schaffen ein einladendes, von Licht belebtes Ambiente.

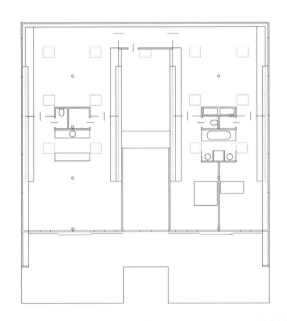

COUNTRY / LAND	**AUSTRIA / ÖSTERREICH**	HOUSE NAME / BEZEICHNUNG DES HAUSES	SLOPE HOUSE HINTERSDORF
LOCATION (CITY/REGION) / LAGE (STADT/REGION)			HINTERSDORF
ARCHITECT / ARCHITEKT	**LICHTBLAU.WAGNER ARCHITEKTEN**	YEAR OF COMPLETION / BAUJAHR	2002
PHOTOGRAPHER / FOTOGRAF	**BRUNO KLOMFAR**	SQUARE FEET / QUADRAT METER	3766 / 350
CITY AND COUNTRY ARCHITECT / STADT UND LAND ARCHITEKT			WIEN, ÖSTERREICH
WEBSITE ARCHITECT / HOMEPAGE ARCHITEKT			WWW.LICHTBLAUWAGNER.COM

X ARCHITEKTEN

LINZ
AUSTRIA / ÖSTERREICH

x architekten is a group of dedicated architects that develops conceptual positions on architecture based on the requirements of the individual designs scenarios. The notion of an "x" as a mathematic variable stands for openness. An "x" also stands for multiplication. The team is structured to avoid hierarchy and to create a substitute for the conventional notion of architects as lone practitioners. Their creative process is enlivened by a balanced concern for critique and self critique that immensely profits from the ideas and impulses provided by all members of the team.

x architekten is composed of varying teams of architects that mostly studied at the Technical Univerity of Graz, Austria. Now, they also teach there and in Vienna, Innsbruck, and Linz. Teaching and working in the profession at the same time has proven to be a major creative motor in the success of x architekten.

Photo: x architekten

x architekten ist eine Gruppe engagierter ArchitektInnen, die in projektbezogener Arbeit konzeptionelle Positionen zur Gegenwartsarchitektur entwickelt. Als mathematische Variable steht das x für Offenheit. Das x fordert die Mehrzahl: Das Team mit flacher Hierarchie ersetzt das Berufsbild des Architekten als Einzelkämpfer. Die Dynamik eines permanenten, zwischen Kreativität und (Selbst)Kritik pendelnden Arbeitsprozesses lässt über das Vermögen des Einzelnen hinausgehende Qualität entstehen.

x architekten sind in wechselnden Gruppierungen und im Austausch mit unterschiedlichen Projektpartnern aus den Zeichensälen der TU Graz hervorgegangen. Die Gleichzeitigkeit von praktischer Tätigkeit und Lehre bzw. Forschung hat sich für ihre Arbeit als förderlich erwiesen.

FALTHAUS

<u>X ARCHITEKTEN</u>

Rather than continuing the traditional house forms and pitched roofs of the surrounding neighbourhood the architects opted instead for creating a building form that translates the hillside landscape into architecture. First, the three levels of this house were precisely fitted into the slope. Then the building functions were skilfully arrayed along the slope.

Anstatt die konventionellen Hausformen und Satteldächer der Umgebung aufzunehmen entschieden sich die Architekten für eine Bauform, welche die Hanglage formal aufgreift. Zuerst wurden alle drei Ebenen des Hauses sorgfältig in den Hang eingepasst, dann wurden die Wohnfunktionen entlang des Hanges angeordnet.

The entire flat roof above the main wing was designed as a roof terrace that is accessed from the living room space below by lightly slanting roof surfaces that both echo and counter the natural slope of the hillside. The floor and roof planes were literally "folded" out of a continuous spatial plane to allow vertical and horizontal planes to merge into an unconventional, dynamic spatial statement.

Das gesamte Flachdach oberhalb des Hauptflügels wurde als Dachterrasse ausgebildet, die vom Wohnzimmer darunter erschlossen wird.. Die Boden- und Deckenebenen sind scheinbar aus einer zusammenhängenden Raumscheibe „gefaltet", so dass die vertikalen und horizontalen Ebenen zu einem unkonventionellen, dynamischen Raumstatement verschmelzen.

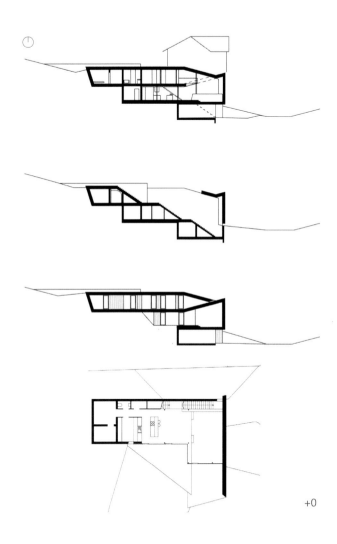

+0

COUNTRY / LAND	AUSTRIA / ÖSTERREICH	HOUSE NAME / BEZEICHNUNG DES HAUSES	FALTHAUS
LOCATION (CITY/REGION) / LAGE (STADT/REGION)			KLOSTERNEUBURG
ARCHITECT / ARCHITEKT		X ARCHITEKTEN YEAR OF COMPLETION / BAUJAHR	2004
PHOTOGRAPHER / FOTOGRAF		X ARCHITEKTEN SQUARE FEET / QUADRAT METER	2152 / 200
CITY AND COUNTRY ARCHITECT / STADT UND LAND ARCHITEKT			LINZ, ÖSTERREICH
WEBSITE ARCHITECT / HOMEPAGE ARCHITEKT			WWW.XARCHITEKTEN.COM

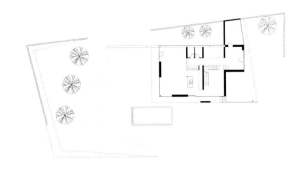

The white, cubic volumes of this home create an exciting counterpoint to the hillside site. Inside, the corridor axis leads directly from the entrance to the informal living/kitchen/dining space and continues outside as a view axis. A generous stair space interconnects the three levels and leads up to the bedroom cube that seems to hover above the plinth formed by the spaces on the lower levels.

Die weißen, kubischen Volumen dieses Hauses schaffen einen spannungsreichen Kontrast zum Hanggrundstück. Die Eingangsachse führt direkt zum informellen Wohn-Essbereich und setzt sich im Freien als Blickachse fort. Ein großzügiger Treppenraum verbindet alle drei Ebenen und führt hinauf zum Schlafkubus, der über den Räumen der unteren Geschosse zu schweben scheint.

+0

VILLA 9003
X ARCHITEKTEN

COUNTRY / LAND	AUSTRIA / ÖSTERREICH	HOUSE NAME / BEZEICHNUNG DES HAUSES	VILLA 9003
LOCATION (CITY/REGION) / LAGE (STADT/REGION)			SCHWERTBERG
ARCHITECT / ARCHITEKT		X ARCHITEKTEN YEAR OF COMPLETION / BAUJAHR	2005
PHOTOGRAPHER / FOTOGRAF		X ARCHITEKTEN SQUARE FEET / QUADRAT METER	2959 / 275
CITY AND COUNTRY ARCHITECT / STADT UND LAND ARCHITEKT			LINZ, ÖSTERREICH
WEBSITE ARCHITECT / HOMEPAGE ARCHITEKT			WWW.XARCHITEKTEN.COM

FLOATING HOUSE
HOLODECK.AT

The conventional connection between building and ground plane was effectively dissolved here. The ground floor is recessed underneath the seemingly massive, carved block of the upper level. Both levels are fully glazed toward the view out to fields and a nearby wooded hill. The forms are consciously variegated and modulated to translate the surrounding topography into built form, not contrast it.

Die herkömmliche Verbindung zwischen Bauwerk und Boden wurde bei diesem Haus effektiv aufgelöst. Das Erdgeschoss ist unter dem scheinbar massiven, ausgeschnitzten Block des Obergeschosses zurückgesetzt. Beide Wohnebenen sind voll verglast und geben den Blick frei auf Felder und Hügel. Die Formen sind bewußt moduliert und variiert, um die umliegende Topografie in gebaute Form zu übersetzten.

COUNTRY / LAND	AUSTRIA / ÖSTERREICH	HOUSE NAME / BEZEICHNUNG DES HAUSES	FLOATING HOUSE
LOCATION (CITY/REGION) / LAGE (STADT/REGION)			SIEGENFELD
ARCHITECT / ARCHITEKT		HOLODECK.AT YEAR OF COMPLETION / BAUJAHR	2005
PHOTOGRAPHER / FOTOGRAF		HERTHA HURNAUS SQUARE FEET / QUADRAT METER	4724 / 439
CITY AND COUNTRY ARCHITECT / STADT UND LAND ARCHITEKT			WIEN, ÖSTERREICH
WEBSITE ARCHITECT / HOMEPAGE ARCHITEKT			WWW.HOLODECK.AT

SHIFTHOUSE
HOLODECK.AT

To incorporate the gentle slope of the site the spaces of this house were shifted onto two levels. A central stair mediates between the levels and interconnects all of the various spaces. The exterior form expresses the spatial shift inside with a balcony on two levels that extends out to shade the completely glazed walls of the ground floor living spaces.

Um den leichten Hang des Grundstückes zu berücksichtigen wurden die Räume dieses Hauses in auf zwei Grundebenen verteilt. Eine zentrale Treppe verbindet die unterschiedlichen Wohnräume. Die Außenform nimmt die versetzten Ebenen des Inneren durch einen zweigeschossigen Balkon auf. Dieser kragt weit aus, um die komplett verglasten Wände der Wohnbereiche im Erdgeschoss zu verschatten.

COUNTRY / LAND	AUSTRIA / ÖSTERREICH	HOUSE NAME / BEZEICHNUNG DES HAUSES	SHIFTHOUSE
LOCATION (CITY/REGION) / LAGE (STADT/REGION)			KLAGENFURT
ARCHITECT / ARCHITEKT		HOLODECK.AT YEAR OF COMPLETION / BAUJAHR	2004
PHOTOGRAPHER / FOTOGRAF		VERONIKA HOFINGER SQUARE FEET / QUADRAT METER	5165 / 480
CITY AND COUNTRY ARCHITECT / STADT UND LAND ARCHITEKT			WIEN, ÖSTERREICH
WEBSITE ARCHITECT / HOMEPAGE ARCHITEKT			WWW.HOLODECK.AT

The central space of this house serves not only as a representative, two-storey living and dining room - it also doubles as a passive solar collector that collects warmth for the adjoining rooms. The "tube" that contains the bedrooms on the upper level hovers like a spaceship above the extensively glazed walls of the lower levels.

Der zentrale Raum dieses Hauses dient nicht nur als repräsentativer, zweigeschossiger Hallenraum - er fungiert zudem als passiver Solarkollektor, der Wärme für die angrenzenden Räume sammelt. Die Röhre, die Schlafzimmer im oberen Geschoss beinhaltet, schwebt wie ein Raumschiff über den vielfach verglasten Wänden der unteren Geschosse. Licht gelangt über große Glaspanelle im Fußboden bis in das untere Geschoss.

SOLAR TUBE
GEORG DRIENDL

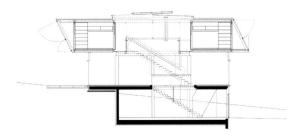

Light flows down from the central space all the way down to the ground floor via large glass floor panels. Closed wall niches modulate the glazed wall surfaces and serve as book walls in the living room. The kitchen nook is separated from the living room space by an open stair that graciously rises up the central hall space to the upper level. The clear building volumes form a transparent, high-tech contrast to the surroundings and at the same time merge the interior spaces with the stand of old trees and the existing natural landscape.

Geschlossene Wandnischen modulieren die verglasten Wandebenen und dienen im Wohnzimmer als Bücherwände. Die Küchennische wird durch eine offene Treppe, die grazil auf die obere Ebene führt, vom Wohnraum getrennt. Die klaren Bauformen schaffen einen transparenten, technisch wirkenden Kontrast zur Umgebung und ermöglichen zugleich die Verschmelzung der Innenräume mit dem alten Baumbestand und der vorgefundenen Landschaft.

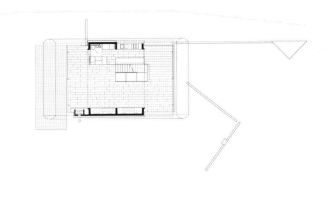

COUNTRY / LAND	AUSTRIA / ÖSTERREICH	HOUSE NAME / BEZEICHNUNG DES HAUSES	SOLAR TUBE
LOCATION (CITY/REGION) / LAGE (STADT/REGION)			WIEN
ARCHITECT / ARCHITEKT	GEORG DRIENDL	YEAR OF COMPLETION / BAUJAHR	2001
PHOTOGRAPHER / FOTOGRAF	BRUNO KLOMFAR, LEW RODIN	SQUARE FEET / QUADRAT METER	3228 / 300
CITY AND COUNTRY ARCHITECT / STADT UND LAND ARCHITEKT			WIEN, ÖSTERREICH
WEBSITE ARCHITECT / HOMEPAGE ARCHITEKT			WWW.DRIENDL.AT

The dynamic forms of this house are wrapped in a continuous, weatherproof shell. The black matting was wrapped around the rounded edges of the sculpturally variegated forms. Inside, white surfaces and large windows contrast with the dark exterior skin and underscore the informal, modern atmosphere that pervades throughout.

Die dynamischen Formen dieses Hauses wurden in eine homogene, wetterfeste Hülle eingepackt. Die schwarzen Matten sind um die runden Kanten der plastischen Baukörper gewickelt. Im Inneren schaffen weiße Flächen und große Fenster einen Kontrast zur dunklen Außenhülle und unterstreichen die informelle, moderne Atmosphäre, die das Haus durchdringt.

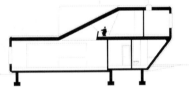

HAUS FÜR EVA & FRITZ

HOBBY A.
SCHUSTER & MAUL

COUNTRY / LAND AUSTRIA / ÖSTERREICH   HOUSE NAME / BEZEICHNUNG DES HAUSES HAUS FÜR EVA & FRITZ

LOCATION (CITY/REGION) / LAGE (STADT/REGION) BERGHEIM, SALZBURG

ARCHITECT / ARCHITEKT HOBBY A. SCHUSTER & MAUL   YEAR OF COMPLETION / BAUJAHR 2003

PHOTOGRAPHER / FOTOGRAF WALTER SCHUSTER   SQUARE FEET / QUADRAT METER 2066 / 192

CITY AND COUNTRY ARCHITECT / STADT UND LAND ARCHITEKT SALZBURG, ÖSTERREICH

WEBSITE ARCHITECT / HOMEPAGE ARCHITEKT WWW.HOBBY-A.AT

NOMADHOME
HOBBY A.
SCHUSTER & MAUL

The Nomadhome is constructed of prefabricated modules that can be combined to create various forms and floor plans. The curved segments were combined to create an L-shaped floor plan here. The garden elevation is entirely glazed whereas green panels completely close the entrance façade. The curved exterior corners are continued inside and create a virtual merging of the wall, floor, and ceiling surfaces.

Das „Nomadhome" besteht aus vorfabrizierten Modulen, die beliebig kombiniert werden können. Hier wurden die gekrümmten Segmente so angeordnet, dass ein L-förmiger Grundriss entsteht. Die Gartenfassaden sind verglast und stehen im Kontrast zu den grünen Panellen der Eingangsseite, die eine geschlossene Front bilden. Die abgerundeten Außenecken setzen sich im Inneren fort wo sie eine räumliche Verschmelzung der Boden-, Wand- und Deckenflächen bewirken.

COUNTRY / LAND	AUSTRIA / ÖSTERREICH	HOUSE NAME / BEZEICHNUNG DES HAUSES	NOMADHOME
LOCATION (CITY/REGION) / LAGE (STADT/REGION)			SEEKIRCHEN, SALZBURG
ARCHITECT / ARCHITEKT	HOBBY A. SCHUSTER & MAUL	YEAR OF COMPLETION / BAUJAHR	2005
PHOTOGRAPHER / FOTOGRAF	MARC HAADER	SQUARE FEET / QUADRAT METER	829 / 77
CITY AND COUNTRY ARCHITECT / STADT UND LAND ARCHITEKT			SALZBURG, ÖSTERREICH
WEBSITE ARCHITECT / HOMEPAGE ARCHITEKT			WWW.HOBBY-A.AT

HOBBY A.
SCHUSTER & MAUL

SALZBURG
AUSTRIA / ÖSTERREICH

Walter Schuster / Wolfgang Maul were born 1966 in Upper Austria and Franken respectively and studied in Graz, Austria und Coburg, Germany.
They gained work experience in Dublin, Ireland and Zürich, Switzerland. After that they formed project partnerships with one room, Salzburg and Halle 1, Salzburg before founding their present firm, hobby a., in 2002.

The Nomadhome; a prefabricated, enlargeable and transportable house, was conceived in 2003-2006.
In 2005 they were awarded the „Das beste Haus 2005" award in Salzburg for their residential project "Haus für Eva & Fritz".
The firm has participated in exhibitions in New York, Vienna, Shanghai, Peking and Salzburg
Their work has been published in France, Switzerland, Germany and Austria.

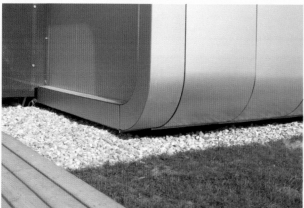

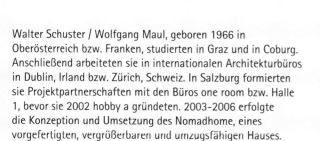

Photo: Katharina Gossow

Walter Schuster / Wolfgang Maul, geboren 1966 in
Oberösterreich bzw. Franken, studierten in Graz und in Coburg.
Anschließend arbeiteten sie in internationalen Architekturbüros
in Dublin, Irland bzw. Zürich, Schweiz. In Salzburg formierten
sie Projektpartnerschaften mit den Büros one room bzw. Halle
1, bevor sie 2002 hobby a gründeten. 2003-2006 erfolgte
die Konzeption und Umsetzung des Nomadhome, eines
vorgefertigten, vergrößerbaren und umzugsfähigen Hauses.

2005 erhielten Schuster und Maul den Architekturpreis „Das
beste Haus 2005" im Bundesland Salzburg für das Haus für Eva
& Fritz.
Ihre Werke wurden durch Ausstellungsbeteiligungen in New York,
Wien und Salzburg einer breiten Öffentlichkeit vorgestellt.
Ihre Arbeiten wurden bereits in Frankreich, Schweiz, Deutschland,
Shanghai, Peking und Österreich veröffentlicht.

HAUS SONNDORF

YES-ARCHITECTURE

Wedge-formed in both plan and section, this house graces a mountainside above a wide Austrian valley. From the entrance side, the wedge appears as a single story, rock-clad façade. From the upper entrance level, where the bedrooms are located, a stair leads down to the main level. The architects utilized the hillside site to maximum advantage.

Keilförmig sowohl im Grundriss als auch im Schnitt, steht dieses Haus auf einem Berghang oberhalb eines weiten Tals. Frontal zeigt sich der Keil als eine eingeschossige, in Stein verkleidete Fassade. Von der Eingangsebene, wo die Schlafzimmer sich befinden, führt die Treppe auf die Hautwohnebene herunter. Die Architekten nahmen die Hanglage zum Anlass, eine spannende Raumkomposition zu kreieren.

They placed the long plan parallel to the slope to create a two-story building volume that culminates in the double height living room with its panoramic view out onto the Alpine landscape. The low-slung, closed wedge of the entrance side transforms into a representative, almost monumental arch on the valley side. Various materials are used to underscore this effect: the slanting end façade is clad in steel panels whereas the entrance and garden facades in stone and glass are played off each other.

Der Baukörper wurde parallel zum Hang angeordnet, um ein zweigeschossiges Volumen zu schaffen, das im hohen Saal des Wohnzimmers kulminiert. Der lang gestreckte Keil der Eingangsseite transformiert sich auf der Talseite in ein repräsentatives, beinahe monumentales, Tor. Verschiedenartige Materialien werden eingesetzt um diesen Effekt zu erhöhen: die schräge Endfassade ist mit Stahlpanellen verkleidet während die Eingangs- und Gartenfassade jeweils in Stein und Glas von einander abgesetzt sind.

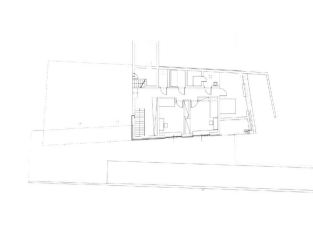

+0

COUNTRY / LAND	AUSTRIA / ÖSTERREICH	HOUSE NAME / BEZEICHNUNG DES HAUSES	HAUS SONNDORF
LOCATION (CITY/REGION) / LAGE (STADT/REGION)			HAFNING
ARCHITECT / ARCHITEKT	YES-ARCHITECTURE	YEAR OF COMPLETION / BAUJAHR	2002
PHOTOGRAPHER / FOTOGRAF	CROCE & WIR	SQUARE FEET / QUADRAT METER	2260 / 210
CITY AND COUNTRY ARCHITECT / STADT UND LAND ARCHITEKT			GRAZ, ÖSTERREICH
WEBSITE ARCHITECT / HOMEPAGE ARCHITEKT			WWW.YES-ARCHITECTURE.COM

HAUS STÜRZ
GOHM & HIESSBERGER

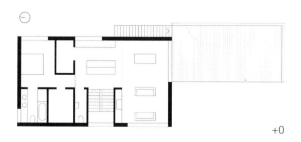

+0

A remote Alpine valley is the site for this exercise in abstraction. The black house form integrates age-old building forms found in this region but transcends them with an architectural language of poetic reduction. Inside, the white surfaces and double-story spaces continue the play with contradiction and Minimalism while at the same time retaining a comfortable sense of country living.

Ein abgelegenes Alpental ist der Standort für diese Übung in Abstraktion. Der schwarze Baukörper integriert uralte Bauformen der Region und überhöht sie zugleich mit einer Architektursprache der poetischen Reduktion. Im Inneren setzten die weißen Ebenen und zweigeschossige Räume das Spiel mit Kontradiktion und Minimalismus fort, ohne jedoch eine angenehm lockere Atmosphäre des ländlichen Lebens außer Acht zu lassen.

COUNTRY / LAND	AUSTRIA / ÖSTERREICH	HOUSE NAME / BEZEICHNUNG DES HAUSES	HAUS STÜRZ
LOCATION (CITY/REGION) / LAGE (STADT/REGION)			DALAAS, VORARLBERG
ARCHITECT / ARCHITEKT	GOHM & HIESSBERGER	YEAR OF COMPLETION / BAUJAHR	2005
PHOTOGRAPHER / FOTOGRAF	BRUNO KLOMFAR	SQUARE FEET / QUADRAT METER	1463 / 136
CITY AND COUNTRY ARCHITECT / STADT UND LAND ARCHITEKT			FELDKIRCCH, ÖSTERREICH
WEBSITE ARCHITECT / HOMEPAGE ARCHITEKT			XXX

HAUS KÖNIG
GOHM & HIESSBERGER

+1

One corner of the clear rectangle floor plan was hollowed out to create a double-height covered patio space that extends inside in the living room hall space. A bridge spans alongside the living room hall to connect the stair with the bedroom wing on the first floor. The seemingly simple building envelope demonstrates surprising potentials for creating generous, dynamic spaces both inside and out.

Eine Ecke des rechteckigen Grundrisses wurde ausgehöhlt, um einen zweigeschossigen Terrassenraum zu schaffen, der sich im geräumigen Saal des Wohnzimmers im Inneren fortsetzt. Eine Brücke spannt entlang des Wohnsaals, um die Treppe mit dem Schlafzimmertrakt zu verbinden. Die scheinbar einfache Bauhülle zeigt sich sowohl im Innen- als auch im Außenbereich überraschend gut dazu geeignet, großzügige und dynamische Räume zu definieren.

137

COUNTRY / LAND	AUSTRIA / ÖSTERREICH	HOUSE NAME / BEZEICHNUNG DES HAUSES	HAUS KÖNIG
LOCATION (CITY/REGION) / LAGE (STADT/REGION)			FELDKIRCH
ARCHITECT / ARCHITEKT		GOHM & HIESSBERGER YEAR OF COMPLETION / BAUJAHR	2001
PHOTOGRAPHER / FOTOGRAF		ALBRECHT SCHNABEL SQUARE FEET / QUADRAT METER	1872 / 174
CITY AND COUNTRY ARCHITECT / STADT UND LAND ARCHITEKT			FELDKIRCCH, ÖSTERREICH
WEBSITE ARCHITECT / HOMEPAGE ARCHITEKT			XXX

An existing house core on a mountain slope above Bregenz was skilfully extended and transformed with this sculptural composition. The old house was extended with a new wing of rooms on the ground level that serves as a massive plinth for the emphatically cantilevered living/dining room spaces on the upper level.

Ein bestehender Hauskern an einem Hang oberhalb von Bregenz wurde gekonnt mit dieser skulpturartigen Komposition gekonnt erweitert und modifiziert. Das alte Haus wurde durch einen neuen Flügel im Erdgeschoss ergänzt, der als ein Sockel für den darüber auskragenden Wohn-Essbereich dient.

HOUSE LUTZ
PHILIP LUTZ ARCHITEKTUR

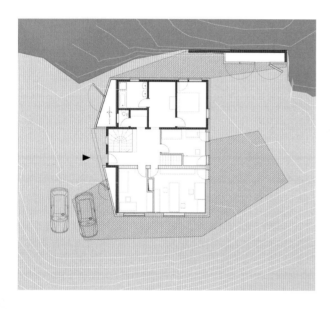

To counter the rigidity and conventionality of the existing building, the architect introduced lightly angled, seemingly folded spatial planes that imbue the forms with lightness and informality. The light-coloured wood shingle siding used to clad the exteriors forms demonstrates that time-proven regional building methods can be implemented to create unique, memorable forms. Wood panelling was used on many of the walls inside to create an engaging synthesis of interior and exterior surfaces.

Um die Rigidität und Konventionalität des Altbaus zu brechen führte der Architekt eine Komposition aus leicht abgewinkelten, scheinbar gefalteten Raumebenen ein, die den Formen Leichtigkeit und Informalität verleihen. Die hellen Holzschindeln der Außenverkleidung setzen eine uralte Bautradition der Region fort und zeigen, dass man hieraus einmalige, einprägsame Formen schaffen kann. Holzpanelle wurden als Verkleidung zahlreicher Innenwände eingesetzt, um eine Synthese von Innen- und Außenebenen herzustellen.

COUNTRY / LAND	AUSTRIA / ÖSTERREICH	HOUSE NAME / BEZEICHNUNG DES HAUSES	HOUSE LUTZ
LOCATION (CITY/REGION) / LAGE (STADT/REGION)			BREGENZ
ARCHITECT / ARCHITEKT	PHILIP LUTZ ARCHITEKTUR	YEAR OF COMPLETION / BAUJAHR	2003
PHOTOGRAPHER / FOTOGRAF	OLIVER HEISSNER	SQUARE FEET / QUADRAT METER	1937 / 180
CITY AND COUNTRY ARCHITECT / STADT UND LAND ARCHITEKT			LOCHAU, ÖSTERREICH
WEBSITE ARCHITECT / HOMEPAGE ARCHITEKT			WWW.PHILIPLUTZ.AT

HOUSE HEINZLE
PHILIP LUTZ ARCHITEKTUR

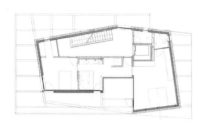

This house is located on a gently falling slope. The upper level opens out to a commanding view of Lake Constance. Therefore the goal was to elevate the living / dining level with its generous terraces as high as possible. This cantilevered "tree house" is constructed of wood and steel. The load bearing plinth is made of beige coloured in-situ concrete and anchors into the site, bordered on two sides by the swimming pool.

Dieses Wohnhaus liegt an einem leicht geneigten Hang. Das zweite Obergeschoß gibt einen Ausblick frei. Daher war es das Ziel, das Wohn- und Essgeschoß mit seinen Terrassen so hoch wie möglich anzuordnen. Dieses auskragende „Baumhaus" ist aus Holz und Stahl gebaut, der tragende Sockel aus beige eingefärbtem Sichtbeton fußt im Gelände, auf zwei Seiten vom Schwimmbecken umgeben.

COUNTRY / LAND	AUSTRIA / ÖSTERREICH	HOUSE NAME / BEZEICHNUNG DES HAUSES	HOUSE HEINZLE
LOCATION (CITY/REGION) / LAGE (STADT/REGION)			BREGENZ
ARCHITECT / ARCHITEKT		PHILIP LUTZ ARCHITEKTUR YEAR OF COMPLETION / BAUJAHR	2002
PHOTOGRAPHER / FOTOGRAF		OLIVER HEISSNER SQUARE FEET / QUADRAT METER	xxx
CITY AND COUNTRY ARCHITECT / STADT UND LAND ARCHITEKT			LOCHAU, ÖSTERREICH
WEBSITE ARCHITECT / HOMEPAGE ARCHITEKT			WWW.PHILIPLUTZ.AT

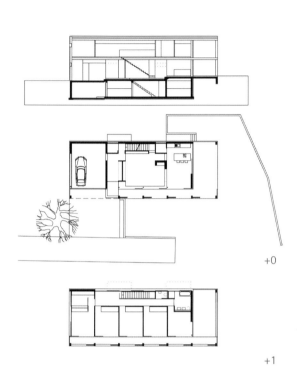

+0

+1

The seemingly simple rectilinear form is defined by a six axis long structural frame. This neutral spatial framework elegantly houses all of the various functions, including a double garage and a covered terrace. The focus of the ground floor is formed by the living room/kitchen/dining area that extends out onto the covered terrace and is delineated by subtle level changes that lead down three steps to the living room. Sliding wooden shutter elements allow closing the entire southern façade for solar and view protection.

Die scheinbar einfache Rechteckform wird durch ein sechs Achsen langes Rahmenwerk definiert. Dieses beherbergt die diversen Bereiche, inklusive einer Doppelgarage und einer überdachten Terrasse. Als Fokalpunkt im Erdgeschoß erstreckt sich der Wohn-, Ess-, Kochbereich bis auf die Terrasse ins Freie. Subtile Höhensprünge wie die drei Stufen, die zum tiefer gelegenen Wohnzimmer führen, bereichern den Raum. Schiebeelemente aus Holz erlauben es, die gesamte Südfassade zu schließen, um die dahinter liegenden Räume vor Sonne und Einblicken zu schützen.

HAUS TEUFEL
ELMAR LUDESCHER

145

COUNTRY / LAND	AUSTRIA / ÖSTERREICH	HOUSE NAME / BEZEICHNUNG DES HAUSES	HAUS TEUFEL
LOCATION (CITY/REGION) / LAGE (STADT/REGION)			FELDKIRCH
ARCHITECT / ARCHITEKT		ELMAR LUDESCHER · YEAR OF COMPLETION / BAUJAHR	2003
PHOTOGRAPHER / FOTOGRAF		BRUNO KLOMFAR · SQUARE FEET / QUADRAT METER	1883 / 175
CITY AND COUNTRY ARCHITECT / STADT UND LAND ARCHITEKT			LAUTERACH, ÖSTERREICH
WEBSITE ARCHITECT / HOMEPAGE ARCHITEKT			XXX

The trapezoidal-shaped site with a street to the south and access from the west is located in the busy town centre. In response to these restraints, the home for a four-person family answers with an assertive building volume. A seemingly monolithic "hammer" clad in dark-gray fibre-cement panels contains the recessed ground floor with living and kitchen spaces and the cantilevered upper floor with the bedrooms.

Ein trapezförmiges Grundstück, im Süden die Straße, im Westen die Zufahrt – mitten im Ortskern. Der Beengtheit des Grundstückes entgegnet das Einfamilienhaus mit einer starken Volumetrie. Ein monolithisch anmutender „Hammer" in anthrazitfarbener Eternithaut beherbergt Erdgeschoss mit Wohn- und Küchenräumen und das auskragende Obergeschoss mit Schlafräumen.

+0

KOSNJAK HOUSE
ELMAR LUDESCHER

146

COUNTRY / LAND	AUSTRIA / ÖSTERREICH	HOUSE NAME / BEZEICHNUNG DES HAUSES	KOSNJAK HOUSE
LOCATION (CITY/REGION) / LAGE (STADT/REGION)			LAUTERACH
ARCHITECT / ARCHITEKT	ELMAR LUDESCHER	YEAR OF COMPLETION / BAUJAHR	2003
PHOTOGRAPHER / FOTOGRAF	HARALD GMEINER	SQUARE FEET / QUADRAT METER	1291 / 120
CITY AND COUNTRY ARCHITECT / STADT UND LAND ARCHITEKT			LAUTERACH, ÖSTERREICH
WEBSITE ARCHITECT / HOMEPAGE ARCHITEKT			XXX

HAUS MORCOTE
MARKUS WESPI
JÉRÔME DE MEURON

The clear forms of traditional Alpine architecture were further reduced here to create a modern home embedded in tradition. Nestled to the steep slope, the rooms on the lower levels orient out through small windows in the massive walls. The upper floor contains the living room under the pitched roof that frames a view out to the nearby Alpine lake landscape.

Die klaren Formen der traditionellen Architektur der Schweizer Alpen wurden hier noch weiter reduziert, um ein modernes Haus zu schaffen, das in der Tradition beheimatet ist. Angelehnt an den Steilhang, sind die Räume in den unteren Geschossen mit kleineren Fenstern in den massiven Wänden ausgestattet. Der Wohnbereich im OG befindet sich unter dem Satteldach, das den Ausblick auf die alpine Seenlandschaft einrahmt.

COUNTRY / LAND	SWITZERLAND / SCHWEIZ	HOUSE NAME / BEZEICHNUNG DES HAUSES	HAUS MORCOTE
LOCATION (CITY/REGION) / LAGE (STADT/REGION)			MORCOTE, TESSIN
ARCHITECT / ARCHITEKT	MARKUS WESPI JÉRÔME DE MEURON ARCHITECTS	YEAR OF COMPLETION / BAUJAHR	2003
PHOTOGRAPHER / FOTOGRAF		HANNES HENZ SQUARE FEET / QUADRAT METER	1592 / 148
CITY AND COUNTRY ARCHITECT / STADT UND LAND ARCHITEKT			CAVIANO + ZÜRICH, SCHWEIZ
WEBSITE ARCHITECT / HOMEPAGE ARCHITEKT			WWW.WESPIDEMEURON.CH

HAUS SCAIANO
MARKUS WESPI JÉRÔME DE MEURON

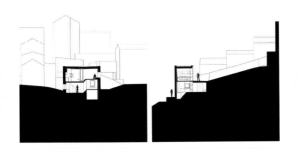

The rugged quality of Swiss mountain villages was integrated into the design language implemented here. Outside, exposed stonework reminiscent of medieval houses creates a durable, place-sensitive hull for the cool abstractness of the interiors where smooth concrete and plaster surfaces define spaces that redefine the rugged exteriors in modern austerity.

Die naturnahe Schroffheit von Gebirgsdörfern in der Schweiz wurde in der Entwurfssprache dieses Hauses berücksichtigt. Außen bildet Sichtmauerwerk - wie es in mittelalterlichen Häusern schon verwendet wurde - eine standfeste, ortsbezogene Hülle für die kühle Abstraktheit der Innenräume. Diese zeichnen sich durch glatte Beton- und Putzflächen aus, welche die Schroffheit der Außenflächen in moderne Schlichtheit im Inneren übersetzen.

COUNTRY / LAND	SWITZERLAND / SCHWEIZ	HOUSE NAME / BEZEICHNUNG DES HAUSES	HAUS SCAIANO
LOCATION (CITY/REGION) / LAGE (STADT/REGION)			SCAIANO
ARCHITECT / ARCHITEKT	MARKUS WESPI JÉRÔME DE MEURON ARCHITECTS	YEAR OF COMPLETION / BAUJAHR	2005
PHOTOGRAPHER / FOTOGRAF		HANNES HENZ SQUARE FEET / QUADRAT METER	753 / 70
CITY AND COUNTRY ARCHITECT / STADT UND LAND ARCHITEKT			CAVIANO + ZÜRICH, SCHWEIZ
WEBSITE ARCHITECT / HOMEPAGE ARCHITEKT			WWW.WESPIDEMEURON.CH

A trapezoidal red hull wraps around to enclose the variously dimensioned interior spaces. The form rises to enclose the living room on the upper floor with its large window that frames a view out to the surrounding landscape. Economical materials- such as the exposed plywood sheathing used for interior walls - were deployed to keep costs as low as possible.

Eine trapezförmige rote Hülle wickelt sich um das Haus und definiert dabei unterschiedlich dimensionierte Innenräume. Die Figur steigt an, um das Wohnzimmer mit dem großen Panoramafenster im OG zu betonen. Wirtschaftliche Materialien –wie die sichtbar gelassenen OSB-Platten der Innenwände- wurden eingesetzt, um die Kosten so gering wie möglich zu halten.

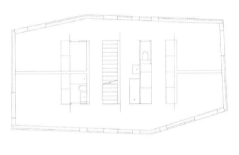

+0

FAMILY HOUSE LENZ
BEAT ROTHEN

151

COUNTRY / LAND	SWITZERLAND / SCHWEIZ	HOUSE NAME / BEZEICHNUNG DES HAUSES	FAMILY HOUSE, LENZ
LOCATION (CITY/REGION) / LAGE (STADT/REGION)			HINWIL
ARCHITECT / ARCHITEKT		BEAT ROTHEN	YEAR OF COMPLETION / BAUJAHR	2005
PHOTOGRAPHER / FOTOGRAF		GASTON WICKY	SQUARE FEET / QUADRAT METER	xxx
CITY AND COUNTRY ARCHITECT / STADT UND LAND ARCHITEKT			WINTERTHUR, SCHWEIZ
WEBSITE ARCHITECT / HOMEPAGE ARCHITEKT			WWW.ROTHEN-ARCHITEKT.COM

FAMILY HOUSE WALSER-ZUBLER
BEAT ROTHEN

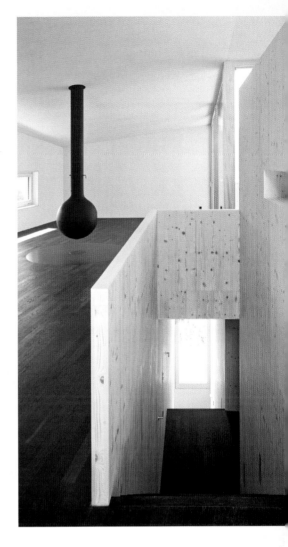

Accessed from the upper level, this home accommodates all the various functions on three levels that are sensitively embedded into a steep hillside. The seemingly simple building volume is skilfully sculpted with recesses such as the ground floor entrance or the roof level terrace that are carved out of the basic volume. The main stair steps down the slope in two long sections that echo the exterior topography inside.

Vom Eingang auf der obersten Ebene aus werden die drei Ebenen dieses in einem Steilhang eingebetteten Hauses betreten. Die scheinbar einfache Bauform wird bildhauerisch behandelt. Rücksprünge wie der Eingang im Erdgeschoss oder die Dachterrasse erscheinen so, als wären sie aus der soliden Hausmasse geschnitzt. Die Haupttreppe staffelt sich analog zum Hang und spiegelt somit die Topographie im Inneren.

153

COUNTRY / LAND	SWITZERLAND / SCHWEIZ	HOUSE NAME / BEZEICHNUNG DES HAUSES	FAMILY HOUSE, WALSER-ZUBLER
LOCATION (CITY/REGION) / LAGE (STADT/REGION)			WINTERTHUR
ARCHITECT / ARCHITEKT		BEAT ROTHEN YEAR OF COMPLETION / BAUJAHR	2005
PHOTOGRAPHER / FOTOGRAF		GASTON WICKY SQUARE FEET / QUADRAT METER	xxx
CITY AND COUNTRY ARCHITECT / STADT UND LAND ARCHITEKT			WINTERTHUR, SCHWEIZ
WEBSITE ARCHITECT / HOMEPAGE ARCHITEKT			WWW.ROTHEN-ARCHITEKT.COM

The building mass here was treated as a sculptural form composed of block-like parts that create a geometric composition that stands in marked contrast to the sloping site. To heighten this perception the first level cantilevers far out to create a covered terrace on the ground floor and the windows were set deep into the façade planes to intensify the play of shadow and light.

Die Baumasse hier wurde als eine skulpturale Form konzipiert, deren block-ähnliche Einzelteile eine geometrische Komposition schaffen, die in markantem Kontrast zur Hangtopografie steht. Um diesen Eindruck zu verstärken ließen die Architekten das Obergeschoss weit über die Terrasse im Erdgeschoss auskragen. Die Fenster wurden tief in die Fassadenebene gesetzt, um das Spiel von Licht und Schatten zu verstärken.

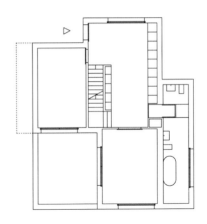

+0

MAISON D.
FRUNDGALLINA SA

COUNTRY / LAND	SWITZERLAND / SCHWEIZ	HOUSE NAME / BEZEICHNUNG DES HAUSES	MAISON D.
LOCATION (CITY/REGION) / LAGE (STADT/REGION)			NEUCHÂTEL
ARCHITECT / ARCHITEKT		FRUNDGALLINA SA YEAR OF COMPLETION / BAUJAHR	2004
PHOTOGRAPHER / FOTOGRAF		GASTON WICKY SQUARE FEET / QUADRAT METER	1614 / 150
CITY AND COUNTRY ARCHITECT / STADT UND LAND ARCHITEKT			NEUCHÂTEL, SCHWEIZ
WEBSITE ARCHITECT / HOMEPAGE ARCHITEKT			WWW.FRUNDGALLINA.CH

VILLA BLED
<u>OFIS ARHITEKTI</u>

A historic villa high above the mountain lake was completely restructured on the ground level with fully glazed, curved façade elements that create a stark contrast to the old structure. The handsome façades of the upper levels were carefully refurbished and seem to hover above the hyper-modern, transparent forms of the plinth level.

Eine historische, hoch über einem Gebirgssee gelegene Villa wurde im Erdgeschoss mit voll verglasten, gekrümmten Fassaden komplett umhüllt, um einen starken Kontrast zum alten Bauwerk herauszubilden. Die wohlproportionierten Fassaden der Obergeschosse des Altbaus wurden aufwendig instand gesetzt. Sie scheinen über den hyper-modernen, transparenten Formen des Erdgeschosses zu schweben.

The historic ground floor plan was completely altered. A spiral stair ramp is the focus of the interior composition. It winds up through the ground floor and offers a variety of visual interconnecting axes, both to the surrounding interior spaces and the exterior gardens and mountain landscape outside. The conventional plaster rendering of the historic villa is contrasted by wood and glass - the formative materials used throughout the interiors and exteriors of this astounding transformation.

Der historische Erdgeschoßgrundriss wurde komplett verändert. Eine spiralförmige Rampe bildet den Fokus der Komposition im Inneren. Sie windet sich hoch ins Obergeschoss und erschließt dabei vielfältige Durch- und Ausblicke, sowohl in die Innenräume, als auch auf die Gebirgslandschaft. Dem konventionellen Putz der Altbaufassaden werden Materialien wie Holz und Glas entgegengesetzt, um eine erstaunliche Transformation der vorgefundenen Gebäudesubstanz zu bewerkstelligen.

COUNTRY / LAND	SLOVENIA / SLOWENIEN	HOUSE NAME / BEZEICHNUNG DES HAUSES	VILLA BLED
LOCATION (CITY/REGION) / LAGE (STADT/REGION)		BLED
ARCHITECT / ARCHITEKT	OFIS ARHITEKTI	YEAR OF COMPLETION / BAUJAHR	2004
PHOTOGRAPHER / FOTOGRAF	TOMAZ GREGORIC	SQUARE FEET / QUADRAT METER	13773 / 1280
CITY AND COUNTRY ARCHITECT / STADT UND LAND ARCHITEKT		LJUBLJANA, SLOVENIA
WEBSITE ARCHITECT / HOMEPAGE ARCHITEKT		WWW.OFIS-A.SI

OFIS ARHITEKTI

LJUBLJANA
SLOVENIA / SLOWENIEN

Ofis arhitekti, based in Ljubljana, Slovenia was formed by partners Rok Oman (born 1970) and Spela Videcnik (born 1971) after they finished their studies at the Architectural Association in London and returned to Slowenia in 2000. They have since emerged as one of the most creative new firms to achieve notoriety in former Yugoslavia.

Their work is characterized by a fresh attitude toward architecture that is strengthened by a convincing command of materials and architectural detailing. In addition to residential works such as the project featured here they are working on projects that range in size from 30 – 50,000 square meters, including performing arts facilities, and projects focusing on global design issues.

Photo: Tomaz Gregovic

Ofis arhitekti, eine junge Architekturfirma aus Ljubljana, Slowenien, wurde von den Partnern Rok Oman (geboren 1970) und Spela Videcnik (born 1971) nach Abschluss ihrer gemeinsamen Studienzeit an der Architectural Association in London und Rückkehr nach Slowenien in 2000 gegründet. Seitdem gelten sie als eines der kreativsten jungen Architekturbüros aus dem Bereich des ehemaligen Jugoslawiens.

Ihre Arbeit zeichnen sich durch einen frischen Standpunkt zur Architektur aus, der durch den gekonnten Einsatz von Materialien und ausgeklügelten Architekturdetails verstärkt wird. Neben Aufträgen im Bereich Wohnungsbau bearbeiten sie verschiedenste Projekte zwischen 30 und 50.000 Quadratmeter Größe, die auch Kulturbauten und Projekte im Bereich des globalen Designs umfassen.

A two story plinth clad in stone forms a base for the ephemeral white cube of the cantilevered top level. The rectilinear building blocks are countered with organically shaped façade openings that frame views out to the surrounding landscape.

Ein zweigeschossiger, in Stein verkleideter Sockel bildet die Basis für den schwebenden weißen Kubus des ausgekragten Obergeschosses. Organisch anmutende Fassadenöffnungen umrahmen Blicke auf die umliegende Landschaft und mildern die rechtwinkligen Kanten der Baukörper.

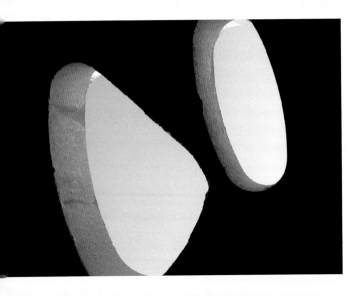

CAPECE VENANZI HOUSE
GIOVANNI VACCARINI

COUNTRY / LAND	ITALY / ITALIEN	HOUSE NAME / BEZEICHNUNG DES HAUSES	CAPECE VENANZI HOUSE
LOCATION (CITY/REGION) / LAGE (STADT/REGION)			GIULIANOVA TERAMO
ARCHITECT / ARCHITEKT	GIOVANNI VACCARINI	YEAR OF COMPLETION / BAUJAHR	2006
PHOTOGRAPHER / FOTOGRAF	xxx	SQUARE FEET / QUADRAT METER	1937 / 180
CITY AND COUNTRY ARCHITECT / STADT UND LAND ARCHITEKT			GUILIANOVA, ITALIEN
WEBSITE ARCHITECT / HOMEPAGE ARCHITEKT			WWW.GIOVANNIVACCARINI.IT

SWING HOUSE
LAURA ROCCA - ROCCATELIER ASSOCIATI

+0

Shifting axes are played off each other here to create dynamic interior spaces organised along a spatial spine. The double-height living/dining space inside is light-filled, welcoming, and informal. The solid massiveness of the ground floor walls is augmented by the light spindly quality of the steel framework that supports the gallery level and the roof planes slanting above.

Verschobene Achsen werden hier gegeneinander gespielt, um eine dynamische Kette von Innenräumen zu schaffen, die entlang eines räumlichen Rückgrats angelegt werden. Der zweigeschossige Eß- bzw. Wohnbereich strahlt in natürlichem Licht und wirkt einladend informell. Die solide Massivität der Erdgeschoßwände wird abgemildert durch das leichte Stahltragwerk, das sowohl die Galerieebene, als auch die schräge Dachkonstruktion darüber trägt.

163

COUNTRY / LAND	ITALY / ITALIEN	HOUSE NAME / BEZEICHNUNG DES HAUSES	SWING HOUSE
LOCATION (CITY/REGION) / LAGE (STADT/REGION)			VIMERCATE, RUGINELLO, MILAN
ARCHITECT / ARCHITEKT	LAURA ROCCA - ROCCATELIER ASSOCIATI	YEAR OF COMPLETION / BAUJAHR	2005
PHOTOGRAPHER / FOTOGRAF	E. SARDELLA & M. PECOL	SQUARE FEET / QUADRAT METER	3228 / 300
CITY AND COUNTRY ARCHITECT / STADT UND LAND ARCHITEKT			MONZA, ITALIA
WEBSITE ARCHITECT / HOMEPAGE ARCHITEKT			WWW.ROCCATELIER.IT

Archaic, local building traditions generated the forms of this house that at the same time emanates a timeless sense of modernity. Private courtyards are formed with exterior walls that remind one of those used for agricultural enclosures in the historic houses on Sardinia.

Archaische, lokale Bautraditionen gaben die Formen dieses Hauses vor, das zugleich eine zeitlose Modernität ausstrahlt. Private Höfe werden durch Außenmauern geschaffen, die an landwirtschaftliche Bauten der Umgebung erinnern.

PRIVATE BEACH HOUSE
ANTONIO CITTERIO AND PARTNERS

+1

The rooms on three sides of the house orient to these private exterior courtyard spaces while the seaside front opens out onto the view of the Mediterranean Sea.

Die Räume auf drei Seiten des Hauses orientieren sich zu diesen privaten Hofräumen während die zum Meer hin gelegene Front sich zum Blick auf das Mittelmeer öffnet.

COUNTRY / LAND	ITALY / ITALIEN	HOUSE NAME / BEZEICHNUNG DES HAUSES	PRIVATE BEACH
LOCATION (CITY/REGION) / LAGE (STADT/REGION)			SARDINIA
ARCHITECT / ARCHITEKT	ANTONIO CITTERIO AND PARTNERS	YEAR OF COMPLETION / BAUJAHR	2004
PHOTOGRAPHER / FOTOGRAF		LEO TORRI SQUARE FEET / QUADRAT METER	4842 / 450
CITY AND COUNTRY ARCHITECT / STADT UND LAND ARCHITEKT			MILANO, ITALIEN
WEBSITE ARCHITECT / HOMEPAGE ARCHITEKT			WWW.ANTONIOCITTERIOANDPARTNERS.IT

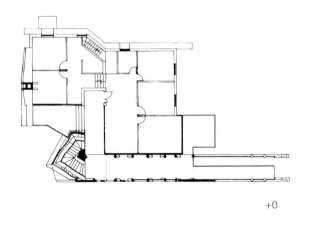

+0

The expressive potential of reinforced concrete was creatively explored in this project. A spine-like building mass rises up to the open stair tower and echoes the geography of the nearby hills. The individual, sculptural form stands out as a welcome and expressive departure from the dreary new houses that dominate in the surroundings.

Das Ausdruckspotential des Betons als Baumaterial wurde in diesem Bauwerk kreativ erschlossen. Eine rückgrat-ähnliche Baumasse erhebt sich zu einem Treppenturm hin und spiegelt die Struktur der nahen Hügel. Die eigenwillige, skulpturartige Form schafft einen willkommenen Kontrast zu den eintönigen neuen Häusern der Umgebung.

SINGLE-FAMILY HOUSE
<u>SOUTHCORNER</u>

COUNTRY / LAND	ITALY / ITALIEN	HOUSE NAME / BEZEICHNUNG DES HAUSES	SINGLE-FAMILY HOUSE
LOCATION (CITY/REGION) / LAGE (STADT/REGION)			ALTAVILLA SILENTINA, CAMPANIA
ARCHITECT / ARCHITEKT	SOUTHCORNER / ANTONIO CUONO E NELLA TARANTINO	YEAR OF COMPLETION / BAUJAHR	2003
PHOTOGRAPHER / FOTOGRAF	CUONO, TARANTINO, ELIA SICA	SQUARE FEET / QUADRAT METER	4541 / 422
CITY AND COUNTRY ARCHITECT / STADT UND LAND ARCHITEKT			AGROPOLI, ITALIA
WEBSITE ARCHITECT / HOMEPAGE ARCHITEKT			WWW.SOUTHCORNER.IT

MAISON L
ISABELLE RICHARD ET FREDERIC SCHOELLER

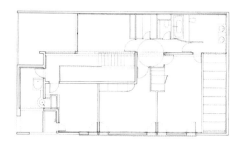

This home in a Parisian suburb is skilfully oriented about the living room space. By placing a glass strip above the floor and carving a light well to the upper level the architects created a sense of generosity and expansiveness on a tight suburban site parcel. The creative, intricate interweaving of spaces allows the home to seem much larger than it actually is.

Dieses Haus in einem Pariser Vorort wurde gekonnt um den zentralen Wohnraum angelegt. Mit einem Glasstreifen direkt oberhalb des Fußbodens und einem Luftraum zum Obergeschoss hin sprengten die Architekten das herkömmliche Maßstabsempfinden und schufen Großzügigkeit auf einem engen Vorstadtgrundstück.

169

COUNTRY / LAND	FRANCE / FRANKREICH	HOUSE NAME / BEZEICHNUNG DES HAUSES	MAISON L
LOCATION (CITY/REGION) / LAGE (STADT/REGION)			VANVES
ARCHITECT / ARCHITEKT	ISABELLE RICHARD ET FREDERIC SCHOELLER	YEAR OF COMPLETION / BAUJAHR	2000
PHOTOGRAPHER / FOTOGRAF		AGENCE SQUARE FEET / QUADRAT METER	2690 / 250
CITY AND COUNTRY ARCHITECT / STADT UND LAND ARCHITEKT			PARIS, FRANCE
WEBSITE ARCHITECT / HOMEPAGE ARCHITEKT			WWW.RICHARD-SCHOELLER.COM

MAISON S
ISABELLE RICHARD ET FREDERIC SCHOELLER

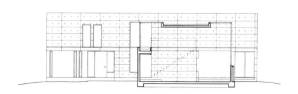

This home also documents the potential for integrating concrete in current residential designs. The gently undulating concrete wall surfaces were left exposed to create an effective merge of inside and outside spaces and interconnect the home with the natural setting of the Bretagne in a fresh architectural statement. The double-height entrance hall receives light from above to assume an almost sacred character.

Dieses Haus dokumentiert das Potential von Beton als Baumaterial für zeitgenössische Wohnlösungen. Die leicht gewellten Wandflächen aus Beton wurden sichtbar gelassen und schaffen eine effektive Verbindung zwischen dem Interieur und der felsigen Naturlandschaft der Bretagne. Die zweigeschossige Eingangshalle erhält durch das Oberlicht einen beinah sakral wirkenden Charakter.

COUNTRY / LAND	FRANCE / FRANKREICH HOUSE NAME / BEZEICHNUNG DES HAUSES	MAISON S
LOCATION (CITY/REGION) / LAGE (STADT/REGION)		CARANTEC
ARCHITECT / ARCHITEKT	ISABELLE RICHARD ET FREDERIC SCHOELLER YEAR OF COMPLETION / BAUJAHR	2000
PHOTOGRAPHER / FOTOGRAF	AGENCE SQUARE FEET / QUADRAT METER	4304 / 400
CITY AND COUNTRY ARCHITECT / STADT UND LAND ARCHITEKT		PARIS, FRANCE
WEBSITE ARCHITECT / HOMEPAGE ARCHITEKT		WWW.RICHARD-SCHOELLER.COM

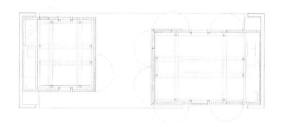

+0

Interspersed on a hillside between old trees, the architects here explored the possibilities for creating a simple, yet comfortable model for living in direct connection with nature. The warm climate allows the diverse spaces of the home to be contained in separate house cubes that are accessed via a common wooden deck. The use of wood throughout gives the architecture a sense of unity both in itself and in relation to the surrounding landscape.

Zwischen den alten Bäumen dieser Hügellage erforschten die Architekten die Möglichkeiten des einfachen, doch gemütlichen Wohnens inmitten der Natur. Das warme Klima erlaubt es, die diversen Räume des Hauses in getrennten Hauswürfeln unterzubringen, die über ein gemeinsames Holzdeck miteinander verbunden sind. Die durchgehende Verwendung von Holz verschafft der Architektur ein Gefühl von Einheit, sowohl für sich selbst, als auch im Bezug zur umliegenden Landschaft.

VILLA BOISSEAU
ATELIER
FERNANDEZ & SERRES

COUNTRY / LAND	FRANCE / FRANKREICH	HOUSE NAME / BEZEICHNUNG DES HAUSES	VILLA BOISSEAU
LOCATION (CITY/REGION) / LAGE (STADT/REGION)			BOULOURIS, SAINT-RAPHAËL
ARCHITECT / ARCHITEKT	ATELIER FERNANDEZ & SERRES	YEAR OF COMPLETION / BAUJAHR	2005
PHOTOGRAPHER / FOTOGRAF	JEAN-MICHEL LANDECY	SQUARE FEET / QUADRAT METER	473 / 44
CITY AND COUNTRY ARCHITECT / STADT UND LAND ARCHITEKT			AIX EN PROVENCE, FRANCE
WEBSITE ARCHITECT / HOMEPAGE ARCHITEKT			WWW.FERNANDEZ-SERRES.COM

VILLA CHALET
ATELIER
FERNANDEZ & SERRES

This mountain cabin offered the architects a chance to create a semi-rustic wooden exterior reminiscent of traditional Alpine farm buildings that is contrasted by the clear the white design vocabulary employed on the interior of the simple structure. Unhandled wood, prefab concrete panels and large plate glass window elements are the formative materials of the hillside retreat.

Diese Gebirgshütte bot den Architekten die Chance, eine rustikale Außenhülle aus Holz, die an ländlicher Alpinarchitektur erinnert, mit einer hellen, schlichten Formensprache im Inneren des einfachen Bauwerks zu kontrastieren. Unbehandeltes Holz, vorgefertigte Betonelemente und große Glaselemente sind die formgebenden Materialien dieses am Hang gelegenen Bauwerks.

173

COUNTRY / LAND	FRANCE / FRANKREICH	HOUSE NAME / BEZEICHNUNG DES HAUSES	VILLA CHALET
LOCATION (CITY/REGION) / LAGE (STADT/REGION)			LIEU DIT DU VIGON
ARCHITECT / ARCHITEKT	ATELIER FERNANDEZ & SERRES	YEAR OF COMPLETION / BAUJAHR	2004
PHOTOGRAPHER / FOTOGRAF	ATELIER FERNANDEZ & SERRES	SQUARE FEET / QUADRAT METER	2690 / 250
CITY AND COUNTRY ARCHITECT / STADT UND LAND ARCHITEKT			AIX EN PROVENCE, FRANCE
WEBSITE ARCHITECT / HOMEPAGE ARCHITEKT			WWW.FERNANDEZ-SERRES.COM

G.HOUSE
FRANK SALAMA

The tight urban site near Paris made it necessary to compact the building mass into a clear formal composition. A fully glazed plinth contains the living room and kitchen/dining areas and the bedrooms and private spaces hover above in a more closed building envelope. To allow as much light as possible into the living room the street-side wall behind the stair rising to the upper level was executed in matte glass.

Das beengte Grundstück unweit von Paris verlangte die kompakte Unterbringung der Raumbereiche in einer klaren Komposition. Das komplett verglaste Erdgeschoss beherbergt Wohnzimmer, Küche und Essbereich. Darüber schwebt der Schlafzimmertrakt in einem stärker abgeschlossenen Baukörper. Um ein Maximum an Licht in das Wohnzimmer zu führen wurde die straßenseitige Außenwand hinter der in das Obergeschoss führende Treppe in Milchglas ausgeführt.

COUNTRY / LAND	FRANCE / FRANKREICH	HOUSE NAME / BEZEICHNUNG DES HAUSES	G.HOUSE
LOCATION (CITY/REGION) / LAGE (STADT/REGION)			NEAR PARIS
ARCHITECT / ARCHITEKT	FRANK SALAMA	YEAR OF COMPLETION / BAUJAHR	2006
PHOTOGRAPHER / FOTOGRAF	HERVÉ ABBADIE	SQUARE FEET / QUADRAT METER	1582 / 147
CITY AND COUNTRY ARCHITECT / STADT UND LAND ARCHITEKT			PARIS, FRANCE
WEBSITE ARCHITECT / HOMEPAGE ARCHITEKT			XXX

Two building masses are juxtaposed here to create a convincing residential composition. The living room wing on the ground floor is inserted on a cross axis sliced across the bedroom wing on the upper level. Within the living room an upper level rises up to the deck level outside and showcases the central fireplace with its characteristic cone chimney.

Zwei Baumassen wurden hier ineinander geschachtelt, um eine überzeugende Wohnkomposition zu schaffen. Der Wohnraumflügel im Erdgeschoss durchschneidet den Schlafzimmerflügel im Obergeschoss in einer Querachse. Innerhalb des Wohnzimmers entstand eine Zwischenebene, die zur Terrassenebene führt und den Kamin mit dem charakteristischen Schornsteinkegel in den Mittelpunkt rückt.

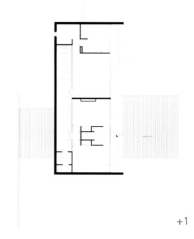

+1

CONSTRUCTION D'UNE MAISON
SCP BOYER PERCHERON ASSUS

COUNTRY / LAND	FRANCE / FRANKREICH	HOUSE NAME / BEZEICHNUNG DES HAUSES	CONSTRUCTION D'UNE MAISON
LOCATION (CITY/REGION) / LAGE (STADT/REGION)			MONTPELLIER
ARCHITECT / ARCHITEKT	SCP BOYER PERCHERON ASSUS	YEAR OF COMPLETION / BAUJAHR	2004
PHOTOGRAPHER / FOTOGRAF	DIDIER BOY DE LA TOUR	SQUARE FEET / QUADRAT METER	1937 / 180
CITY AND COUNTRY ARCHITECT / STADT UND LAND ARCHITEKT			MONTPELLIER, FRANCE
WEBSITE ARCHITECT / HOMEPAGE ARCHITEKT			XXX

BELLWE HOUSE
RCR ARANDA PIGEM VILALTA ARQUITECTES

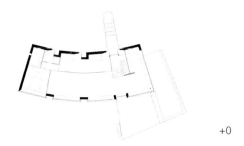

+0

The architects here created an uncompromising, individual house form that is enlivened by the dichotomy of white, closed walls on two sides and glazed walls on the other two sides. The circular segment of the plan makes the interior spaces seem larger than they are and allows the sun to shine into the spaces on its course all through the day.

Die Architekten schufen ein kompromissloses, individuelles Haus, das von der Spannung zwischen fast völlig verschlossenen und verglasten Wänden belebt wird. Der auf ein Kreissegment basierende Grundriss schafft es, die Räume größer wirken zu lassen und die Sonne im Laufe des Tages gekonnt durch das Hausinnere zu leiten.

COUNTRY / LAND	SPAIN / SPANIEN	HOUSE NAME / BEZEICHNUNG DES HAUSES	BELLWE HOUSE
LOCATION (CITY/REGION) / LAGE (STADT/REGION)			LES PRESS, GIRONA
ARCHITECT / ARCHITEKT	RCR ARANDA PIGEM VILALTA ARQUITECTES	YEAR OF COMPLETION / BAUJAHR	2001
PHOTOGRAPHER / FOTOGRAF	EUGENI PONS	SQUARE FEET / QUADRAT METER	2808 / 261
CITY AND COUNTRY ARCHITECT / STADT UND LAND ARCHITEKT			OLOT, GIRONA, ESPANA
WEBSITE ARCHITECT / HOMEPAGE ARCHITEKT			WWW.RCRARQUITECTES.ES

A seemingly simple, symmetrical floor plan reveals itself to be an amazingly refined and thoughtful statement on austerity and courageous design. Closed façade surfaces clad in grey-painted steel mesh stand in heightened contrast to the completely glazed transparency of the central living room space. Two spatial cavities are recessed into the building mass to allow light into the bedrooms located on the house ends.

Ein scheinbar einfacher, symmetrischer Grundriss entpuppt sich als ein erstaunlich raffiniertes und durchdachtes Statement zum Thema Sachlichkeit und als äußerst mutiges Design. Geschlossene Fassadenflächen, verhüllt in grau beschichteten Streckmetallpanellen, stehen in erhöhtem Kontrast zur komplett verglasten Transparenz des zentralen Wohnzimmerraumes. Zwei Raumschneisen wurden aus der Baumasse gehöhlt, um Licht in die Schlafzimmer an den Hausenden zu führen.

M-LIDIA HOUSE
RCR ARANDA PIGEM VILALTA
ARQUITECTES

The entrance sequence into the house occurs via one of these recesses where an exterior stair leads up to the entrance from a lower level where the garage is located. The kitchen/living room space is united within the open plan with the kitchen arrayed along the long back wall of the space. Movable partition elements allow separating the kitchen niche from the main space as necessary. Roll-down blinds integrated into the ceiling similarly allow both visual separation between the adjacent bedrooms and the central space and for protection from views and sun on the exterior.

Die Erschließung des Hauses verläuft über eine dieser Schneisen über eine Treppe, die von der unteren Ebene zum Eingang führt. Wohnraum und Küche wurden als eine zusammenhängende Fläche konzipiert. Die Küche ist entlang der Längswand angeordnet und kann durch bewegliche Wandelemente abgetrennt werden. Rolljalousien wurden in die Decken eingebaut um eine visuelle Trennung zwischen den Schlafzimmern und dem Wohnraum und Sicht- und Sonnenschutz der verglasten Flächen zu gewährleisten.

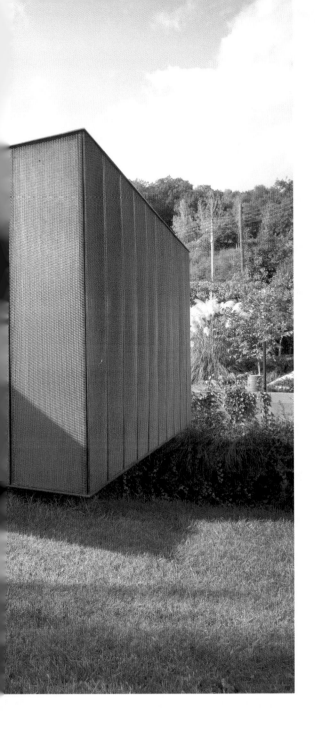

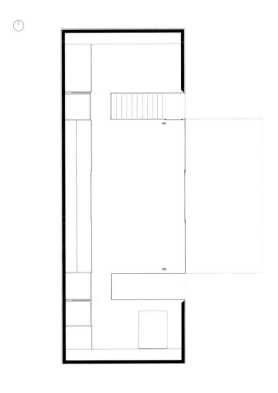

+0

COUNTRY / LAND	SPAIN / SPANIEN	HOUSE NAME / BEZEICHNUNG DES HAUSES	M-LIDIA HOUSE
LOCATION (CITY/REGION) / LAGE (STADT/REGION)			MONTAGUT, GIRONA
ARCHITECT / ARCHITEKT	RCR ARANDA PIGEM VILALTA ARQUITECTES	YEAR OF COMPLETION / BAUJAHR	2003
PHOTOGRAPHER / FOTOGRAF	EUGENI PONS	SQUARE FEET / QUADRAT METER	1840 / 171
CITY AND COUNTRY ARCHITECT / STADT UND LAND ARCHITEKT			OLOT, GIRONA, ESPANA
WEBSITE ARCHITECT / HOMEPAGE ARCHITEKT			WWW.RCRARQUITECTES.ES

HOUSE BLACKSMITH / HAIRDRESSER
RCR ARANDA PIGEM
VILALTA ARQUITECTES

In stark contrast to the traditional forms of the surrounding suburban, country houses the architects opted for creation of a simple white house cube that is modulated by an elongated copper-clad volume inserted on the upper level. This volume imbues the form with clear horizontality and interconnects the house with the ground plane of the rural valley location. Inside, views out onto the rolling green hills are framed by generously dimensioned window strips.

In deutlichem Kontrast zu den traditionellen Formen der ländlichen Vororthäuser entschieden sich die Architekten für einen einfachen, weißen Hauskubus, der durch einen in Kupfer gehüllten, in das Obergeschoss eingeschobenen Körper gegliedert wird. Dieser Körper verstärkt die Horizontalität des Bauwerkes und schafft somit auch eine Korrespondenz zur Topografie Profil des Tales. Im Inneren werden Blicke auf die grünen Hügel durch großzügig bemessene Fensterbänder eingerahmt.

COUNTRY / LAND	SPAIN / SPANIEN	HOUSE NAME / BEZEICHNUNG DES HAUSES	HOUSE BLACKSMITH
LOCATION (CITY/REGION) / LAGE (STADT/REGION)			LA CANYA, GIRONA
ARCHITECT / ARCHITEKT	RCR ARANDA PIGEM VILALTA ARQUITECTES	YEAR OF COMPLETION / BAUJAHR	2000
PHOTOGRAPHER / FOTOGRAF		EUGENI PONS	SQUARE FEET / QUADRAT METER	3056 / 284
CITY AND COUNTRY ARCHITECT / STADT UND LAND ARCHITEKT			OLOT, GIRONA, ESPANA
WEBSITE ARCHITECT / HOMEPAGE ARCHITEKT			WWW.RCRARQUITECTES.ES

The tight suburban site dictated a creative solution. By creating horizontal joint strips in the facades the architects create the impression that this is a normal two-story home. But by hollowing out the site and arraying the section they created a four-story home. Service rooms, the garage and bathrooms are located on the lowest sub-street level, the living room with adjacent pool and the master bedroom is on the ground floor and the shimmering white central tower rises up another two levels to contain additional bedrooms and office spaces.

Das beengte Vorstadtgrundstück forderte von den Architekten eine kreative Lösung. Horizontale Fassadenstreifen lassen den Eindruck entstehen, dass es sich um ein zweigeschossiges Haus handelt. Doch durch aushöhlen des Grundstückes und einen intelligenten Gebäudeschnitt wurden hier vier Wohnebenen geschaffen. Die Garage sowie Wellnessbereiche befinden sich unter Straßenniveau im Tiefgeschoss, darüber befindet sich das EG mit Wohnraum und anschließendem Pool.

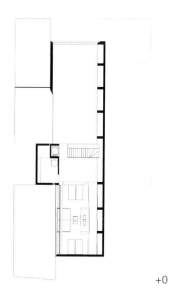

+0

PUBLISHER HOUSE

RCR ARANDA PIGEM VILALTA ARQUITECTES

COUNTRY / LAND	SPAIN / SPANIEN	HOUSE NAME / BEZEICHNUNG DES HAUSES	PUBLISHER HOUSE
LOCATION (CITY/REGION) / LAGE (STADT/REGION)			SPAIN
ARCHITECT / ARCHITEKT	RCR ARANDA PIGEM VILALTA ARQUITECTES	YEAR OF COMPLETION / BAUJAHR	2000
PHOTOGRAPHER / FOTOGRAF		EUGENI PONS SQUARE FEET / QUADRAT METER	5864 / 545
CITY AND COUNTRY ARCHITECT / STADT UND LAND ARCHITEKT			OLOT, GIRONA, ESPANA
WEBSITE ARCHITECT / HOMEPAGE ARCHITEKT			WWW.RCRARQUITECTES.ES

RCR – ARANDA PIGEM VILALTA ARQUITECTES

186

Rafael Aranda, Carme Pigem and Ramon Vilalta finished their studies in Architecture at Escuela Técnica Superior de Arquitectura del Vallès in 1987. In 1988 they began their own studio in their birthplace, the northern Spanish town of Olot. Their work displays a commitment to architecture as an art form that must also accommodate human needs. They often create abstract forms that skillfully form sculptural compositions.

These forms are tailored to the region, especially to the stark sunlight that bathes their buildings in warmth and light. The sculptural quality of these building compositions is dramatically heightened through a consequential reduction of form. Additionally, RCR's work demonstrates strong compositional qualities that result from clear formulation of the design idea in conceptual sketches that form the basis for the design and building execution process.

Photo: Hisao Suziki

Rafael Aranda, Carme Pigem und Ramon Vilalta haben ihr Studium der Architektur 1987 an der Escuela Técnica Superior de Arquitectura del Vallès abgeschlossen. Ein Jahr später gründeten sie ihr eigenes Büro in ihrer Geburtsstadt Olot im Norden Spaniens. Ihre Arbeit bezeugt ein Verständnis von Architektur als Kunstform, die auch die Bedürfnisse von Menschen berücksichtigen muss. Oftmals kreieren sie abstrakte Formen und setzten sie zu skulpturartigen Kompositionen zusammen.

Diese Formen stehen im klaren Bezug zur Region und ihrem scheinbar immer währenden Sonnelicht. Die Reduktion der Formen führt zu dramatischen, skulpturartigen Baukompositionen. Zudem besitzen ihre Arbeiten starke kompositorische Qualitäten, die auf einer klaren Formulierung der Entwurfsidee in Skizzen und ihrer konsequenten Umsetzung beruhen.

Powerful, cube-like forms characterize the house complex with its white walls that stand in strong contrast to the earthen hues of the landscape. Nonetheless, the home seems in tune with the natural habitat that is dominated by the expansive view of the sea far below.

Kraftvolle, kubische Formen kennzeichnen den Hauskomplex, der mit seinen weißen Wänden im starken Kontrast zu den Erdtönen der Landschaft steht. Dennoch wirkt der Bau im Einklang mit der Umgebung, die vom weiten Blick auf das tief unten gelegene Meer geprägt wird.

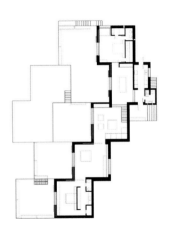

+1

CASA NA XEMENA
RAMON ESTEVE ESTUDIO DE ARQUITECTURA

COUNTRY / LAND	SPAIN / SPANIEN	HOUSE NAME / BEZEICHNUNG DES HAUSES	CASA NA XEMENA
LOCATION (CITY/REGION) / LAGE (STADT/REGION)			IBIZA
ARCHITECT / ARCHITEKT	RAMON ESTEVE ESTUDIO DE ARQUITECTURA	YEAR OF COMPLETION / BAUJAHR	2003
PHOTOGRAPHER / FOTOGRAF	RAMON ESTEVE	SQUARE FEET / QUADRAT METER	5111 / 475
CITY AND COUNTRY ARCHITECT / STADT UND LAND ARCHITEKT			VALENCIA, ESPAÑA
WEBSITE ARCHITECT / HOMEPAGE ARCHITEKT			WWW.RAMONESTEVE.COM

BELOURA HOUSE
A-LDK

+0

The hillside location of this house allowed creation of four levels. A large indoor pool space and garage are located on the lower level. The living room was foreseen with a gallery to connect the ground floor with the first floor. To give scale to the mass, different materials were used to clad the cube-like exterior forms. Aluminum panels stand in cool contrast to wood panels and white rendering. The same palette of materials is continued inside in the metal railings, wood floors and smooth white wall surfaces.

Die Hanglage erlaubte die Schaffung von vier Wohnebenen. Eine große Schwimmhalle befindet sich im Untergeschoss neben der Garage. Das Wohnzimmer wurde mit einer Galerie ausgestattet, die das EG mit dem 1. OG verbindet. Um die Masse des Hauses optisch zu gliedern wurden verschiedene Fassadematerialien als Verkleidung der kubusartigen Formen verwendet. Die Aluminiumelemente, Holzpanelle und ruhigen Putzflächen setzten sich im Inneren bei den Geländern, Fußböden und Wandflächen fort.

COUNTRY / LAND	PORTUGAL	HOUSE NAME / BEZEICHNUNG DES HAUSES	BELOURA HOUSE
LOCATION (CITY/REGION) / LAGE (STADT/REGION)			QUINTA DA BELOURA, SINTRA
ARCHITECT / ARCHITEKT	A-LDK	YEAR OF COMPLETION / BAUJAHR	2004
PHOTOGRAPHER / FOTOGRAF	RUI MORAIS DE SOUSA	SQUARE FEET / QUADRAT METER	6456 / 600
CITY AND COUNTRY ARCHITECT / STADT UND LAND ARCHITEKT			LISBON, PORTUGAL
WEBSITE ARCHITECT / HOMEPAGE ARCHITEKT			WWW.A-LDK-STUDIO.COM

190

The imminent material of the region – field stone – was used to create this small house that seems at once of the land and austerely modern. While the simple rectangular forms echo the traditional farmhouses and agricultural buildings found in the vicinity the interiors of this home have a light-filled, modern ambience that seems to be light years beyond the dank old farmhouses nearby.

Das vorherrschende Material dieser Region – Feldstein – wurde verwendet um sich hier gleichzeitig dem regionalen Stil anzupassen und eine ausgeprägte Modernität zu erreichen. Obwohl die einfachen Formen die lokale Bauweise adaptieren, herrscht im Inneren des Hauses ein helles, freundliches Ambiente, das Lichtjahre von den feuchten alten Bauernhäusern der Umgebung entfernt ist.

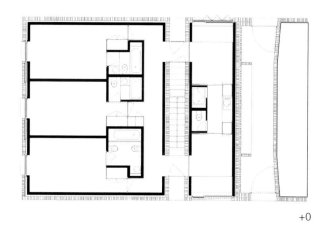

+0

CASA DO LOIVO
CHRISTINA GUEDES

COUNTRY / LAND	PORTUGAL	HOUSE NAME / BEZEICHNUNG DES HAUSES	CASA DO LOIVO
LOCATION (CITY/REGION) / LAGE (STADT/REGION)			VILA NOVA DE CERVEIRA
ARCHITECT / ARCHITEKT		CHRISTINA GUEDES YEAR OF COMPLETION / BAUJAHR	2002
PHOTOGRAPHER / FOTOGRAF		CRISTIAN RICHTERS SQUARE FEET / QUADRAT METER	2798 / 260
CITY AND COUNTRY ARCHITECT / STADT UND LAND ARCHITEKT			PORTO, PORTUGAL
WEBSITE ARCHITECT / HOMEPAGE ARCHITEKT			WWW.MENOSEMAIS.COM

This house's organization reacts precisely to the given qualities of the site with its dune-like topography. A private wing of rooms with bedrooms and bathrooms was embedded into the dune landscape. The gently slanting glazed box form of the living space rises above this plinth and opens to the sea beyond.

Die Organisation des Hauses geht präzise auf die Gegebenheiten des Ortes und die Topographie ein. Der private Flügel mit Schlaf- und Badezimmern wurde in die Dünenlandschaft eingebettet. Darüber erhebt sich die schräg ansteigende, sich zum Meer hin öffnende Glaskiste des Wohnbereiches.

CASA DE OFIR
JOSÉ FERNANDO GONÇALVES
CHRISTINA GUEDES

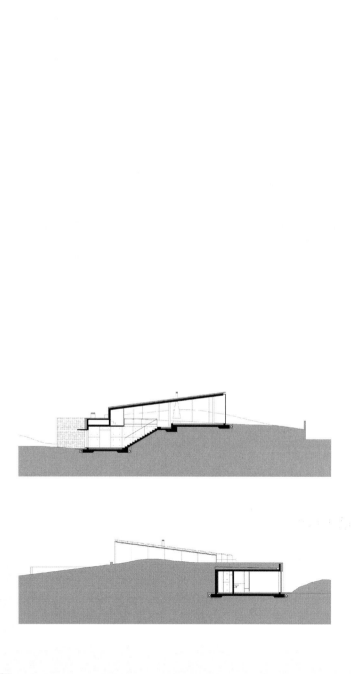

This creative deployment of functions in two wings minimizes environmental impact. Walkers on the nearby beach scarcely notice the house and the inhabitants enjoy an especially close interconnection to the natural surroundings. In-situ concrete, slate, marble, wood, steel, and glass form a palette of materials that harmonizes well with the natural surroundings.

Der Eingriff in die Natur wird durch diesen kreativen Umgang mit den Gebäudemassen minimiert. So bemerken Strandgänger das Haus kaum und die Bewohner leben in Nähe zum umliegenden Naturraum. Sichtbeton, Schiefer, Marmor, Holz, Stahl und Glas bilden eine Materialienpalette, die in Harmonie zur umliegenden Landschaft steht.

COUNTRY / LAND	**PORTUGAL** HOUSE NAME / BEZEICHNUNG DES HAUSES	**CASA DE OFIR**
LOCATION (CITY/REGION) / LAGE (STADT/REGION)		**OFRI / ATLANTIC COAST**
ARCHITECT / ARCHITEKT	JOSÉ FERNANDO GONÇALVES, CHRISTINA GUEDES YEAR OF COMPLETION / BAUJAHR	**2003**
PHOTOGRAPHER / FOTOGRAF	ALESSANDRA CHEMOLLO SQUARE FEET / QUADRAT METER	**2798 / 260**
CITY AND COUNTRY ARCHITECT / STADT UND LAND ARCHITEKT		**PORTO, PORTUGAL**
WEBSITE ARCHITECT / HOMEPAGE ARCHITEKT		**WWW.MENOSEMAIS.COM**

196

The steep hillside site inspired the architect to distribute the house functions down the slope and interconnect them with a stair that connects the multiple levels. Stepping the building mass down the slope allows for multiple windows that bring light into every level. The exterior walls are made of exposed concrete that effectively translates the surrounding rocky landscape into a new architectural solution.

Der Steilhang inspirierte den Architekten dazu, die Hausfunktionen entlang des Hangs anzuordnen und mit einer dem Hang folgenden Treppe zu verbinden. Die abgestuften Bauformen erlauben die Anordnung von zahlreichen Fenstern, über die das Innere des Hauses großzügig belichtet wird. Die Außenwände wurden in Sichtbeton ausgeführt, einem Material, das die felsige Umgebung gekonnt in eine neue Architektursprache übersetzt.

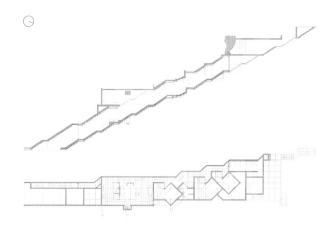

CASA TOLÓ
ÁLVARO LEITE SIZA VIERA

COUNTRY / LAND	**PORTUGAL**	HOUSE NAME / BEZEICHNUNG DES HAUSES	**CASA TOLÓ**
LOCATION (CITY/REGION) / LAGE (STADT/REGION)			**ALVITE**
ARCHITECT / ARCHITEKT	**ÁLVARO LEITE SIZA VIERA**	YEAR OF COMPLETION / BAUJAHR	**2005**
PHOTOGRAPHER / FOTOGRAF	**FERNANDO GUERRA**	SQUARE FEET / QUADRAT METER	**1270 / 118**
CITY AND COUNTRY ARCHITECT / STADT UND LAND ARCHITEKT			**PORTO, PORTUGAL**
WEBSITE ARCHITECT / HOMEPAGE ARCHITEKT			**XXX**

By carefully integrating the building mass into the hillside site the architects created a composition that reminds of the simplicity and austerity of the archaic architecture found in Greece and the eastern Mediterranean region. Several building wings are dispersed across a plateau embedded into the dry hillside. The main house is stone clad and rises two levels up from the plateau whereas a dining pavilion with an outdoor dining space is housed in a white plaster enclosure.

Durch das vorsichtige Integrieren der Baumasse in den Hang schufen die Architekten eine Komposition, die an die Monumentalität der archaischen Architektur im östlichen Mittelmeerraum erinnert. Diverse Flügel und Bauteile wurden auf einem Plateau angeordnet, das in den Hang eingebettet wurde. Das Haupthaus wurde mit Stein verkleidet und erhebt sich zweigeschossig aus dem Plateau. Der Küchenpavillon daneben wurde in weißem Putz ausgeführt und mit einem Essplatz im Freien ausgestattet.

KRATIR
DECAARCHITECTURE

A stair between these structures leads down to a hillside path that accesses a separate retreat space located further down the mountain. A separate guest house located on the central plateau forms a spatial border for the plaza-like space with its pool that extends across the entire length of the plateau to cool the interior and exterior spaces. Especially thick walls were constructed and the buildings were partially embedded in the hillside to protect them from the brutal summer heat that prevails in this region.

Eine Treppe zwischen den beiden Bauteilen führt den Hang hinab zu einem in den Hang eingebetteten Rückzugsraum. Ein separates Gästehaus bildet eine Raumkante am anderen Ende des Plateaus. Dort befindet sich eine lang gestreckte Poolanlage, die kühlende Luft für die Außen- und Innenräume heranschafft. Besonders dicke Wände wurden vorgesehen, um sie vor der brutalen Sommerhitze der Region zu schützen.

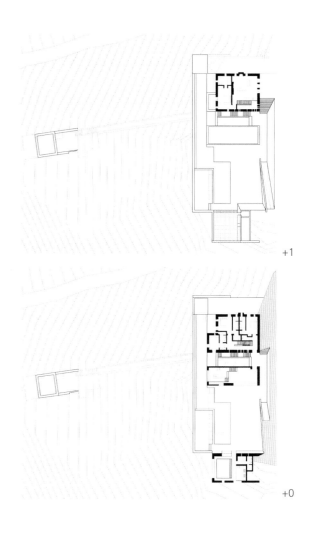

+1

+0

COUNTRY / LAND	GREECE / GRIECHENLAND	HOUSE NAME / BEZEICHNUNG DES HAUSES	KRATIR
LOCATION (CITY/REGION) / LAGE (STADT/REGION)			ANTIPAROS
ARCHITECT / ARCHITEKT		DECAARCHITECTURE YEAR OF COMPLETION / BAUJAHR	2004
PHOTOGRAPHER / FOTOGRAF		KYLE JAMES GUDSELL SQUARE FEET / QUADRAT METER	6133 / 570
CITY AND COUNTRY ARCHITECT / STADT UND LAND ARCHITEKT			ATHEN, GREECE
WEBSITE ARCHITECT / HOMEPAGE ARCHITEKT			XXX

After years of destruction and war a new generation of architects has set itself to the task of rebuilding Beirut and Lebanon to its former splendor. The intelligent floor plan of this home creates a spatial focus by stepping down the living room space three steps. A connecting hall extends out to the garden terrace to form a semi enclosed private outdoor space. Glossy white panels make the walls and the house itself seem like furniture pieces

Nach Jahren der Zerstörung und des Kriegs hat sich eine neue Architektengeneration die Restauration des ehemaligen Glanzes von Beirut zum Ziel gesetzt. Der intelligente Grundriss dieses Hauses erzeugt einen räumlichen Fokus durch die Absenkung des Wohnraums um drei Stufen. Ein Verbindungsgang auf der oberen Ebene erstreckt sich zur Terrasse und bildet dort einen geschützten Außenraum. Glänzend weiße Wandpanelle verschaffen den Eindruck als wären Haus und Wände Möbelstücke.

NBK RESIDENCE
BERNARD KHOURY

COUNTRY / LAND	LEBANON / LIBANON	HOUSE NAME / BEZEICHNUNG DES HAUSES	NBK RESIDENCE
LOCATION (CITY/REGION) / LAGE (STADT/REGION)			LEBANON
ARCHITECT / ARCHITEKT		BERNARD KHOURY	YEAR OF COMPLETION / BAUJAHR	2000
PHOTOGRAPHER / FOTOGRAF		BERNARD KHOURY ARCHITECTS	SQUARE FEET / QUADRAT METER	1722 / 160
CITY AND COUNTRY ARCHITECT / STADT UND LAND ARCHITEKT			BEIRUT, LEBANON
WEBSITE ARCHITECT / HOMEPAGE ARCHITEKT			WWW.BERNARDKHOURY.COM

M.HOUSE
ADA KARMI-MELAMEDE

+0

The street-side façade with its protected entrance forecourt is largely closed with small windows. A rounded, vertical tower element in the corner marks the entrance door. The garden façade is mostly glazed with elegant metal windows that allow ample light inside and open out to the garden patio.

Die Straßenfront mit dem geschützten Eingangsvorhof ist recht verschlossen und weist nur kleine Fensteröffnungen auf. Ein abgerundeter Turm in der Ecke markiert den Eingang. Die Gartenfassade hingegen ist weitgehend mit eleganten Metallfenstern versehen, die viel Licht ins Innere führen und den Blick auf den Garten eröffnen.

COUNTRY / LAND	ISRAEL	HOUSE NAME / BEZEICHNUNG DES HAUSES	M.HOUSE
LOCATION (CITY/REGION) / LAGE (STADT/REGION)			TEL-AVIV
ARCHITECT / ARCHITEKT		ADA KARMI-MELAMEDE YEAR OF COMPLETION / BAUJAHR	2003
PHOTOGRAPHER / FOTOGRAF		TAL KARMI SQUARE FEET / QUADRAT METER	2700 / 251
CITY AND COUNTRY ARCHITECT / STADT UND LAND ARCHITEKT			TEL-AVIV, ISRAEL
WEBSITE ARCHITECT / HOMEPAGE ARCHITEKT			WWW.ADAKARMIMELAMADE.COM

Working within the oeuvre of Modernism the architect here creates a generous light-filled quality that further develops and redefines the Modern architecture propagated by architects who immigrated to Israel over 60 years ago. Horizontal window strips, elegant metal window frames, and white plaster surfaces inside and out are the hallmarks of this timeless architecture.

Mit den Mitteln der klassischen Moderne arbeitend schafft die Architektin hier eine helle Großzügigkeit, welche die in den 1930er Jahren nach Israel gelangte Moderne weiterentwickelt und neu definiert. Horizontal lagernde Fensterstreifen, elegante Metallfensterrahmen und weiße Putzflächen im Inneren und Äußeren kennzeichnen diese zeitlose Architektursprache.

G.HOUSE
ADA KARMI-MELAMEDE

COUNTRY / LAND	ISRAEL	HOUSE NAME / BEZEICHNUNG DES HAUSES	G.HOUSE
LOCATION (CITY/REGION) / LAGE (STADT/REGION)			TEL-AVIV
ARCHITECT / ARCHITEKT		ADA KARMI-MELAMEDE	YEAR OF COMPLETION / BAUJAHR	2005
PHOTOGRAPHER / FOTOGRAF		ARDON BAR-HAMA	SQUARE FEET / QUADRAT METER	3500 / 325
CITY AND COUNTRY ARCHITECT / STADT UND LAND ARCHITEKT			TEL-AVIV, ISRAEL
WEBSITE ARCHITECT / HOMEPAGE ARCHITEKT			WWW.ADAKARMIMELAMADE.COM

Distributing the spaces of this house on three levels opened
up the possibility to create a generous two-level gallery
that interconnects the kitchen/dining area on the ground
floor with the main living room space on the first level. The
curving wall shell of the living/dining area extends up to the
ceiling of the first level to form a dynamic enclosure for the
spacious composition.

Die Verteilung der Nutzungen auf drei Ebenen eröffnete
die Möglichkeit, eine zweigeschossige Halle auszubilden,
welche den Koch-/Essbereich im EG mit dem Wohnsaal
im 1. OG verbindet. Die gekrümmte Wandschale des Ess-
/Wohnbereiches erstreckt sich bis zur Decke unter dem 2.
OG und schafft eine dynamische Raumbegrenzung für die
großzügige Komposition.

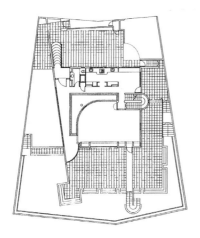

+0

K.HOUSE
ADA KARMI-MELAMEDE

COUNTRY / LAND	ISRAEL	HOUSE NAME / BEZEICHNUNG DES HAUSES	K.HOUSE
LOCATION (CITY/REGION) / LAGE (STADT/REGION)			TEL-AVIV
ARCHITECT / ARCHITEKT	ADA KARMI-MELAMEDE	YEAR OF COMPLETION / BAUJAHR	2002
PHOTOGRAPHER / FOTOGRAF	TAL KARMI	SQUARE FEET / QUADRAT METER	3800 / 353
CITY AND COUNTRY ARCHITECT / STADT UND LAND ARCHITEKT			TEL-AVIV, ISRAEL
WEBSITE ARCHITECT / HOMEPAGE ARCHITEKT			WWW.ADAKARMIMELAMADE.COM

The warm climate allowed separating the spaces of this house into two wings that are connected by a spacious colonnade that also serves to create a spatial barrier to the neighbouring site. The buildings define a private courtyard garden space with tropical vegetation onto which all major rooms – such as the living/dining room in the front wing and bedroom/studio spaces in the back wing – are oriented.

Das warme Klima erlaubte es, die diversen Räume dieses Hauses in zwei Flügeln unterzubringen, die durch eine Kolonnade miteinander verbunden werden, die eine schützende Begrenzung zum Nachbargrundstück herstellt. Die Bauten definieren einen privaten Hof zu dem sich alle Haupträume des Hauses, wie der Wohn-/Essbereich im vorderen Flügel und die Schlaf- und Arbeitszimmer im hinteren Flügel – orientieren.

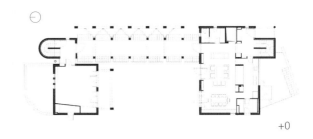

⊖

+0

L-2 HOUSE
SCHOCKEN ASSAYAG
ARCHITECTS

COUNTRY / LAND	ISRAEL	HOUSE NAME / BEZEICHNUNG DES HAUSES	L-2 HOUSE
LOCATION (CITY/REGION) / LAGE (STADT/REGION)			JERUSALEM
ARCHITECT / ARCHITEKT	SCHOCKEN ASSAYAG ARCHITECTS	YEAR OF COMPLETION / BAUJAHR	2002
PHOTOGRAPHER / FOTOGRAF	YAKI ASSAYAG	SQUARE FEET / QUADRAT METER	7532 / 700
CITY AND COUNTRY ARCHITECT / STADT UND LAND ARCHITEKT			JERUSALEM, ISRAEL
WEBSITE ARCHITECT / HOMEPAGE ARCHITEKT			WWW.SCHOCKEN-ARCHITECTS.COM

Pearl Bay House - Yzerfontein, South Africa - Stefan Antoni Olmesdahl Truen Architects - Photographer Stefan Antoni

AFRICA / AFRIKA

225 • 218-224

214, 230 • 226

Situated at Constantia Nek, on the upper slopes of the Vlakkenberg, a former livestock farm was redeveloped into a small scale vineyard with a main residence, a meditation pavilion, and a guest cottage. The physical and conceptual centre of the main residence house is the double volume kitchen and dining-family room, the 'heart of the house' around which all the external courtyards and the various living and bedroom functions gravitate. The intention was to depart entirely from an architecture of punctured walls with attached roof and pursue another type of composition altogether. 'Floating elements' are combined to create a unified whole. This strategy was pursued to erode the solidity of the 'dwelling' and allow the landscape to dominate.

Eine ehemalige Rinderfarm, die am oberen Bereich des Vlakkenbergs gelegene Constantia Nek, wurde in ein kleines Weingut mit Haupthaus, einem Meditationspavillon und einem Gästehaus umgewandelt. Die zweigeschossige Halle des Wohn-, Koch- und Essraumes bildet das physische und konzeptionelle Zentrum des Haupthauses. Um diese Halle gruppieren sich die Höfe, Wohnräume und Schlafbereiche. Der Entwurfsansatz sah vor, sich ganz von massiven Lochfassaden zu lösen. „Schwebende Elemente" werden zu einem einheitlichen Ganzen zusammengeführt. Angestrebt wurde die Auflösung der herkömmlichen Solidität des „Hauses" und somit einen Verzahnung der Räume mit der umliegenden Landschaft.

BEAU CONSTANCE
<u>METROPOLIS</u>

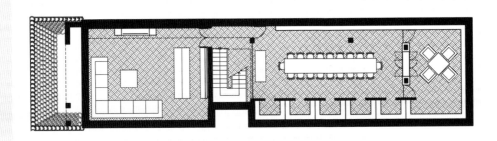

+0

216

The meditation pavilion comprises a space for individual and small group activities (such as yoga), a brine pool, a sauna, and a changing area. The design intention was to create a harmonious space in total contact with the surrounding beautiful landscape, but at the same time to maintain a serene centre of calm & containment. The visitor's cottage is sited on a narrow platform with spectacular views of the valley and mountains all round. A grove of well developed trees shields it from the house and the pavilion.

Der Meditationspavillon schafft einen Raum für Einzel- und Gruppenaktivitäten (wie Yoga) und beherbergt zudem ein Salzwasserbecken, eine Sauna und einen Umkleidebereich. Hier ist ein besonders harmonischer Raum in unmittelbarem Kontakt zur Natur entstanden. Das Gästehaus steht auf einer schmalen Plattform und verfügt über Ausblicke ins Tal und auf die umliegenden Berge. Ein Hain mit alten Bäumen formt einen Puffer zwischen Gästehaus und Haupthaus bzw. dem Meditationspavillon.

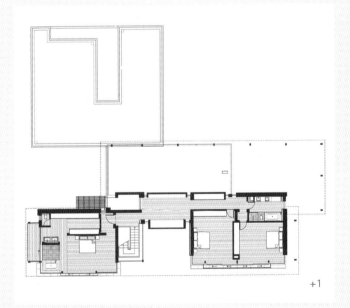

+1

COUNTRY / LAND	SOUTH AFRICA / SÜDAFRIKA	HOUSE NAME / BEZEICHNUNG DES HAUSES		BEAU CONSTANCE
LOCATION (CITY/REGION) / LAGE (STADT/REGION)				CAPE TOWN
ARCHITECT / ARCHITEKT		METROPOLIS	YEAR OF COMPLETION / BAUJAHR	2004
PHOTOGRAPHER / FOTOGRAF		WIELAND GLEICH	SQUARE FEET / QUADRAT METER	9684 / 900
CITY AND COUNTRY ARCHITECT / STADT UND LAND ARCHITEKT				CAPE TOWN, SOUTH AFRICA
WEBSITE ARCHITECT / HOMEPAGE ARCHITEKT				WWW.METROPOLISDESIGN.CO.ZA

HOUSE STEYN

THOMAS GOUWS
ARCHITECTS

Situated east of Pretoria, the house nestles on a rocky outcrop on a generous, densely vegetated plot. Barn-like masonry structures are grouped around a courtyard and open outward towards views and private enclaves claimed from the landscape. Sheet metal roofs with deep overhangs are supported on articulated steel and timber columns and are often separated from solid planes with substantial glazing. Taking inspiration from its context, the volumes, materials and details are assembled sensitively and simply, reflecting the origins of the owners and reinterpreting the spirit of South African rural architecture.

Das östlich von Pretoria gelegene Haus schmiegt sich an einen felsigen Hang auf einem großen, dicht bewachsenen Grundstück. Scheunenähnliche Mauerwerksbauten gruppieren sich um einen zentralen Hof und öffnen sich zur umliegenden Landschaft. Metalldächer mit weiten Dachüberständen werden durch Stahl- und Holzstützen getragen und heben sich oftmals von geschlossenen Ebenen durch Glasstreifen ab. Mit sensibler Rücksicht auf die Umgebung entstand ein Haus, dessen Baukörper, Materialien und Details die Herkunft der Bauherrschaft reflektieren und damit den Geist der südafrikanischen Architektur neu interpretieren.

COUNTRY / LAND	SOUTH AFRICA / SÜDAFRIKA	HOUSE NAME / BEZEICHNUNG DES HAUSES		HOUSE STEYN
LOCATION (CITY/REGION) / LAGE (STADT/REGION)				PRETORIA
ARCHITECT / ARCHITEKT		THOMAS GOUWS ARCHITECTS	YEAR OF COMPLETION / BAUJAHR	2004
PHOTOGRAPHER / FOTOGRAF		SASCHA LIPKA, THOMAS GOUWS	SQUARE FEET / QUADRAT METER	5595 / 520
CITY AND COUNTRY ARCHITECT / STADT UND LAND ARCHITEKT				PRETORIA, SOUTH AFRICA
WEBSITE ARCHITECT / HOMEPAGE ARCHITEKT				XXX

Designed in four phases, the house is an ongoing project – an organic building that grows over time. The children's quarters act as a prototype which duplicates as a second phase, completing the family hub. A more formal extension includes a "performance" stage adjoining the garage, which doubles as an auditorium. The design challenges one to abandon associations and explore the raw quality of space. Daylight projected onto curved walls guides one through a series of unexpected rooms, opening into double volumes and vertical progressions. Unconventional circulation routes and multi-level experiences remind of a three-dimensional labyrinth, enhancing a subconscious child-like spontaneity.

In vier Phasen entworfen, stellt dieses Haus ein in ständiger Entwicklung begriffenes Projekt dar – ein organisches Bauwerk, das im Laufe der Zeit anwächst. Der Kinderbereich dient als Prototyp der Anlage und wird in der zweiten Bauphase dupliziert, um den Bereich der Familie zu komplettieren. Ein Anbau umfasst eine Bühne neben der Garage, die zugleich als Auditorium fungiert. Die gekrümmten Wände führen durch eine eigenwillige Sequenz unterschiedlichster Räume, die auch durch Zweigeschossigkeit vertikal ausgebildet werden. Die ungewöhnliche Erschließung erinnert an ein Labyrinth und soll eine beinah kindliche Unbekümmertheit ausstrahlen.

HOUSE STEENKAMP
ELMO SWART

222

Governed by a tight budget, the project was undertaken
by a friend of the architect with no building experience.
Communication was done via an extensive 3D model and on-site
sketches. Each craftsman was allowed a hands-on approach.
Brick-layers had to adapt their perceptions as they were given
liberty to contour their brick courses, resulting in an enigmatic
process fuelled by intuition and dialogue between architect,
owner and craftsman.

Aufgrund des engen finanziellen Rahmens erfolgten Teile des
Ausbaus durch den Eigentümer selbst, der im Bauen unerfahren
war. Der Entwurf entstand mit Hilfe eines 3D Modells bzw. durch
vor Ort gefertigte Skizzen. Die hier tätigen Handwerker wurden
dazu aufgefordert, eigene Lösungsansätze einzubringen, so
dass das Haus im Dialog zwischen Architekt, Bauherr und den
Handwerkern entstand.

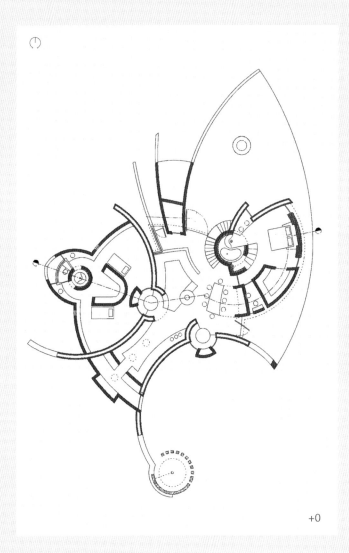

+0

COUNTRY / LAND	SOUTH AFRICA / SÜDAFRIKA	HOUSE NAME / BEZEICHNUNG DES HAUSES	HOUSE STEENKAMP
LOCATION (CITY/REGION) / LAGE (STADT/REGION)			PRETORIA
ARCHITECT / ARCHITEKT		ELMO SWART YEAR OF COMPLETION / BAUJAHR	2005
PHOTOGRAPHER / FOTOGRAF		ELMO SWART SQUARE FEET / QUADRAT METER	3658 / 340
CITY AND COUNTRY ARCHITECT / STADT UND LAND ARCHITEKT			PRETORIA, SOUTH AFRICA
WEBSITE ARCHITECT / HOMEPAGE ARCHITEKT			XXX

Designed around a loose brief, the clients' specification was an open living area with lots of light, and an industrial feel. The rooms were grouped around a ritual space with a fireplace in the middle – a node around which accommodation is arranged. The multi-volume living area is open and light whereas the bedrooms, by contrast, are isolated capsules that provide intimate retreat spaces.

Der Bauherr gab dem Architekten großzügigen Spielraum, er forderte lediglich einen offenen, von Licht durchfluteten Wohnbereich mit einem eher industriellen Ambiente. Die Räume sind um den zentralen Bereich mit dem offenen Kamin angeordnet. Der mehrgeschossige Wohnbereich ist offen und hell. Die Schlafzimmer werden hingegen eher als abgeschiedene, intime Raumzonen entwickelt.

+0

HOUSE VAN DYK
ELMO SWART

224

COUNTRY / LAND	SOUTH AFRICA / SÜDAFRIKA	HOUSE NAME / BEZEICHNUNG DES HAUSES		HOUSE VAN DYK
LOCATION (CITY/REGION) / LAGE (STADT/REGION)				PRETORIA
ARCHITECT / ARCHITEKT		ELMO SWART	YEAR OF COMPLETION / BAUJAHR	2004
PHOTOGRAPHER / FOTOGRAF		ELMO SWART	SQUARE FEET / QUADRAT METER	6671 / 620
CITY AND COUNTRY ARCHITECT / STADT UND LAND ARCHITEKT				PRETORIA, SOUTH AFRICA
WEBSITE ARCHITECT / HOMEPAGE ARCHITEKT				XXX

HOUSE ERASMUS
HUGO HAMITY ARCHITECTS

+1

This project was commissioned by a client with the need to build a newly starting family home flexible to allow for many years of growth and changes. The aim was to maximise the open public area in the house while keeping the street relationship intact and in accordance with the general design parameters of the residential estate guidelines.

Dieses Projekt entstand im Auftrag einer neu gegründeten Familie, die ein Zuhause benötigte, welches in den kommenden Jahren wachsen und sich verändern kann. Das Ziel war es, den Anteil an offenen Gemeinschaftsflächen zu maximieren und gleichzeitig einen Straßenraum so zu definieren, wie dies in der Gestaltungssatzung des Wohnviertels vorgeschrieben wurde.

225

COUNTRY / LAND	SOUTH AFRICA / SÜDAFRIKA	HOUSE NAME / BEZEICHNUNG DES HAUSES	HOUSE ERASMUS
LOCATION (CITY/REGION) / LAGE (STADT/REGION)			JOHANNESBURG
ARCHITECT / ARCHITEKT	HUGO HAMITY ARCHITECTS	YEAR OF COMPLETION / BAUJAHR	2004
PHOTOGRAPHER / FOTOGRAF	KARIN BRADY	SQUARE FEET / QUADRAT METER	5434 / 505
CITY AND COUNTRY ARCHITECT / STADT UND LAND ARCHITEKT			JOHANNESBURG, SOUTH AFRICA
WEBSITE ARCHITECT / HOMEPAGE ARCHITEKT			WWW.HUGOHAMITY.CO.ZA

PEARL BAY

STEFAN ANTONI OLMESDAHL
TRUEN ARCHITECTS

The beachside site inspired the architects to create an uncompromising residence of engaging austerity that nonetheless remains residential and comfortable. The L-shaped plan accommodates the various spaces with relaxed ease. The lower level contains the living room, kitchen and dining area whereas the entire bedroom wing is located on the upper level. The living room / dining / kitchen zone forms the spatial conclusion of the composition and orients parallel to the beach, providing views of the distant horizon.

Das strandnahe Grundstück inspirierte die Architekten dazu, ein kompromisslos einfaches Haus zu kreieren, das gleichzeitig wohnlich und bequem ist. Der L-förmige Grundriss beherbergt die unterschiedlichen Raumzonen auf lockere, ungezwungene Weise. Im Erdgeschoss befinden sich die Wohnbereiche, der komplette Schlaftrakt liegt im Obergeschoss. Der Wohn-, Eß-, und. Kochbereich bildet den räumlichen Abschluss der Komposition und orientiert sich parallel zum Strand, um Ausblicke auf den fernen Horizont zu optimieren.

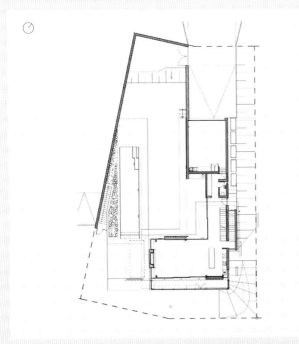

+0

A more informal living room zone accesses a protected poolside courtyard. Large glass doors and sliding façade panels can be opened to transform the ground floor into an generous indoor/ outdoor space. A limited palette of materials was employed: white plaster exterior walls, exposed concrete on the floors, and wooden façade panels combine to merge the residence with the surrounding dune landscape.

Eine zweite, informelle Wohnzimmerzone öffnet sich zum geschützten Hof mit Schwimmbecken. Große Glastüren und bewegliche Fassadenpanelle lassen sich öffnen, um das Erdgeschoss in einen großzügigen Innen-Außenbereich zu transformieren. Eine begrenzte Materialienpalette wurde eingesetzt: weißverputzte Wände, sichtbar belassener Estrichfußboden und Fassadenelemente aus Holz werden gekonnt kombiniert, um das Haus nahtlos mit der umliegenden Dünenlandschaft verschmelzen zu lassen.

COUNTRY / LAND	SOUTH AFRICA / SÜDAFRIKA	HOUSE NAME / BEZEICHNUNG DES HAUSES	PEARL BAY
LOCATION (CITY/REGION) / LAGE (STADT/REGION)			YZERFONTEIN
ARCHITECT / ARCHITEKT	STEFAN ANTONI OLMESDAHL TRUEN ARCHITECTS	YEAR OF COMPLETION / BAUJAHR	2006
PHOTOGRAPHER / FOTOGRAF		STEFAN ANTONI	SQUARE FEET / QUADRAT METER	3777 / 351
CITY AND COUNTRY ARCHITECT / STADT UND LAND ARCHITEKT			CAPE TOWN, SOUTH AFRICA
WEBSITE ARCHITECT / HOMEPAGE ARCHITEKT			WWW.SAOTA.COM

The diverse spaces of this large home are arrayed on three levels to skilfully maximize views and integrate the building mass into the hillside topography. The lower, poolside level contains all functions necessary to serve as an independent residential unit for guests or visiting family members.

Die diversen Raumbereiche dieses großen Hauses befinden sich auf drei Ebenen, um die atemberaubenden Ausblicke zu maximieren und die Baumasse in die Hangtopographie zu integrieren. Das untere Niveau, das an den Pool direkt anschließt, beherbergt einen kompletten eigenen Wohnbereich, der alle Funktionen einer eigenen Wohnung für Gäste oder Familienmitglieder bietet.

AVENUE ST. LEON

STEFAN ANTONI OLMESDAHL
TRUEN ARCHITECTS

The middle, entrance level serves as main living zone where a large kitchen, informal, formal and outdoor dining and living zones, an office wing, and a bedroom tract are located. The upper level contains the master bedroom suite that commands an expansive view out onto the Indian Ocean. In spite of the large floor area contained within the home, it seems well-scaled and at one with the site due to the special care taken by the architects to modulate the impressive building masses and embed the forms in the natural environment of the seaside bluffs.

Das mittlere Eingangsniveau dient als Hauptebene, auf der sich eine große Küche, informelle und formelle Eß- und Wohnbereiche, ein Büroflügel und ein Schlaftrakt befinden. Das Obergeschoss umfasst den repräsentativen Bereich, der über einen umfassenden Ausblick auf das Meer verfügt. Trotz der großen Wohnfläche des Hauses wirkt es dank der Bemühungen der Architekten, die Masse zu modulieren und in die Landschaft einzubetten, maßstäblich und im Einklang mit der umliegenden Naturlandschaft.

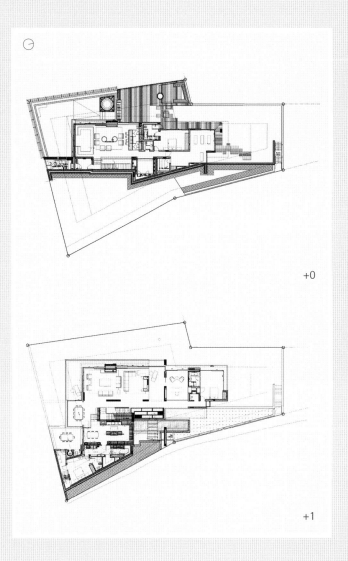

+0

+1

COUNTRY / LAND	SOUTH AFRICA / SÜDAFRIKA	HOUSE NAME / BEZEICHNUNG DES HAUSES	AVENUE ST. LEON
LOCATION (CITY/REGION) / LAGE (STADT/REGION)			BANTRY BAY, CAPE TOWN
ARCHITECT / ARCHITEKT	STEFAN ANTONI OLMESDAHL TRUEN ARCHITECTS	YEAR OF COMPLETION / BAUJAHR	2004
PHOTOGRAPHER / FOTOGRAF	STEFAN ANTONI	SQUARE FEET / QUADRAT METER	8931 / 830
CITY AND COUNTRY ARCHITECT / STADT UND LAND ARCHITEKT			CAPE TOWN, SOUTH AFRICA
WEBSITE ARCHITECT / HOMEPAGE ARCHITEKT			WWW.SAOTA.COM

STEFAN ANTONI OLMESDAHL TRUEN ARCHITECTS

CAPE TOWN
SOUTH AFRICA / SÜDAFRIKA

Stefan Antoni Olmesdahl Truen Architects is considered one of the most interesting firms among South Africa's new generation of architects. They strive to promote services marked by excellence both in their buildings and in addressing the needs of their clients, with the focus on high standards and elegance. The importance of a balance between the interests of business and architecture is stressed by the partners, and is evidenced in the number of clients who have achieved significant returns from their buildings, as well as numerous repeat commissions.

The philosophy of the practice is embodied in the spirit of enquiry that flourishes amongst its staff and the desire to seek new solutions that are generated by the challenges of new projects that are unique to South Africa's evolving character. The buildings are born out of the dynamics of site and context and are infused with the subtle poetry. Light, views, water, and landscaping are all combined to provide an elegant backdrop for the drama of life, displayed objects and art.

235

Stefan Antoni Olmesdahl Truen Architekten werden als eines der interessantesten Büros der neuen Generation in Südafrika angesehen. Das Büro strebt danach, für die jeweilige Bauherrschaft einen hochwertigen Baustandard unter Berücksichtigung der Nutzerwünsche zu gewährleisten, und gleichzeitig eine harmonische Eleganz zu erzielen. Wichtig dabei ist es, eine Balance zwischen geschäftlichen und architektonischen Gesichtspunkten zu haltend.

Die Philosophie des Büros betont den Geist des Hinterfragens. Die Herausforderungen, welche neue Projekte bieten, werden angenommen, um Lösungsansätze zu entwickeln, die dem sich wandelnden Charakter Südafrikas entsprechen. Die Bauwerke nehmen Bezug auf die Besonderheiten der Bauorte, um eine subtile, poetische Qualität zu erreichen. Licht und Ausblicke, Wasser und Landschaft werden alle zusammengeführt, um einen eleganten Hintergrund für das Drama des Lebens, der ausgestellten Objekte und Kunst zu inszenieren.

Horizon House - Atami, Japan - Shinichi Ogawa & Associates - Photographer Nacasa & Partners Inc., Koichi Torimura

ASIA / ASIEN

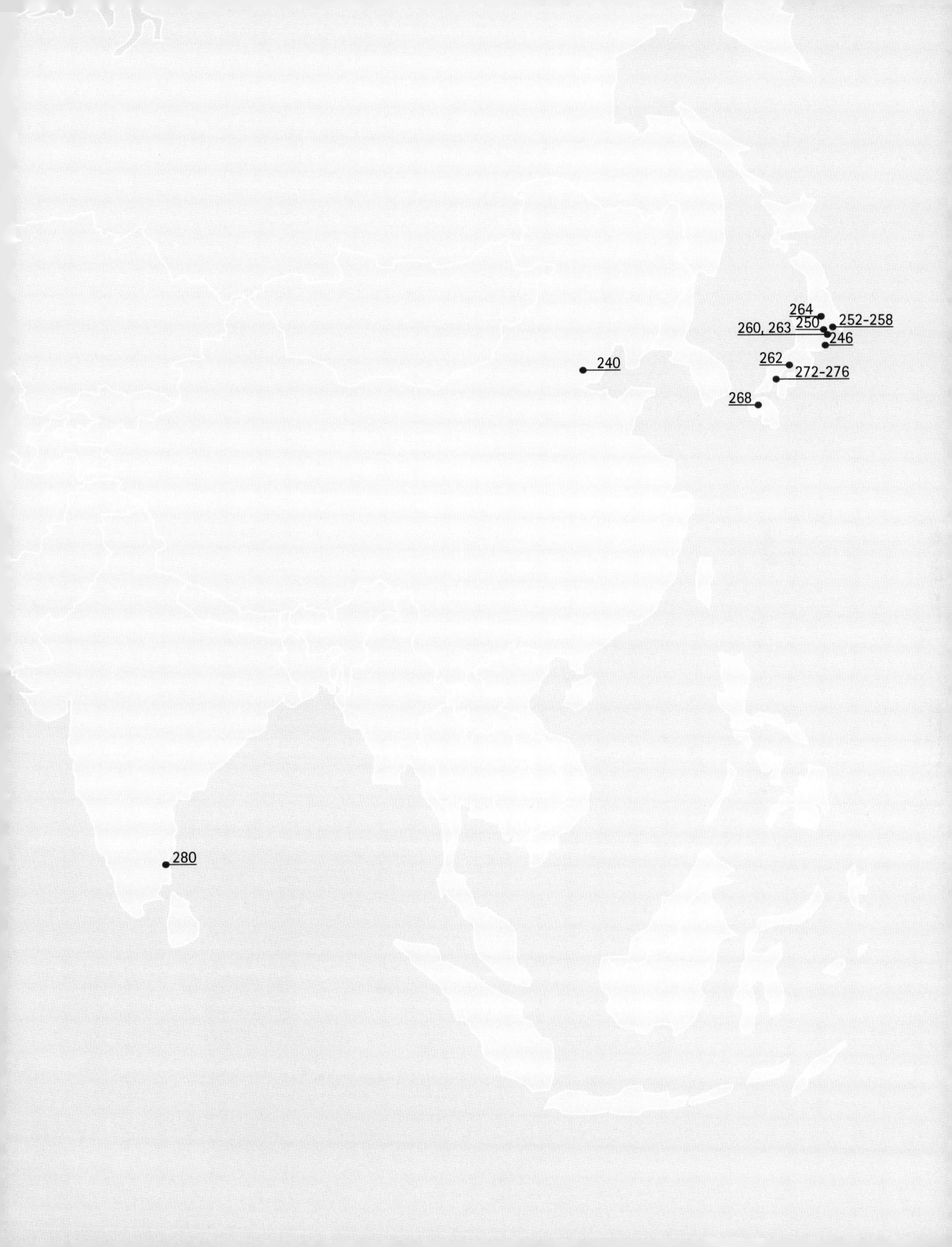

264
252–258
260, 263
250
246
240
262
272–276
268
280

Most of the rising stars on the vital Chinese architectural scene pay scarce attention to local tradition and regional architectural precedents. Their source of inspiration is Western architecture and since many of the most successful new Chinese architects studied in the West they are well versed in the history of Modernism. Le Corbusier's early villas served as the architectural role model for this striking suburban villa composition for two neighbouring homes that form a unified composition.

Die aufstrebenden neuen Architekten der recht lebendigen chinesischen Szene orientieren sich wenig an lokalen Traditionen oder regionalen Vorbildern. Ihre Inspiration holen Sie doch eher bei westlichen Vorbildern, nicht zuletzt weil viele Architekten der erfolgreichen jungen Generation im Westen studiert haben und die Geschichte der modernen Architektur geradezu verinnerlicht haben. Die frühen Villen Le Corbusiers dienten als das Vorbild für diese Anlage, die aus zwei Villen besteht, die eine einheitliche Komposition bilden.

LUSHI VILLA A+B
ATELIER FRONTI

The architect created rectangular, white buildings from which interior courtyards and the broad exterior stair were hollowed out. Villa A is two-storied and emphasizes the horizontal ground plane whereas three-storey Villa B creates a vertical, tower-like focal point. The brilliant white surfaces extend from the exterior wall surfaces to the interior walls inside. Black metal window frames form a stark contrast to the wall surfaces and underscore the Minimalist approach pursued throughout the house.

Der Architekt schuf rechteckige weiße Baukörper aus denen Innenhöfe und Treppen ausgehöhlt wurden. Villa A weist zwei Geschosse auf und wurde horizontal gestreckt, um die Linie der Topografie zu betonen. Villa B setzt einen vertikal en Akzent dagegen und erhebt sich mit drei Geschossen gegen den Himmel. Die strahlend weißen Außenwände setzen sich in den Innenräumen fort. Schwarze Fensterrahmen aus Metall bilden einen starken Kontrast zu den weißen Wandebenen und unterstreichen den minimalistischen Ansatz, der im ganzen Hause konsequent verfolgt wurde.

COUNTRY / LAND	CHINA	HOUSE NAME / BEZEICHNUNG DES HAUSES	LUSHI VILLA A+B
LOCATION (CITY/REGION) / LAGE (STADT/REGION)			SHIJINGSHAN DISTRICT, BEIJING
ARCHITECT / ARCHITEKT	ATELIER FRONTI	YEAR OF COMPLETION / BAUJAHR	2005
PHOTOGRAPHER / FOTOGRAF	WANG YUN	SQUARE FEET / QUADRAT METER	17216 / 1600
CITY AND COUNTRY ARCHITECT / STADT UND LAND ARCHITEKT			BEIGJING, CHINA
WEBSITE ARCHITECT / HOMEPAGE ARCHITEKT			WWW.FRONTO.CN

ATELIER FRONTI

SHIJINGSHAN DISTRICT, BEIJING
CHINA

After studying in Tokyo until 1999 Wang Yun founded Atelier Fronti in Beijing in 2002. During the past 5 years Atelier Fronti has designed a diverse range of buildings in China ranging from housing and schools to office buildings. A broad spectrum of theoretical considerations provides a framework within which Atelier Fronti operates. These include the notions of "Foreshortened Figure and Geometry", "Dimensionality and Abstraction" and "White and Disappearance".

Wang Yun Ph. D.
Associate Prof. Peking University, Chief architect Atelier Fronti.
1985 Graduated from Beijing institute of Civil Engineering and Architecture.
1995 Graduated from University of Tokyo, Master Degree.
1999 Graduated from University of Tokyo, Ph. D.
20th NISSHINKOGYO Architecture competition, Japan, 2nd prize
4th SxL housing design competition, Japan, 1st prize

Photo: Ning Jing

Nach seinem bis 1999 dauernden Studium in Tokio gründete
Wang Yun 2002 das Atelier Fronti in Beijing. In den letzten
fünf Jahren hat Atelier Fronti in China ein breites Spektrum
an Bauwerken errichtet, das Wohnungsbauten, Schulen und
Bürobauten umfassen. Philosophische Grundsätze wie „Verkürzte
Figur und Geometrie", „Dimensionalität und Abstraktion" sowie
„Weiß und Verschwinden" verdeutlichen den anspruchsvollen
theoretischen Ansatz des jungen Büros.

Wang Yun Ph. D.
Professor an der Universität Beijing
Geschäftsführender Architekt im Atelier Fronti.[Punkt streichen]
1985 Diplom des TU Beijing
1995 Masters- Abschluss der Universität Tokio
1999 Doktor-Abschluss an der Universität Tokio
20. NISSHINKOGYO Wettbewerb, Japan, 2. Preis

HORIZON HOUSE
<u>SHINICHI OGAWA & ASSOCIATES</u>

The site presented an opportunity seldom found in Japan: the design of a
residence with an unimpeded view of the sea. The architect responded to
this challenge with uncompromising consequence. The salient line of the far
horizon was directly translated into architecture. The living room and the
large bathroom on the entrance level were foreseen with a dramatic ribbon
window that creates a radical horizontality.

Der Bauplatz bietet die in Japan seltene Gelegenheit, ein Haus mit
ungehindertem Meerblick zu verwirklichen. Der Architekt antwortete auf
diese Herausforderung mit einer kompromisslosen Konsequenz.
Die ruhende Linie des weiten Horizonts wurde zum Hauptmotiv des
Entwurfs. Die Wohnräume und das große Bad im Eingangsgeschoss des
Hanghauses erhielten ein durchgehendes Fensterband, das eine radikale
Horizontalität erzeugt.

248

Sliding glass window wall elements here allow the inhabitants to completely open the seaside facade. The bathing pool was set into the floor to heighten the sense of bathing in nature, a quality encountered in Japan's traditional "onsen" spas.

Gläserne Wandelemente ermöglichen einen uneingeschränkten Meerblick. Ein Pool wurde in den Boden eingelassen, um ein Gefühl vom Baden in der Natur zu verstärken – so, wie in den traditionellen „Onsen"-Bädern Japans.

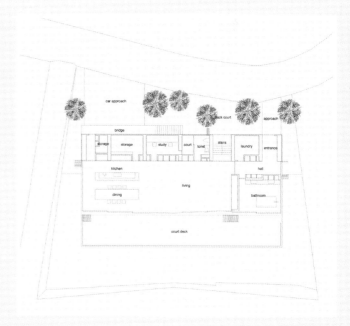

COUNTRY / LAND	JAPAN	HOUSE NAME / BEZEICHNUNG DES HAUSES	HORIZON HOUSE

LOCATION (CITY/REGION) / LAGE (STADT/REGION)   ATAMI, SHIZUOKA / PACIFIC COAST

ARCHITECT / ARCHITEKT	SHINICHI OGAWA & ASSOCIATES	YEAR OF COMPLETION / BAUJAHR	2005
PHOTOGRAPHER / FOTOGRAF	NACÁSA & PARTNERS INC., KOICHI TORIMURA	SQUARE FEET / QUADRAT METER	11 / 1

CITY AND COUNTRY ARCHITECT / STADT UND LAND ARCHITEKT   TOKYO / HIROSHIMA, JAPAN

WEBSITE ARCHITECT / HOMEPAGE ARCHITEKT   WWW.SHINICHIOGAWA.COM

Wood, Japan's most traditional building material, was employed here to create an airy lightness and warm ambience that reminds one of ancient Japanese temples and at the same time seems fresh and contemporary. The wooden deck that surrounds the house defines an exterior zone that is additionally delineated by the cantilevered roof framework.

Holz, das traditionellste Baumaterial Japans, wurde hier verwendet, um eine luftige Leichtigkeit und warmes Ambiente zu erzeugen, das an uralten japanischen Tempel erinnert und zugleich frisch und zeitgenössisch wirkt. Die Holzterrasse, die das Haus umgibt, definiert einen zum Haus gehörigen Außenbereich, der zusätzlich durch das auskragende Holzskelett der Dachkonstruktion betont wird

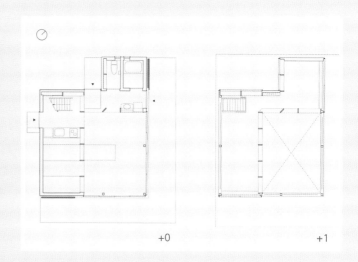

+0   +1

HUT T
<u>KAZUNARI SAKAMOTO</u>

COUNTRY / LAND	JAPAN	HOUSE NAME / BEZEICHNUNG DES HAUSES	HUT T
LOCATION (CITY/REGION) / LAGE (STADT/REGION)			YAMANAKAKO-MURA, YAMANASHI
ARCHITECT / ARCHITEKT	KAZUNARI SAKAMOTO ARCHITECTURAL LABORATORY	YEAR OF COMPLETION / BAUJAHR	2001
PHOTOGRAPHER / FOTOGRAF	KAZUNARI SAKAMOTO	SQUARE FEET / QUADRAT METER	646 / 60
CITY AND COUNTRY ARCHITECT / STADT UND LAND ARCHITEKT			TOKYO, JAPAN
WEBSITE ARCHITECT / HOMEPAGE ARCHITEKT			HTTP://CYCLOPS.ARCH.TITECH.AC.JP/SAKAMOTO_LAB/

Surrounded by a neighbourhood of normal pitched-roof houses this home stands apart as a unique sculptural object. The bright white surfaces fold up to continue up to the peak of the steeply pitched roof. Inside, well-proportioned living spaces were intricately stacked underneath the slanted roof planes.

Umgeben von einer Nachbarschaft, die zumeist aus normalen Satteldachhäusern besteht, wirkt dieses Haus wie ein skulpturales Objekt. Die hellen, weißen Außenwandflächen werden am Knickpunkt zum Dach gefaltet und steigen dann als steil geneigte Dachflächen gen Himmel. Im Inneren locken gut proportionierte Räume, die gekonnt gestapelt wurden und bis in die Dachspitze steigen.

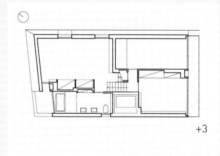

+3

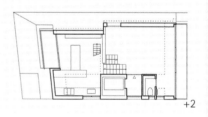

+2

QUICO JINGUMAE
KAZUNARI SAKAMOTO

COUNTRY / LAND	JAPAN	HOUSE NAME / BEZEICHNUNG DES HAUSES	QUICO JINGUMAE
LOCATION (CITY/REGION) / LAGE (STADT/REGION)			SHIBUYA-KU, TOKYO
ARCHITECT / ARCHITEKT	KAZUNARI SAKAMOTO ARCHITECTURAL LABORATORY	YEAR OF COMPLETION / BAUJAHR	2005
PHOTOGRAPHER / FOTOGRAF		KAZUNARI SAKAMOTO	SQUARE FEET / QUADRAT METER	4196 / 390
CITY AND COUNTRY ARCHITECT / STADT UND LAND ARCHITEKT			TOKYO, JAPAN
WEBSITE ARCHITECT / HOMEPAGE ARCHITEKT			HTTP://CYCLOPS.ARCH.TITECH.AC.JP/SAKAMOTO_LAB/

HOUSE ON MUSHASHINO-HILLS
K.ASSOCIATES / ARCHITECTS

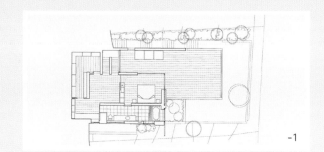

To take advantage of the view the architect opted for placing the major living spaces on the upper level. Here, the kitchen opens onto a combined living-dining space that was foreseen with floor to ceiling glazing that extends around the corner to offer a panoramic view of the cityscape beyond.

Um den Ausblick optimal auszunutzen entschied sich der Architekt für eine Anordnung der Hauptwohnräume dieses Hauses auf der oberen Ebene. Hier öffnet sich die Küche zum kombinierten Wohn-Essraum, der mit einer komplett verglasten Stirnseite versehen wurde, durch die sich der Panoramablick auf die darunter liegende Stadtlandschaft öffnet.

COUNTRY / LAND	JAPAN	HOUSE NAME / BEZEICHNUNG DES HAUSES		HOUSE ON MUSHASHINO-HILLS
LOCATION (CITY/REGION) / LAGE (STADT/REGION)				TOKYO
ARCHITECT / ARCHITEKT		K.ASSOCIATES / ARCHITECTS	YEAR OF COMPLETION / BAUJAHR	2005
PHOTOGRAPHER / FOTOGRAF		HIROSHI UEDA	SQUARE FEET / QUADRAT METER	1636 / 152
CITY AND COUNTRY ARCHITECT / STADT UND LAND ARCHITEKT				KYOTO, JAPAN
WEBSITE ARCHITECT / HOMEPAGE ARCHITEKT				HTTP://K-ASSOCIATES.COM

256

Inspired by traditional Japanese elements such as "onsen" outdoor baths and Machiya courtyard houses, the architects created a house where interior spaces extend directly into enclosed private terrace spaces outside. Separated by the courtyard, the living/dining wing is linked to the sleeping/bathroom wing via a glass corridor. It subdivides the courtyard into a patio terrace and a private outdoor bath reminiscent of an "onsen". Sliding cloth canopies in the courtyard allow creating of both intimate outdoor rooms and, when fully opened, a generous terrace connected to the sky.

Inspiriert von traditionellen japanischen Elementen wie „onsen"-Naturbädern und Machiya-Hofhäusern schufen die Architekten ein Gefüge nahtlos ineinander übergehender Innen- und Außenräume. Die getrennten Flügel mit Wohn-/Essnutzung bzw. Schlafzimmer/Bad werden über den Hof mit einem gläsernen Korridor verbunden. Dieser definiert eine offene, nicht einsehbare Terrasse und eine private, „onsen"-ähnliche Badezone im Freien. Verschiebbare Stoffbahnen über dem Hof erlauben es, niedrige Außenräume zu schaffen. Wenn sie beiseite geschoben werden, orientiert sich der Hofraum völlig offen zum Himmel hin.

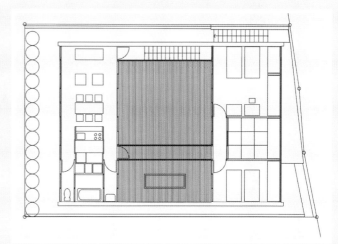

MACHIYA HOUSE
TAKAHARU + YUI TEZUKA

COUNTRY / LAND	JAPAN	HOUSE NAME / BEZEICHNUNG DES HAUSES	MACHIYA HOUSE
LOCATION (CITY/REGION) / LAGE (STADT/REGION)			TOKYO
ARCHITECT / ARCHITEKT	TAKAHARU + YUI TEZUKA / TEZUKA ARCHITECTS	YEAR OF COMPLETION / BAUJAHR	2000
PHOTOGRAPHER / FOTOGRAF	KATSUHISA KIDA	SQUARE FEET / QUADRAT METER	1065 / 99
CITY AND COUNTRY ARCHITECT / STADT UND LAND ARCHITEKT			SETAGAYA-KU, JAPAN
WEBSITE ARCHITECT / HOMEPAGE ARCHITEKT			WWW.TEZUKA-ARCH.COM

The entire side wall of the elongated house can be opened via sliding glass window elements to extend the space seamlessly out into the narrow garden courtyard. A backbone of cupboards, kitchen units, and shelves extends along the back wall up to the window sill of the clerestory window ribbon that directs even more light into the innovative space.

Die gesamte Seitenwand des langen Hauses kann mittels Schiebefenster geöffnet werden, um den Raum nahtlos mit dem schmalen Gartenhof zu verbinden. Ein Rückgrat aus Schränken, Kücheneinbauten und Regalen erstreckt sich entlang der Rückwand bis an die Unterkante des Oberlichtbandfensters, das zusätzliches Licht und Luft in den innovativ gestalteten Raum einführt.

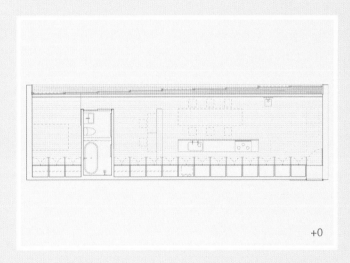

+0

ENGAWA HOUSE
TAKAHARU + YUI TEZUKA

COUNTRY / LAND	JAPAN	HOUSE NAME / BEZEICHNUNG DES HAUSES	ENGAWA HOUSE
LOCATION (CITY/REGION) / LAGE (STADT/REGION)			ADACHI-KU, TOKYO
ARCHITECT / ARCHITEKT	TAKAHARU + YUI TEZUKA / TEZUKA ARCHITECTS	YEAR OF COMPLETION / BAUJAHR	2003
PHOTOGRAPHER / FOTOGRAF	KATSUHISA KIDA	SQUARE FEET / QUADRAT METER	796 / 74
CITY AND COUNTRY ARCHITECT / STADT UND LAND ARCHITEKT			TOKYO, JAPAN
WEBSITE ARCHITECT / HOMEPAGE ARCHITEKT			WWW.TEZUKA-ARCH.COM

THIN ROOF HOUSE
TAKAHARU + YUI TEZUKA

The repertoire of the traditional Japanese house has fascinated generations of Western architects. "Shojis", wood-framed sliding walls with translucent rice paper panels, allow both spatial flexibility and open connection between interior and exterior spaces, which also responds to the humid tropical climate. This house extension is based in this tradition, yet transcends it effectively. Changing the spanning direction of the rafters to run parallel, not perpendicular, to the eaves creates a virtually column-less perimeter and achieves a perfect union between architecture and nature.

Das Repertoire des traditionellen japanischen Wohnhauses hat bereits Generationen von westlichen Architekten in seinen Bann gezogen. Schiebewände aus Reispapier, „shoji" genannt, erlauben hier die Verschmelzung von Innen- und Außenraum, was jedoch auch als Antwort auf das extrem schwüle Monsun-Klima entstanden ist. Bei diesem Anbau entsann man sich der Tradition, übertraf sie aber, indem die Spannrichtung der Dachbalken nicht quer, sondern parallel zur Längsseite verläuft. Dies schafft eine stützenfreie Sicht auf den Garten und somit die vollkommene Vereinigung von Architektur und Natur.

COUNTRY / LAND	JAPAN	HOUSE NAME / BEZEICHNUNG DES HAUSES		THIN ROOF HOUSE
LOCATION (CITY/REGION) / LAGE (STADT/REGION)				KANAGAWA
ARCHITECT / ARCHITEKT	TAKAHARU + YUI TEZUKA / TEZUKA ARCHITECTS		YEAR OF COMPLETION / BAUJAHR	2001
PHOTOGRAPHER / FOTOGRAF		KATSUHISA KIDA	SQUARE FEET / QUADRAT METER	484 / 45
CITY AND COUNTRY ARCHITECT / STADT UND LAND ARCHITEKT				SETAGAYA-KU, JAPAN
WEBSITE ARCHITECT / HOMEPAGE ARCHITEKT				WWW.TEZUKA-ARCH.COM

The free-spanning roof slab seemingly floats above the ribbon of spaces contained in this home. Sliding glass wall elements were uncompromisingly employed all around the entire house to allow complete opening of the spaces out to the surrounding gardens. Wooden floorboards and built-in closets are played off the white surface of the ceiling to create a welcoming residential ambience.

Die frei spannende Dachscheibe scheint regelrecht über dem Raumband der aneinander gereihten Zimmer dieses Hauses zu schweben. Schiebewandelemente aus Glas wurden kompromisslos um das ganze Haus angeordnet, um die komplette Öffnung aller Räume zu den umliegenden Gärten hin zu gewährleisten. Fußböden und Schrankeinbauten aus Holz ergänzen die weiße Deckenuntersicht um ein einladendes Wohnambiente zu schaffen.

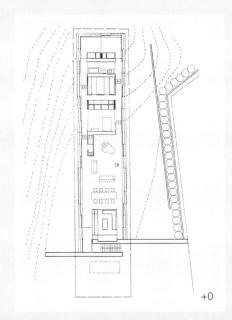

+0

ROOF FLOATING HOUSE
TAKAHARU + YUI TEZUKA

COUNTRY / LAND		JAPAN	HOUSE NAME / BEZEICHNUNG DES HAUSES		ROOF FLOATING HOUSE
LOCATION (CITY/REGION) / LAGE (STADT/REGION)					OKAYAMA-SHI
ARCHITECT / ARCHITEKT	TAKAHARU + YUI TEZUKA / TEZUKA ARCHITECTS		YEAR OF COMPLETION / BAUJAHR		2005
PHOTOGRAPHER / FOTOGRAF		KATSUHISA KIDA	SQUARE FEET / QUADRAT METER		3110 / 289
CITY AND COUNTRY ARCHITECT / STADT UND LAND ARCHITEKT					TOKYO, JAPAN
WEBSITE ARCHITECT / HOMEPAGE ARCHITEKT					WWW.TEZUKA-ARCH.COM

BIG WINDOW HOUSE
TAKAHARU + YUI TEZUKA

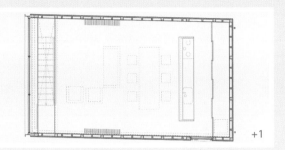

The box-like building form was carefully oriented to provide visual protection from the directly adjacent street and at the same time contain a generous double-storey space with an upper gallery level where the kitchen-dining zone is located. The large main window can be completely sunk on side-mounted tracks to create an expansive façade opening that allows fresh air and light inside.

Der kistenartige Baukörper ist sensibel gestaltet worden, um visuellen Schutz zur vor der angrenzenden Straße zu erzielen und dennoch einen großzügigen zweigeschossigen Wohnraum mit Küche-Essplatz auf der oberen Galerieebene zu ermöglichen. Das große Hauptfenster lässt sich im Boden versenken, um eine große Öffnung zu schaffen, die Licht und frische Luft in das Haus führt

COUNTRY / LAND	JAPAN	HOUSE NAME / BEZEICHNUNG DES HAUSES		BIG WINDOW HOUSE
LOCATION (CITY/REGION) / LAGE (STADT/REGION)				YOKOHAMA, KANAGAWA
ARCHITECT / ARCHITEKT	TAKAHARU + YUI TEZUKA / TEZUKA ARCHITECTS	YEAR OF COMPLETION / BAUJAHR		2004
PHOTOGRAPHER / FOTOGRAF	KATSUHISA KIDA	SQUARE FEET / QUADRAT METER		516 / 48
CITY AND COUNTRY ARCHITECT / STADT UND LAND ARCHITEKT				TOKYO, JAPAN
WEBSITE ARCHITECT / HOMEPAGE ARCHITEKT				WWW.TEZUKA-ARCH.COM

FOREST HOUSE
<u>TAKAHARU + YUI TEZUKA</u>

Traditional Japanese architecture is renowned for the intricate interconnection of built and natural elements. Transparency between inside and outside is one method commonly employed to achieve this quality. Another possibility often explored is the use of natural building materials such as wood that echoes the materials of the surrounding landscape and thus effectively extends it into the house. Both methods were further refined in this forest pavilion.

Die traditionelle japanische Architektur ist bekannt dafür, gebaute Formen mit den Elementen der Natur eindrucksvoll zu verbinden. Transparenz zwischen Innen und Außen ist ein Mittel, das oftmals eingesetzt wurde, um diese Synthese zu erreichen. Eine weitere Möglichkeit besteht darin, aus der Natur kommende Baumaterialien wie Holz zu verwenden, um den umgebenden Naturraum in die Architektur übergehen zu lassen. Beide Methoden wurden bei diesem Waldpavillon weiterentwickelt

+0

The angular composition avoids bland rectilinear lines and creates unique exterior forms and dynamic interior spaces. Glass walls on both ends of the house create transparency and allow the small spaces to seem larger than they are. Wood was used as the main structural material, to sheathe the exterior walls and to heighten the connection to the surrounding natural forest setting.

Die schrägen Linien der Komposition kommen ganz ohne rigide Rechtwinkligkeit aus und schaffen einprägsame äußere Formen und dynamische Innenräume. Glaswände an beiden Enden des Hauses schaffen Transparenz und lassen die kleinen Räume großer erscheinen. Holz wurde als das Hauptmaterial der Tragkonstruktion und als Fassadenmaterial eingesetzt um die Verschmelzung mit der umliegenden Waldlandschaft zu vervollkommnen.

COUNTRY / LAND	JAPAN	HOUSE NAME / BEZEICHNUNG DES HAUSES	FOREST HOUSE
LOCATION (CITY/REGION) / LAGE (STADT/REGION)			CHINO-SHI, NAGANO
ARCHITECT / ARCHITEKT	TAKAHARU + YUI TEZUKA / TEZUKA ARCHITECTS	YEAR OF COMPLETION / BAUJAHR	2004
PHOTOGRAPHER / FOTOGRAF	KATSUHISA KIDA	SQUARE FEET / QUADRAT METER	872 / 81
CITY AND COUNTRY ARCHITECT / STADT UND LAND ARCHITEKT			TOKYO, JAPAN
WEBSITE ARCHITECT / HOMEPAGE ARCHITEKT			WWW.TEZUKA-ARCH.COM

By handling the building as a sculptural form the architect created a unique home that both stands out in its surroundings as a special place and also boasts special interior spaces. The tilted exterior walls fold up to create the pitched roof that faintly echoes the roofs of the nearby homes. This merging of wall and roof surfaces is underscored with the metal panels used to sheathe the complete exterior hull.

Durch Behandlung des Baukörpers als ein bildhauerisches Objekt schuf der Architekt ein einprägsames Zuhause, das sich angenehm von der öden Architektur der Umgebung absondert und zudem spannende Innenräume beherbergt. Die gekippten Außenwände sind gefaltet und setzen sich als Dachflächen fort. Diese Verschmelzung der Wand- und Dachflächen wird durch den Einsatz einer durchgehenden Außenverkleidung aus Metallpaneelen unterstrichen.

HOUSE IN KURUME
TANIJIRI MAKOTO

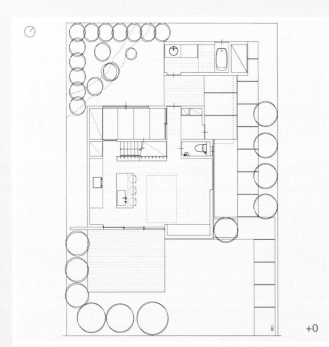

+0

The double-height living-dining space opens via folding doors onto a wooden deck that visually extends the floor plane of the space on the exterior. In a bold, unusual move the living room ceiling was also clad with wood. The tatami room, a common feature of Japanese homes where tatami mats serve as flooring, orients out to the quiet back garden and serves as a space for meditation or tea ceremonies. The dark brown tones employed throughout contrast well with the bright white wall surfaces and imbue the surfaces and spaces with a touch of nature.

Der zweigeschossige Wohn-Essraum öffnet sich über Falttüren zur Terrasse. Die Verwendung von Holz als Bodenmaterial im Wohnzimmer und auf der Terrasse lässt den Innenraum optisch wesentlich größer wirken lassen. Das für japanische Häuser typische Tatami-Zimmer mit Tatamimatten als Bodenbelag zum Sitzen orientiert sich zum ruhigen hinteren Garten hin und dient als Ort der Meditation. Die dunklen Brauntöne der Naturmaterialien wie Metall und Holz, die durchgehend verwendet werden, kontrastieren mit den hellen Wand- und Deckenebenen.

COUNTRY / LAND	JAPAN	HOUSE NAME / BEZEICHNUNG DES HAUSES	HOUSE IN KURUME
LOCATION (CITY/REGION) / LAGE (STADT/REGION)			FUKUOKA, KURUME
ARCHITECT / ARCHITEKT	TANIJIRI MAKOTO	YEAR OF COMPLETION / BAUJAHR	2005
PHOTOGRAPHER / FOTOGRAF	YANO YUKINORI	SQUARE FEET / QUADRAT METER	968 / 90
CITY AND COUNTRY ARCHITECT / STADT UND LAND ARCHITEKT			HIROSHIMA, JAPAN
WEBSITE ARCHITECT / HOMEPAGE ARCHITEKT			WWW.SUPPOSE.JP

HOUSE IN OONO
TANIJIRI MAKOTO

Perched on a low suburban embankment above a commuter train track and busy road, this house demonstrates the potentials inherent in urban sites often thought unsuited for building and proves that just such difficult sites can lead to the most exciting architectural soliutions. Rather than closing the house to the noisy street/train line the architect opted for a dramatic, fully glazed façade that frames the view of the passing trains.

Hoch über eine Bahntrasse und nah an einer Schnellstraße gelegen beweist dieses Haus, dass schwierige, bisher für nicht bebaubar gehaltene Grundstücke großes Potential für hochqualitative Wohnlösungen aufweisen. Anstatt die Fassade vor den störenden Lärmquellen der Bahn und der Straße zu schließen, ergriff der Architekt die Flucht nach vorne und öffnete die Gebäudefront auf dramatische Weise mit einer Vollverglasung, welche den Ausblick auf die vorbeifahrenden Vorortzüge einrahmt.

Cantilevering out the house mass from the hillside allows it to seemingly float above the site like a large sculpture piece. A split-level floor plan creates a tight-knit network of interior spaces dispersed on various levels. The exterior lines of the sculptural building volume directly follow and underscore the innovative floor plan layout and sensitively augment the natural topography with a memorable, enigmatic statement.

Die gewagte Auskragung des Hauses oberhalb der Hanglinie lässt es scheinbar schweben und wie eine große Skulptur wirken. Der Grundriss mit halb versetzten Ebenen schafft ein verwobenes Raumgefüge aus Innenräumen, die je nach Nutzungsart überzeugend angeordnet wurden. Die Linien der Außenform der skulpturartigen Baumasse folgen dem innovativen Grundriss im Inneren und gehen sensibel auf die vorhandene Topographie ein, um einen einprägsamen Akzent zu setzen.

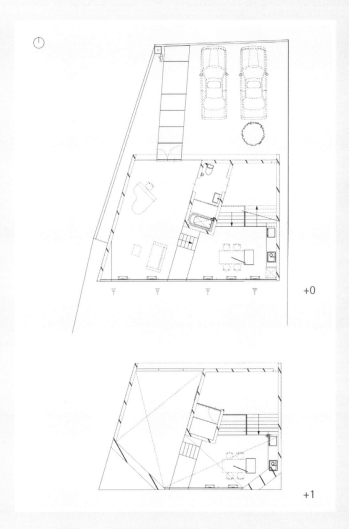

+0

+1

COUNTRY / LAND	JAPAN	HOUSE NAME / BEZEICHNUNG DES HAUSES	HOUSE IN OONO
LOCATION (CITY/REGION) / LAGE (STADT/REGION)			HIROSHIMA, OONO
ARCHITECT / ARCHITEKT	TANIJIRI MAKOTO	YEAR OF COMPLETION / BAUJAHR	2004
PHOTOGRAPHER / FOTOGRAF	YANO YUKINORI	SQUARE FEET / QUADRAT METER	958 / 89
CITY AND COUNTRY ARCHITECT / STADT UND LAND ARCHITEKT			HIROSHIMA, JAPAN
WEBSITE ARCHITECT / HOMEPAGE ARCHITEKT			WWW.SUPPOSE.JP

HOUSE IN USHITASHINMATI
TANIJIRI MAKOTO

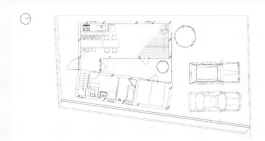

+0

A very tight urban site with directly neighbouring houses on both sides generated a creative solution. The house functions were distributed into two wings and separated by a narrow exterior courtyard onto which all of the spaces of the house orient. Concrete, wood, and aluminium-framed glass façade elements form a dignified palette of materials employed consequently throughout.

Das extreme enge Grundstück mit direkt angrenzenden Nachbarhäusern zu beiden Seiten führte zu einer besonders kreativen Lösung. Die Funktionen wurden in zwei Flügeln angeordnet, die durch einen gemeinsamen Lichthof miteinander verbunden werden. Beton, Holz und Aluminiumfenster stellen eine vornehme Materialienpalette dar, die konsequente Anwendung fand.

COUNTRY / LAND	JAPAN	HOUSE NAME / BEZEICHNUNG DES HAUSES	HOUSE IN USHITASHINMATI
LOCATION (CITY/REGION) / LAGE (STADT/REGION)			HIROSHIMA, USHITASHINMATI
ARCHITECT / ARCHITEKT		TANIJIRI MAKOTO YEAR OF COMPLETION / BAUJAHR	2004
PHOTOGRAPHER / FOTOGRAF		YANO YUKINORI SQUARE FEET / QUADRAT METER	1011 / 94
CITY AND COUNTRY ARCHITECT / STADT UND LAND ARCHITEKT			HIROSHIMA, JAPAN
WEBSITE ARCHITECT / HOMEPAGE ARCHITEKT			WWW.SUPPOSE.JP

TANIJIRI MAKOTO

HIROSHIMA
JAPAN

Makoto Tanijiri was born in Japan's Hiroshima Prefecture in 1974. He worked for Motokane Architects from 1994 to 1999 and for HAL Architects from 1999 until 2000, when he established Suppose Design Office. The successful office is presently staffed with four other young architects and a miniature Dachshund, and is currently working on 20 ongoing projects located mostly in Hiroshima Prefecture. As the projects presented here demonstrate, Suppose Design Office approaches each project with new and experimental design ideas. This assures that their architecture never seems redundant or copied but is rather inventive and refreshing. Tanijiri is the recipient of numerous awards including the JCD Award in 2002 and 2003, the Good Design Award in 2003, and the JCD Award and Urban Design Award in 2004.

Photo: Suppose Design Office

Der japanische Architekt Makoto Tanijiri wurde 1974 nahe Hiroshima geboren. Er arbeitete bei Motokane Architects von 1994-1999, bevor er für den Zeitraum 1999-2000 zu HAL Architects wechselte. Im Jahr 2000 gründete er Suppose Design Office. Das erfolgreiche kleine Büro, das von vier jungen Architekten und einen Dackel unterstützt wird, arbeitet z. Zt. an 20 Projekten im Raum Hiroshima.

Wie die hier dargstellten Projekte bezeugen, geht Suppose Design Office an jedes Projekt mit experimentellen Ideen und Ansätzen heran. Ihre Architektur wirkt nie monoton oder kopiert. Das junge Büro erhielt bereits zahlreiche Preise, u.a. den JCD Award in 2002 und 2003, den Good Design Preis 2003 und den JCD Preis bzw. den Urban Design Preis 2004.

The various spaces of this home were distributed into clearly defined building masses. A narrow, wall-like bedroom wing rises up to create a spatial backbone that is fronted by the living and dining spaces that are contained in pavilion-like structures. A double-height arched vault fronts the wall-like wing and creates a generous, airy exterior living space that interconnects the various building wings.

Die verschiedenen Räume dieses Bauwerks sind auf klar definierte, voneinander getrennte Baukörper verteilt worden. Der schmale, mauerähnliche Schlafzimmerflügel, vor dem die niedrigeren Baukörper der Wohn- und Essbereiche anliegen, erhebt sich zu einem hohen räumlichen Rückgrat. Ein zweigeschossiges Gewölbe verläuft parallel zum mauerähnlichen Flügel und bildet einen großzügigen, luftigen Wohnraum im Freien, der zudem die diversen Raumbereiche untereinander verbindet.

WALL HOUSE
ANUPAMA KUNDOO

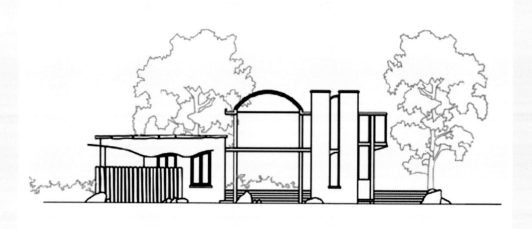

Due to the warm and humid climate exterior spaces play an especially important role in the organisation and daily use. A bridge gallery under the vault covers the exterior dining area and connects the building wings on the upper level. Additionally, the bedroom at the end of the wall-like wing was foreseen with an intimate roof terrace. Massive masonry walls made of narrow red bricks were used in combination with exposed concrete columns throughout.

Aufgrund des warmen und schwülen Klimas spielen die Außenräume eine zentrale Rolle in der Organisation und Nutzung des Hauses. Ein Brückensteg schafft eine zusätzliche Überdachung für den Essplatz im Freien und verbindet die Räume im Obergeschoss. Das Schlafzimmer am Ende des mauerähnlichen Flügels erhielt eine eigene intime Dachterrasse. Massiv gemauerte Wände aus roten Ziegeln bilden in Kombination mit Stützen aus Sichtbeton die stilprägenden Materialien des Hauses.

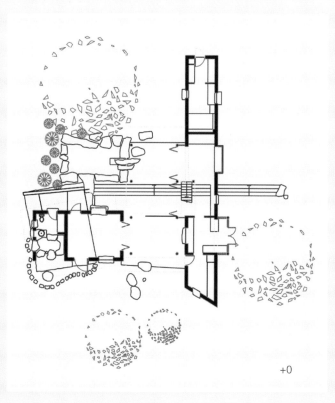

+0

COUNTRY / LAND	INDIA / INDIEN	HOUSE NAME / BEZEICHNUNG DES HAUSES	WALL HOUSE
LOCATION (CITY/REGION) / LAGE (STADT/REGION)			AUROVILLE
ARCHITECT / ARCHITEKT	ANUPAMA KUNDOO	YEAR OF COMPLETION / BAUJAHR	2000
PHOTOGRAPHER / FOTOGRAF	ANDREAS DEFFNER, ANUPAMA KUNDOO	SQUARE FEET / QUADRAT METER	1614 / 150
CITY AND COUNTRY ARCHITECT / STADT UND LAND ARCHITEKT			BERLIN, DEUTSCHLAND
WEBSITE ARCHITECT / HOMEPAGE ARCHITEKT			XXX

Wanaka House - Wanaka, South Island, New Zealand - Paul Clarke in Crosson Clarke Carnachan Architects - Photographer Patrick Reynolds

OCEANIA / OZEANIEN

Der rechteckige Grundriss wurde in drei Zonen unterteilt. Die östliche wird von den Eltern benutzt, die westliche von den Kindern. Die zentrale Zone umfasst Küche, Wohnzimmer und Essbereich. Eine Eingangsplattform mit einem Dach aus Aluminiumlamellen definiert den Eingang und fungiert zugleich als Veranda.

Der rechteckige Grundriss wurde in drei Zonen unterteilt. Die östliche wird von den Eltern benutzt, die westliche von den Kindern. Die zentrale Zone umfasst Küche, Wohnzimmer und Essbereich. Eine Eingangsplattform mit einem Dach aus Aluminiumlamellen definiert den Eingang und fungiert zugleich als eine Veranda.

ROSE HOUSE

IAN MOORE ARCHITECTS

On entering the house the dramatic view of the Pacific down the mountain to the south instantly opens up. Centralizing the living areas and pulling the service cores back from the glazing lines opens up striking diagonal vistas. To minimize the site impact of the building a lightweight steel structure was conceived.

Beim Betreten des Hauses öffnet sich ein freier Blick auf den Pazifik. Das Zusammenlegen der Wohnbereiche und Zurücksetzen der Serviceräume von der Fassade schafft reizvolle Diagonalblicke. Eine leichte Stahlkonstruktion wurde entwickelt, um das Grundstück möglichst wenig anzutasten.

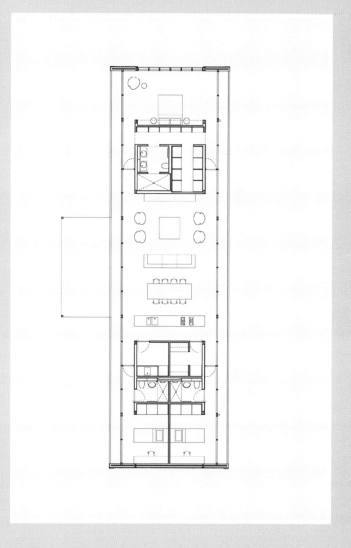

COUNTRY / LAND	AUSTRALIA / AUSTRALIEN	HOUSE NAME / BEZEICHNUNG DES HAUSES	ROSE HOUSE
LOCATION (CITY/REGION) / LAGE (STADT/REGION)			KIAMA / PACIFIC COAST
ARCHITECT / ARCHITEKT	ENGELEN MOORE ARCHITECTS	YEAR OF COMPLETION / BAUJAHR	2005
PHOTOGRAPHER / FOTOGRAF	ROSS HONEYSETT	SQUARE FEET / QUADRAT METER	1722 / 160
CITY AND COUNTRY ARCHITECT / STADT UND LAND ARCHITEKT			SYDNEY, AUSTRALIA
WEBSITE ARCHITECT / HOMEPAGE ARCHITEKT			WWW.IANMOOREARCHITECTS.COM

HAY BARN
IAN MOORE ARCHITECTS

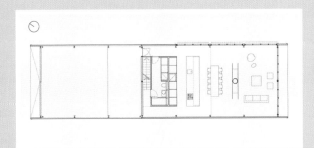

The utilitarian forms of Australian rural architecture are echoed here in a new architectural solution of striking simplicity. In fact, an existing barn that stood here was originally to be retained and extended with a guest cottage. It was finally decided to raze the old structure and to create the new one on the same building footprint. Half of the space is used as a studio whereas the second half serves as a light-filled guest cottage with a sleeping loft under the exposed pitched roof.

Die einfachen Formen australischer Agrararchitektur wurden hier in überzeugender Einfachheit neu interpretiert. Eine bestehende Scheune sollte lediglich durch einen Anbau ergänzt werden. Letztendlich entschied man sich für den Abriss der Scheune und den formgleichen Neubau an gleicher Stelle. Die Hälfte des Bauwerks dient als Atelier, die andere Hälfte als Gasthaus mit einem Schlafpodest unter dem geneigten Dach.

COUNTRY / LAND	AUSTRALIA / AUSTRALIEN	HOUSE NAME / BEZEICHNUNG DES HAUSES		HAY BARN
LOCATION (CITY/REGION) / LAGE (STADT/REGION)				MITTAGONG
ARCHITECT / ARCHITEKT	IAN MOORE ARCHITECTS	YEAR OF COMPLETION / BAUJAHR		2003
PHOTOGRAPHER / FOTOGRAF	ROSS HONEYSETT	SQUARE FEET / QUADRAT METER		2819 / 262
CITY AND COUNTRY ARCHITECT / STADT UND LAND ARCHITEKT				SYDNEY, AUSTRALIA
WEBSITE ARCHITECT / HOMEPAGE ARCHITEKT				WWW.IANMOOREARCHITECTS.COM

This house and studio for an industrial designer is located at the end of a street, hard against a three storey high sandstone cliff, and built within the shell of a 1950's light industrial shed formerly used as a machine shop. The two formative concepts pursued here were: the clear delineation of old and new in response to the code requirement that the existing brick façade be integrated into the new building, and the focus on the cliff face displayed behind glas to compensate for lack of any other view from the site.

Dieses Haus/Atelier für einen Industriedesigner steht am Ende einer Strasse direkt an einer dreigeschossigen Felswand, innerhalb einer Hülle, die durch einen bestehenden Gewerbebau aus den 1950er Jahren vorgegeben wird. Zwei formale Konzepte wurden hier verfolgt. Alte und neue Elemente sind klar gegenüber gestellt als Reaktion auf die Forderung des Planungsamtes, die alte Halle zu erhalten und deren Klinkerfassade in das neue Bauwerk zu integrieren. Zudem wird der Ausblick auf die Felswand betont, denn das Grundstück bot keine anderen Ausblicke.

COHEN HOUSE
IAN MOORE ARCHITECTS

COUNTRY / LAND	AUSTRALIA / AUSTRALIEN	HOUSE NAME / BEZEICHNUNG DES HAUSES		COHEN HOUSE
LOCATION (CITY/REGION) / LAGE (STADT/REGION)				PADDINGTON, SYDNEY
ARCHITECT / ARCHITEKT	IAN MOORE ARCHITECTS	YEAR OF COMPLETION / BAUJAHR		2005
PHOTOGRAPHER / FOTOGRAF	ROCKET MATTLER	SQUARE FEET / QUADRAT METER		2905 / 270
CITY AND COUNTRY ARCHITECT / STADT UND LAND ARCHITEKT				SYDNEY, AUSTRALIA
WEBSITE ARCHITECT / HOMEPAGE ARCHITEKT				WWW.IANMOOREARCHITECTS.COM

IAN MOORE
ARCHITECTS

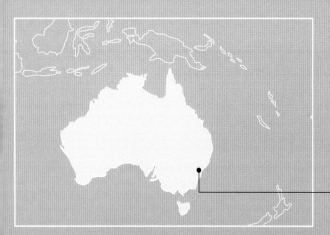

SYDNEY
AUSTRALIA / AUSTRALIEN

The practice's architectural production over the past 15 years has been driven by an optimism in the continuing validity of the 'Modern House' as the vehicle to develop an architectural language for the 21st century dwelling. In this respect, Ian Moore Architects work is clearly not new or ground breaking; it is a development and reworking of principles and prototypes well known to the architectural profession. Adjustments are made to suit the individual circumstances of site, climate, new technology and changing lifestyles, yet principles remain the same.

The majority of the projects to date have been achieved on limited budgets, which lend themselves to a few well chosen ideas, the simpler the better. In each and every project there are three essential ingredients; Space, Light and Ventilation. These three ingredients inform the design process through an integration and layering of a series of architectural devices employed to enrich the inherent simplicity of the initial concepts. There is an overwhelming desire to discard the superfluous and to provide only that which is absolutely necessary. The work is not an exercise in academic theorizing; it is about the act of building.

Photo: Tim Bauer

Die Arbeit des Büros wurde im Laufe der letzten 15 Jahre angetrieben durch einen Optimismus, der in der Überzeugung gründet, dass die Vision des „modernen Hauses" noch Gültigkeit für das Haus des 21. Jahrhunderts hat. So gesehen ist die Arbeit von Ian Moore nicht neu oder bahnbrechend, sie ist vielmehr eine Weiterentwicklung von Prinzipien, die Architekten schon lange beschäftigt haben. Die Entwürfe reagieren auf Ort, Klima, neue Technologien und sich verändernden Lebensstile, die Prinzipien jedoch verbleiben unverändert.

Die Mehrheit der bisherigen Projekte wurde innerhalb begrenzter Budgets realisiert, die nach kreativen Lösungen verlangten, frei nach dem Motto je einfacher, desto besser. Drei Aspekte stellen die Ausgangsbasis eines jeden Projektes dar: Raum, Licht und Durchlüftung. Diese drei Aspekte werden im Laufe des Entwurfs- und Bauprozesses immer wieder in den jeweiligen Arbeitsschritt integriert. Die Arbeiten sind darauf ausgerichtet, auf Überflüssiges soweit als möglichst zu verzichten, um vielmehr das Nötige zu betonen. Architektur ist für Moore nichts Theoretisches, sondern vielmehr der Akt des Bauens.

Two distinct pavilions of differing heights were designed to respond to the topography and height controls set by local building code. The pavilions align themselves to the adjacent site boundaries to create a wedge of space between them. An entry bridge leads to this space from which the indoor pool on the lower level is accessed. The central space is open and transparent whereas the pavilions themselves contain the more private functions and are clad in elegant grey Basalt stone.

Zwei Wohnpavillons von unterschiedlicher Höhe nehmen die Topographie auf und erfüllen zudem die planungsrechtlichen Anforderungen an die Gebäudehöhe. Die Baukörper passen sich dem konischen Verlauf der Grundstücksgrenzen an, dazwischen entstand die keilförmige Eingangshalle, die über einen Holzsteg erschlossen wird und zum Innenpool auf der unteren Ebene führt. Während dieser zentrale Raum offen und transparent gestaltet wurde, beherbergen die in elegantem Basaltstein verkleideten Wohnpavillons die privaten Funktionen des Hauses.

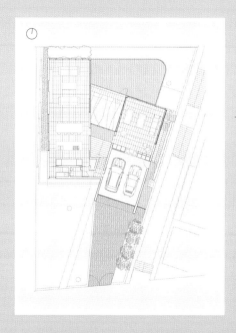

MCASSEY HOUSE

IAN MOORE ARCHITECTS

COUNTRY / LAND	AUSTRALIA / AUSTRALIEN	HOUSE NAME / BEZEICHNUNG DES HAUSES	MCASSEY HOUSE
LOCATION (CITY/REGION) / LAGE (STADT/REGION)			BALMORAL BEACH, SYDNEY
ARCHITECT / ARCHITEKT	IAN MOORE ARCHITECTS	YEAR OF COMPLETION / BAUJAHR	2005
PHOTOGRAPHER / FOTOGRAF	ROCKET MATTLER	SQUARE FEET / QUADRAT METER	3658 / 340
CITY AND COUNTRY ARCHITECT / STADT UND LAND ARCHITEKT			SYDNEY, AUSTRALIA
WEBSITE ARCHITECT / HOMEPAGE ARCHITEKT			WWW.IANMOOREARCHITECTS.COM

DROMANA RESIDENCE
BBP ARCHITECTS

The spaces of this coastal residence were distributed into various building volumes and optimally stacked to take advantage of the view out to the ocean beyond. A stair aligned between the building wings leads dramatically down the view axis from the entrance to the lower level. The deck cantilevers out above the hillside slope to effectively extend the living room with a protected exterior space.

Die Räume dieses Strandhauses sind auf klar gegliederte Volumen verteilt, die so gestapelt wurden, dass sie den Ausblick auf das Meer optimal rahmen. Eine Treppe zwischen den beiden Wohnflügeln führt effektvoll vom Eingang aus zur unteren Ebene und folgt damit der Hangtopographie. Die weit auskragende Terrasse schwebt über dem Hang und erweitert den Wohnraum um einen geschützten Wohnbereich im Freien.

COUNTRY / LAND	AUSTRALIA / AUSTRALIEN	HOUSE NAME / BEZEICHNUNG DES HAUSES		DROMANA RESIDENCE
LOCATION (CITY/REGION) / LAGE (STADT/REGION)				DROMANA
ARCHITECT / ARCHITEKT		BBP ARCHITECTS	YEAR OF COMPLETION / BAUJAHR	2005
PHOTOGRAPHER / FOTOGRAF		SHANIA SHEGEDYN	SQUARE FEET / QUADRAT METER	4089 / 380
CITY AND COUNTRY ARCHITECT / STADT UND LAND ARCHITEKT				MELBOURNE, AUSTRALIA
WEBSITE ARCHITECT / HOMEPAGE ARCHITEKT				WWW.BBPARCHITECTS.COM

DAWESVILLE RESIDENCE
<u>IREDALE PEDERSEN HOOK ARCHITECTS</u>

On his first visit to the site the architect discovered a local, 1950's house typology. These homes were raised above ground to provide protection from insects and dampness, and to maximize cooling winds in the hot climate. On this impulse it was decided to consequently raise the new home above plenum.

Bei seinem Erstbesuch vor Ort entdeckte der Architekt einen hier häufigen Haustyp aus den 50er Jahren. Diese Häuser wurden vom Terrain gelöst, um sie vor Feuchtigkeit, Insekten und Tieren zu schützen und eine kühlende Luftumspülung im heißen Klima zu erreichen. Angeregt hiervon wurde entschieden, das neue Haus ebenfalls vom Grund zu lösen.

302

The dramatic red wedge house seemingly hovers, supported merely by thin steel stilts. The hillside site additionally creates a protected space underneath the house that is used as an exterior living room during the region's long warm season. The innovative home was successfully built within the tight financial budget available.

Hier erfolgt dies auf effektvolle Weise: leichte Stahlstelzen lassen die Masse des Hauses schweben. Durch die Hanglage entsteht unter dem Haus ein überdachtes Wohnzimmer im Freien. Das Haus wurde innerhalb eines engen Finanzrahmens erfolgreich realisiert.

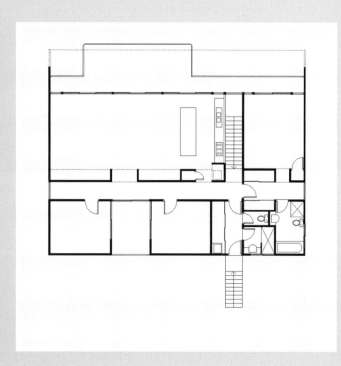

COUNTRY / LAND	AUSTRALIA / AUSTRALIEN	HOUSE NAME / BEZEICHNUNG DES HAUSES	DAWESVILLE RESIDENCE
LOCATION (CITY/REGION) / LAGE (STADT/REGION)			DAWESVILLE, INDIAN OCEAN
ARCHITECT / ARCHITEKT	IREDALE PEDERSEN HOOK ARCHITECTS	YEAR OF COMPLETION / BAUJAHR	2002
PHOTOGRAPHER / FOTOGRAF	TONY NATHAN	SQUARE FEET / QUADRAT METER	2152 / 200
CITY AND COUNTRY ARCHITECT / STADT UND LAND ARCHITEKT			PERTH, AUSTRALIA
WEBSITE ARCHITECT / HOMEPAGE ARCHITEKT			xxx

This house, designed to accommodate four related families, is sited to maximize the full potential of solar gain and heighten protection against prevailing winds. It opens to the north where grassed terraces, a swimming pool and sundeck are protected from the south-western winds. All rooms have views of the surrounding coastlines. Conceptually, the house is both a refuge and a built metaphor of a seabird.

Dieses Haus, das vier Familien als Wochenend- und Feriendomizil dient, wurde unter Einbeziehung des Sonnenlichts und unter Berücksichtigung der starken Windböen entworfen. Es öffnet sich nach Norden zu den mit Dünengras bepflanzten Terrassen, sowie zum Pool und zum Sonnendeck. Diese Bereiche werden durch die Baukörper von harschen Windböen aus dem Südwesten geschützt. Die Formen des Hauses sollen gleichzeitig an ein Refugium, wie an Meeresvögel erinnern

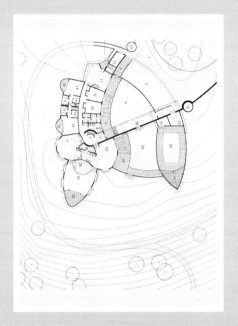

BURRAWORRIN RESIDENCE
GREGORY BURGESS PTY LTD ARCHITECTS

COUNTRY / LAND	AUSTRALIA / AUSTRALIEN	HOUSE NAME / BEZEICHNUNG DES HAUSES	BURRAWORRIN RESIDENCE
LOCATION (CITY/REGION) / LAGE (STADT/REGION)			FLINDERS / INDIAN OCEAN
ARCHITECT / ARCHITEKT	GREGORY BURGESS PTY LTD ARCHITECTS	YEAR OF COMPLETION / BAUJAHR	1999
PHOTOGRAPHER / FOTOGRAF	TREVOR MEIN	SQUARE FEET / QUADRAT METER	6994 / 650
CITY AND COUNTRY ARCHITECT / STADT UND LAND ARCHITEKT			RICHMOND, AUSTRALIA
WEBSITE ARCHITECT / HOMEPAGE ARCHITEKT			WWW.GREGORYBURGESSARCHITECTS.COM.AU

TAPLIN HOUSE
CON BASTIRAS ARCHITECT

The public beach promenade in Gleneig, a suburb of Adelaide, fronts directly onto the site. This led the architect to orient the home both toward the sea and to an inner courtyard with pool. The choice of cool, neutral materials creates a sense of pleasant understatement within which the delicate mix of informal and formal living functions are skilfully integrated.

Die öffentliche Uferpromenade des Adelaide-Vororts Gleneig schließt direkt an das Grundstück an. So entschied der Architekt, das Haus zum Meer und zu einem privaten Wohnhof mit Pool auszurichten. Die zurückhaltende Materialienpalette bildet einen neutralen Rahmen für den Mix aus informellen und repräsentativen Wohnfunktionen.

COUNTRY / LAND	AUSTRALIA / AUSTRALIEN	HOUSE NAME / BEZEICHNUNG DES HAUSES		TAPLIN HOUSE
LOCATION (CITY/REGION) / LAGE (STADT/REGION)				ADELAIDE / INDIAN OCEAN
ARCHITECT / ARCHITEKT	CON BASTIRAS ARCHITECT		YEAR OF COMPLETION / BAUJAHR	2002
PHOTOGRAPHER / FOTOGRAF	TREVOR FOX		SQUARE FEET / QUADRAT METER	5380 / 500
CITY AND COUNTRY ARCHITECT / STADT UND LAND ARCHITEKT				KINGS PARK, AUSTRALIA
WEBSITE ARCHITECT / HOMEPAGE ARCHITEKT				xxx

PANORAMA HOUSE
SJB ARCHITECTS

The typical lifeguard stations at local beaches served as a model for this house near Melbourne. The elevated upper level was foreseen with aluminum-framed windows. Wide eaves protect the windows and the terrace from the sun. The kitchen, dining, and living areas combine into a single space that seems large and generous in spite of its relatively small size.

Die typischen Kanzeln der lokalen Strandaufsichtspavillons dienten als Vorbild für dieses Haus nahe Melbourne. Das angehobene Obergeschoss wurde rundum mit Glaselementen versehen. Ein weiter Dachüberstand schützt die Glasflächen vor der Sonne und spendet Schatten für die große Terrasse. Küche, Essplatz und Wohnecke bilden eine zusammenhängende Raumzone, die trotz der relativ kleinen Fläche großzügig wirkt.

COUNTRY / LAND	AUSTRALIA / AUSTRALIEN	HOUSE NAME / BEZEICHNUNG DES HAUSES	PANORAMA HOUSE
LOCATION (CITY/REGION) / LAGE (STADT/REGION)			MORNINGTON PENINSULA / PACIFIC COAST
ARCHITECT / ARCHITEKT	SJB ARCHITECTS	YEAR OF COMPLETION / BAUJAHR	2003
PHOTOGRAPHER / FOTOGRAF	xxx	SQUARE FEET / QUADRAT METER	2367 / 220
CITY AND COUNTRY ARCHITECT / STADT UND LAND ARCHITEKT			SOUTHBANK, AUSTRALIA
WEBSITE ARCHITECT / HOMEPAGE ARCHITEKT			WWW.SJB.COM.AU

The rectangular plan is divided into three zones. The eastern zone is for the parents, the western zone for the children. The central zone contains the kitchen, living room, and dining area. An entry platform with an aluminium-louvered roof forms the entry to the house as well as a shaded veranda.

Der rechteckige Grundriss wurde in drei Zonen unterteilt. Die östliche wird von den Eltern benutzt, die westliche von den Kindern. Die zentrale Zone umfasst Küche, Wohnzimmer und Essbereich. Die Plattform mit einem Dach aus Aluminiumlamellen definiert den Eingang und fungiert zugleich als Veranda.

FLINDERS HOUSE

JACKSON CLEMENTS
BURROWS ARCHITECTS

310

On entering the house the dramatic view of the Pacific down the mountain to the south instantly opens up. Centralizing the living areas and pulling the service cores back from the glazing lines opens up striking diagonal vistas. To minimize the site impact of the building a lightweight steel structure was conceived.

Beim Betreten des Hauses öffnet sich ein freier Blick auf den Pazifik. Das Zusammenlegen der Wohnbereiche und Zurücksetzen der Servicekerne von der Fassade schafft reizvolle Diagonalblicke. Eine leichte Stahlkonstruktion wurde entwickelt, um das Grundstück möglichst wenig anzutasten.

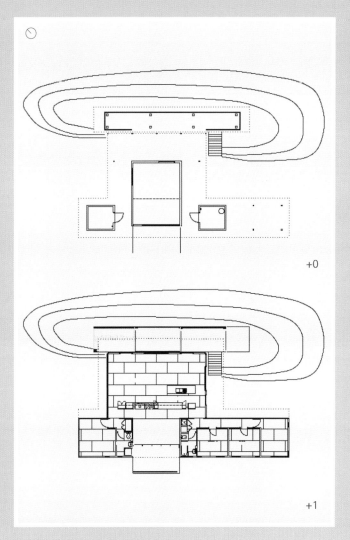

+0

+1

COUNTRY / LAND	AUSTRALIA / AUSTRALIEN	HOUSE NAME / BEZEICHNUNG DES HAUSES	FLINDERS HOUSE
LOCATION (CITY/REGION) / LAGE (STADT/REGION)			VICTORIA / PACIFIC COAST
ARCHITECT / ARCHITEKT	JACKSON CLEMENTS BURROWS PTY LTD ARCHITECTS	YEAR OF COMPLETION / BAUJAHR	2002
PHOTOGRAPHER / FOTOGRAF	EMMA CROSS, GOLLINGS PHOTOGRAPHY	SQUARE FEET / QUADRAT METER	2367 / 220
CITY AND COUNTRY ARCHITECT / STADT UND LAND ARCHITEKT			MELBOURNE, AUSTRALIA
WEBSITE ARCHITECT / HOMEPAGE ARCHITEKT			WWW.JCBA.COM.AU

The first floor plan is configured as three interlocking shells unified by a central "breezeway" corridor. The entry shell comprises a study and garage. The middle shell contains sleeping quarters, bathrooms and laundry. The end shell facing north contains kitchen, informal and formal living spaces. Underneath at ground level are located an additional bedroom, bathroom, alternative living zone and storage areas.

Die Hauptebene dieses Hauses besteht aus drei ineinander verschachtelten Schalen, welche durch einen offenen zentralen Durchgang miteinander verbunden werden. Der Eingangsbauteil besteht aus einem Büroraum und der Garage. Der mittlere Bauteil beherbergt Schlafräume, Badezimmer und einen Hauswirtschaftsraum. Der abschließende, nach Norden gerichtete Bauteil umfasst die Küche sowie informelle und formelle Wohnzimmer.

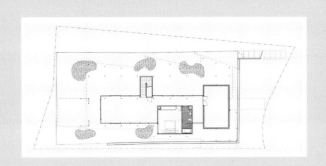

KEW HOUSE

JACKSON CLEMENTS
BURROWS ARCHITECTS

COUNTRY / LAND	AUSTRALIA / AUSTRALIEN	HOUSE NAME / BEZEICHNUNG DES HAUSES		KEW HOUSE
LOCATION (CITY/REGION) / LAGE (STADT/REGION)				MELBOURNE
ARCHITECT / ARCHITEKT	JACKSON CLEMENTS BURROWS ARCHITECTS	YEAR OF COMPLETION / BAUJAHR		2004
PHOTOGRAPHER / FOTOGRAF	JOHN GOLLINGS	SQUARE FEET / QUADRAT METER		xxx
CITY AND COUNTRY ARCHITECT / STADT UND LAND ARCHITEKT				MELBOURNE, AUSTRALIA
WEBSITE ARCHITECT / HOMEPAGE ARCHITEKT				WWW.JCBA.COM.AU

TYSON STREET

<u>JACKSON CLEMENTS</u>
<u>BURROWS ARCHITECTS</u>

The house is built to two boundaries, is two and a half storeys high, located on a site of just 280 square meters and blends in well into the adjacent single storey neighbourhood that is under historic preservation protection. To attain planning permission for demolition of the former structure a photographic image of the former home was applied to the new entrance façade behind which the home spatially unfolds in a series of protected private spaces which embrace a series of city views and the garden.

Dieses zweieinhalbgeschossige Haus überbaut das 280 qm große Grundstück bis an zwei Grundstücksgrenzen und passt sich sehr gut in eine denkmalgeschützte Nachbarschaft aus eingeschossigen Häusern ein. Um die Baugenehmigung zu erlangen, schlugen die Architekten das Anbringen eines Fotos des abgerissenen Vorgängerhauses an die gesamte Eingangsfront des neuen Hauses vor. Dahinter entfalten sich die geschützten Privatbereiche, die sich zu diversen Ausblicken auf die Stadt und den Garten öffnen.

COUNTRY / LAND	AUSTRALIA / AUSTRALIEN	HOUSE NAME / BEZEICHNUNG DES HAUSES	TYSON STREET
LOCATION (CITY/REGION) / LAGE (STADT/REGION)			MELBOURNE
ARCHITECT / ARCHITEKT	JACKSON CLEMENTS BURROWS ARCHITECTS	YEAR OF COMPLETION / BAUJAHR	2005
PHOTOGRAPHER / FOTOGRAF		JOHN GOLLINGS	SQUARE FEET / QUADRAT METER	xxx
CITY AND COUNTRY ARCHITECT / STADT UND LAND ARCHITEKT			MELBOURNE, AUSTRALIA
WEBSITE ARCHITECT / HOMEPAGE ARCHITEKT			WWW.JCBA.COM.AU

WANAKA HOUSE

PAUL CLARKE, IN CROSSON CLARKE CARNACHAN ARCHITECTS

The client requested a holiday home with a contemporary aesthetic, clean lines and seamless connections between inside and out. They also desired materials such as concrete, glass and timber and that the house was to sit comfortably on the land. In response, the architects created a home that immerses the user in the surrounding natural landscape. The house is low slung and nestled into the landscape, wedged into a gentle gully on the site, allowing for privacy from surrounding dwellings and protection from the wind.

Die Bauherrschaft wünschte ein Ferienhaus im zeitgenössischen Stil – mit klaren Gestaltungslinien und nahtlosen Übergänge zwischen Innen- und Außenbereich. Sie schlugen zudem vor, mit Materialien wie Beton, Glas und Holz zu arbeiten. Gewünscht war außerdem, dass das Haus sich in die Landschaft einfügt. Als Antwort auf diese Maßgaben entwarfen die Architekten ein Haus, das den Bewohnern erlaubt, unmittelbar in der Natur zu leben. So entstand das Gebäude als gestreckter Baukörper, der sich in eine Landschaftsmulde fügt, auch um Schutz vor Einblicken und harschen Winden zu gewährleisten.

The garage to the east is disconnected from the main house allowing for a modulation of the built forms in the landscape. This is also the entry point to the house, moving between the timber garage wall along a sculptured gabion wall. Steel sections placed in this wall provide light shafts into the east of the house. The holiday house is enjoyed throughout the year, socially and as a retreat from city life.

Die Garage ist in einem separaten Baukörper untergebracht und ermöglicht so einen geschützten Eingang ins Haus. Der Weg führt zwischen der hölzernen Garagenwand und einer mit Feldsteinen gefüllten Gabionwand zum Eingang. Die Gabionwand erhielt Aussparungen, durch die Licht gekonnt in das Hausinnere geführt wird. Das Ferienhaus wird das ganze Jahr über als Ort des Rückzugs von der Stadt sowie als geselliger Ort für Treffen mit Freunden geschätzt.

COUNTRY / LAND	NEW ZEALAND / NEUSEELAND	HOUSE NAME / BEZEICHNUNG DES HAUSES		WANAKA HOUSE
LOCATION (CITY/REGION) / LAGE (STADT/REGION)				WANAKA, SOUTH ISLAND
ARCHITECT / ARCHITEKT	PAUL CLARKE IN CROSSON CLARKE CARNACHAN	YEAR OF COMPLETION / BAUJAHR		2005
PHOTOGRAPHER / FOTOGRAF	PATRICK REYNOLDS	SQUARE FEET / QUADRAT METER		2432 / 226
CITY AND COUNTRY ARCHITECT / STADT UND LAND ARCHITEKT				AUCKLAND, NEW ZEALAND
WEBSITE ARCHITECT / HOMEPAGE ARCHITEKT				WWW.CCCA.CO.NZ

COROMANDEL PENINSULA HOUSE

CROSSON CLARKE CARNACHAN
ARCHITECTS

The house was conceived as a habitable container. Crafted in wood, it expresses structure, cladding, and joinery in a unique way. The unadorned natural timber creates a connection to nature. The decks can be hoisted to a closed position and become walls when the cabin is uninhabited.

Das Haus wurde als bewohnbarer Container konzipiert. Die Primärkonstruktion, Schalung und Böden wurden komplett aus Holz gefertigt, was eine eindrucksvolle Verbindung zur Natur schafft. Die Terrassen können hoch gekippt werden, um geschlossene Wandflächen zu bilden.

321

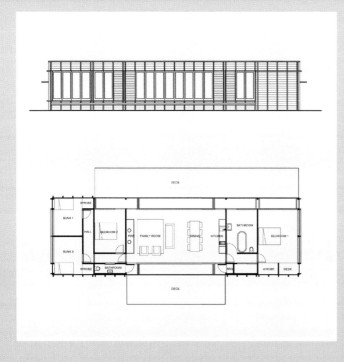

The simple rectangular building reminds one of a rural shed, facing north and the view. The living room is open to the outside and the sun, a metaphorical tent, while the bunkrooms are enclosed and cool. The fireplace allows winter occupation and the open bathroom and moveable bath allow the ritual of bathing to become an experience connected to nature.

Das einfache Rechteck mit Nordorientierung zum Meer hin erinnert an eine Scheune. Das Wohnzimmer öffnet sich zur Landschaft und zur Sonne und erinnert an ein Zelt. Der offene Kamin ermöglicht auch eine Winternutzung. Das Bad kann zur Natur hin geöffnet werden, um ein Baden im Freien zu ermöglichen.

COUNTRY / LAND	NEW ZEALAND / NEUSEELAND	HOUSE NAME / BEZEICHNUNG DES HAUSES	COROMANDEL PENINSULA HOUSE
LOCATION (CITY/REGION) / LAGE (STADT/REGION)			PACIFIC COAST
ARCHITECT / ARCHITEKT	CROSSON CLARKE CARNACHAN ARCHITECTS	YEAR OF COMPLETION / BAUJAHR	2001
PHOTOGRAPHER / FOTOGRAF	PATRICK REYNOLDS	SQUARE FEET / QUADRAT METER	1377 / 128
CITY AND COUNTRY ARCHITECT / STADT UND LAND ARCHITEKT			AUCKLAND, NEW ZEALAND
WEBSITE ARCHITECT / HOMEPAGE ARCHITEKT			xxx

CROSSON CLARKE
CARNACHAN
ARCHITECTS

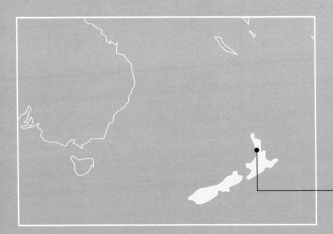

AUCKLAND
NEW ZEALAND / NEUSEELAND

Crosson Clarke Carnachan emphasizes the importance of listening to people's needs. A skilled and dedicated team supports the design output; their backgrounds and interests are diverse and yet their communication expertise allows them to progress in a cohesive and efficient partnership. Simon Carnachan has been widely recognized as one of New Zealand's foremost architects. Ken Crosson has won numerous local and national awards for architecture. Paul Clarke has been a director of Crosson Clarke Architects since 1999. Paul and Ken worked together for 6 years before the recent merge with Simon Carnachan.

Each project is analyzed for its special requirements and opportunities; the end result being not a preconceived idea but a combination of the client's requirements and desires, the site and the budget. Crosson Clarke Carnachan Architects strives for the highest standards of client service, design and documentation. At the completion of each project the aim is to have achieved a building that is beyond the client's expectations. Crosson Clarke Carnachan Architects believe good design will produce functional and aesthetically pleasing spaces and buildings that have an enduring quality over time.

Photo: James Young

Crosson Clarke Carnachan zeichnen sich durch ihre Bereitschaft aus, die Bedürfnisse ihrer Klienten ernst zu nehmen. Ein qualifiziertes Team unterstützt die Arbeit der Partner, die trotz verschiedenster Hintergründe und Interessen in der Lage sind, kommunikativ nach immer besseren Lösungen zu streben. Simon Carnachan ist einer der meistausgezeichneten Architekten Neuseelands. Ken Crosson erhielt ebenfalls bereits viele lokale und nationale Auszeichnungen für seine Arbeiten. Paul Clarke arbeitete 6 Jahre lang zusammen mit Ken, bevor die beiden sich mit Simon Carnachan zusammen taten.

Jedes Projekt wird als ein spezielles, eigenständiges Bauwerk neu entwickelt. Das Endresultat ist keineswegs eine vorgefertigte Idee, sondern vielmehr das Ergebnis der Berücksichtigung von Nutzerwünschen, dem Bauplatz und des finanziellen Rahmens. Am Beginn eines jeden Projektes steht das Ziel im Raum, ein Bauwerk geschaffen zu haben, das die Erwartungen der Bauherrschaft übertrifft. Die Architekten vertreten die Meinung, dass gutes Architekturdesign zu funktionalen und zugleich ästhetischen Räumen führt, die ihre Gültigkeit auch im Laufe der Zeiten behalten werden.

ISLAND HOUSE

PETE BOSSLEY
ARCHITECTS

The indigenous architecture of the Pacific Islands – simple wooden pole structures with large roofs – was the direct precursor for this design. The linear floor plan descends along the hillside as it slopes down from north to south. The spaces, each of them designed as an individual room under the common roof, were interlinked to form a spatial chain. The prefabricated wooden structural framework and the roof were built first. Interior fitting and mounting of the window glazing were then easily executed under the weather protection provided by the broad roof.

Prämisse war es hier, das Grundbedürfnis nach Obdach auf die elementarste Form zu abstrahieren und daraus eine neuartige Wohnwelt zu schaffen. Vorbilder der Bauform mit ihrem großen, auf Pfeilern lagernden Dach sind in der Volksarchitektur der pazifischen Inseln zu finden. Der lineare Grundriss folgt der von Norden nach Süden abfallenden Geländetopografie. Die Räume wurden kettenartig angelegt, jeder davon betont wie ein Einzelhaus unter dem großen Dach. Zuerst wurde das konstruktive Gerüst und das Dach errichtet, danach erfolgte wettergeschützt der Innenausbau und das Aufstellen der Glaswände.

COUNTRY / LAND	NEW ZEALAND / NEUSEELAND	HOUSE NAME / BEZEICHNUNG DES HAUSES	HEATLEY HOUSE
LOCATION (CITY/REGION) / LAGE (STADT/REGION)			BAY OF ISLANDS / PACIFIC COAST
ARCHITECT / ARCHITEKT	PETE BOSSLEY ARCHITECTS LTD	YEAR OF COMPLETION / BAUJAHR	2001
PHOTOGRAPHER / FOTOGRAF	PATRICK REYNOLDS	SQUARE FEET / QUADRAT METER	3551 / 330
CITY AND COUNTRY ARCHITECT / STADT UND LAND ARCHITEKT			AUCKLAND, NEW ZEALAND
WEBSITE ARCHITECT / HOMEPAGE ARCHITEKT			WWW.BOSSLEYARCHITECTS.CO.NZ

Hill House - Pacific Palisades, California, USA - Johnston Marklee Architects - Photographer Eric Staudenmaier

NORTH AMERICA / NORD AMERIKA

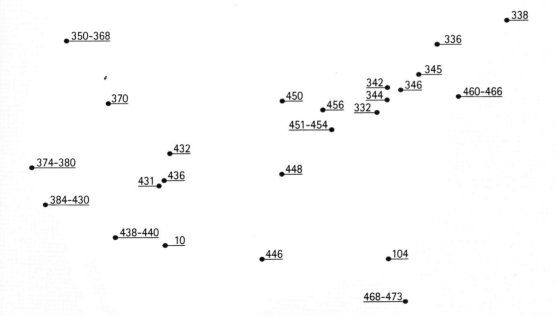

The program for this house was deployed in three interconnected building volumes that form an intimate entrance courtyard from which all three wings are accessed. The floor plan reflects the specific needs of the clients.

Die Funktionen des Hauses wurden in drei miteinander verbundenen Baukörpern untergebracht. Diese definieren einen intimen Eingangshof, von dem aus das zum See hin gelegene Haupthaus betreten wird. Das Raumangebot entspricht den speziellen Bedürfnissen des kinderlosen Besitzerpaars.

LAKE ERIE WEEKEND HOME
EFM DESIGN
EMANUELA FRATTINI MAGNUSSON

Since no children are present, a small kitchen was deemed sufficient in order to create a generous living room with a gallery that opens to the bedroom on the upper level of the lakeside main house wing. Canadian granite was used to create lively interior and exterior wall surfaces. Cedar, galvanized tin, and glass complete the harmonious selection of materials.

Die recht kleine Küche ist abgeschlossen, der Wohn-Essraum wurde dafür großzügig mit einer offenen Galerie zum Schlafzimmer im OG gestaltet. Kanadischer Granit erzeugt stimmungsvolle Wandflächen innen und außen. Cedarholz, Zinkblech und Glas komplettieren die harmonisch abgestimmte Materialienpalette.

COUNTRY / LAND	CANADA / KANADA	HOUSE NAME / BEZEICHNUNG DES HAUSES	LAKE ERIE WEEKEND HOME
LOCATION (CITY/REGION) / LAGE (STADT/REGION)			ONTARIO / LAKE ERIE
ARCHITECT / ARCHITEKT	EFM DESIGN EMANUELA FRATTINI MAGNUSSON	YEAR OF COMPLETION / BAUJAHR	2002
PHOTOGRAPHER / FOTOGRAF	BILL WHITAKER	SQUARE FEET / QUADRAT METER	4089 / 380
CITY AND COUNTRY ARCHITECT / STADT UND LAND ARCHITEKT			NEW YORK, NY, USA
WEBSITE ARCHITECT / HOMEPAGE ARCHITEKT			WWW.EFMDESIGN.COM

The art collector clients wanted a country house in which their collection can be exhibited. The plan contains three distinct realms: a private, a public, and a circulation zone. Wood was used as the main material: structurally it comprises the framing walls and the post-and-beam system; aesthetically it provides warmth and mellowness, inside as well as outside

Die Bauherrschaft - passionierte Kunstsammler - wünschten sich ein Landhaus, das sich insbesondere zur Ausstellung ihrer Kunstsammlung eignen sollte. Der Grundriss definiert drei klare Bereiche: eine private, eine öffentliche und eine Verteilerzone. Holz wurde als Hauptmaterial gewählt. Dies erfolgte nicht nur aufgrund der guten Wirtschaftlichkeit des Materials, sondern auch um eine durchgehende Wärme zu erzeugen, sowohl im Inneren als auch im Äußeren.

+1

RESIDENCE LES ABOUTS
PIERRE THIBAULT ARCHITECTE

COUNTRY / LAND	CANADA / KANADA	HOUSE NAME / BEZEICHNUNG DES HAUSES	RESIDENCE LES ABOUTS
LOCATION (CITY/REGION) / LAGE (STADT/REGION)			SAINT-EDMOND-DE-GRANTHAM, QUÉBEC
ARCHITECT / ARCHITEKT	PIERRE THIBAULT ARCHITECTE	YEAR OF COMPLETION / BAUJAHR	2005
PHOTOGRAPHER / FOTOGRAF	ALAIN LAFOREST	SQUARE FEET / QUADRAT METER	2500 / 232
CITY AND COUNTRY ARCHITECT / STADT UND LAND ARCHITEKT			QUÉBEC, CANADA
WEBSITE ARCHITECT / HOMEPAGE ARCHITEKT			WWW.PTHIBAULT.COM

This home occupies the crown of a hilltop, from which it enjoys a 360 degree view over both the outer ocean and the inland landscape. The bald, exposed hilltop suggested a site strategy that would accommodate an archetypal desire for both prospect and refuge. Both the structures turn outward against the wind but also open to face one another across a courtyard sheltered by low concrete walls. A dynamic relationship is established between the two structures, so that one focuses out to the landscape by ironically looking inward through the court.

Dieses Haus steht am Scheitel eines Hügels und verfügt somit über Ausblicke auf das Meer und die küstennahe Landschaft. Die exponierte Lage auf dem Hügel veranlasste die Architekten dazu, eine Strategie des Öffnens und zugleich des Rückzuges zu entwickeln. Beide Bauteile verschließen sich gegen die harschen Winde, öffnen sich jedoch über einen gemeinsamen, von niedrigen Betonstutzmauern geschützten Hof zueinander. Somit entsteht eine dynamische Beziehung zwischen den Bauteilen, wobei man ironischerweise durch den Hof erst in die weite der Landschaft blickt.

HILL HOUSE
MACKAY-LYONS SWEETAPPLE ARCHITECTS

Both structures have blunt ends which contain two stories of cellular spaces; sleeping quarters and studio in the main house; and guest areas in the barn. Open plan spaces face toward covered decks and the courtyard. The servant functions, including entries, stairs and bathrooms are located on the sides of the plans. Two pin-wheeling concrete walls appear to slide out from under the shingled skins to form the courtyard. A continuous line of cabinetry follows the concrete wall in each structure, becoming a wood storage unit outdoors.

Beide Bauteile sind mit geschlossenen, rumpfartigen Enden versehen worden. Hier befinden sich gestapelt die Schlafzimmer bzw. ein Atelier im Haupthaus und die Gastbereiche in der Scheune. Offene Raumbereiche orientieren sich zum Hof. Die „dienenden" Räume wie Eingänge, Treppen und Badezimmer erstrecken sich entlang der Seiten des Grundrisses. Zwei niedrige Betonstützmauer schieben sich aus den Keilen und definieren den zentralen Hof.

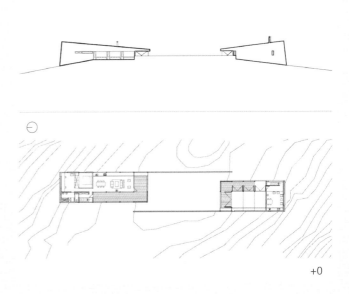

+0

COUNTRY / LAND	CANADA / KANADA	HOUSE NAME / BEZEICHNUNG DES HAUSES	HILL HOUSE
LOCATION (CITY/REGION) / LAGE (STADT/REGION)			NOVA SCOTIA
ARCHITECT / ARCHITEKT	MACKAY-LYONS SWEETAPPLE ARCHITECTS	YEAR OF COMPLETION / BAUJAHR	2004
PHOTOGRAPHER / FOTOGRAF	MACKAY-LYONS SWEETAPPLE ARCHITECTS	SQUARE FEET / QUADRAT METER	XXX
CITY AND COUNTRY ARCHITECT / STADT UND LAND ARCHITEKT			HALIFAX, CANADA
WEBSITE ARCHITECT / HOMEPAGE ARCHITEKT			WWW.MLARCHITECTS.CA

Since the owners entertain up to 15 guests per night in the summers they wished a private sleeping space as a separate private cabin removed from the main residence. Floor to ceiling glass walls on three sides allow views onto the lake through the veil of wooden slats. The cabin contains a bedroom, an enclosed toilet and an outdoor sink/shower space.

Da die Bauherrschaft im Sommer bis zu 15 Gästen im Haupthaus beherbergen, wünschten sie einen privaten Schlafbereich in einem abgelegenen Gebäudeteil. Glaselemente wurden an drei Seiten des Baues angeordnet. Sie öffnen den Blick auf den nahe gelegenen See, der durch einen Schleier aus Holzlamellen gefiltert wird. Das separate Häuschen verfügt über ein Schlafzimmer und einen Toilettenraum; Dusche und Waschtisch befinden sich im Freien.

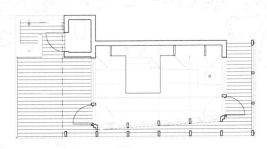

+0

SUNSET CABIN
TAYLOR_SMYTH ARCHITECTS

COUNTRY / LAND	CANADA / KANADA	HOUSE NAME / BEZEICHNUNG DES HAUSES	SUNSET CABIN
LOCATION (CITY/REGION) / LAGE (STADT/REGION)			LAKE SIMCOE
ARCHITECT / ARCHITEKT		TAYLOR_SMYTH ARCHITECTS	YEAR OF COMPLETION / BAUJAHR 2004
PHOTOGRAPHER / FOTOGRAF		BEN RAHN – AFRAME STUDIO	SQUARE FEET / QUADRAT METER 275 / 26
CITY AND COUNTRY ARCHITECT / STADT UND LAND ARCHITEKT			TORONTO, CANADA
WEBSITE ARCHITECT / HOMEPAGE ARCHITEKT			WWW.TAYLORSMYTH.COM

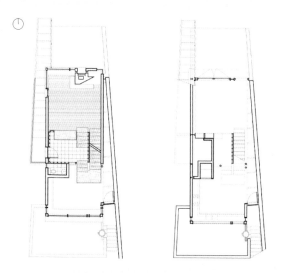

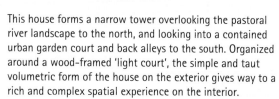

This house forms a narrow tower overlooking the pastoral river landscape to the north, and looking into a contained urban garden court and back alleys to the south. Organized around a wood-framed 'light court', the simple and taut volumetric form of the house on the exterior gives way to a rich and complex spatial experience on the interior.

Dieses Haus bildet einen schmalen Turm, der Ausblicke auf eine Flusslandschaft im Süden, einen städtischen Gartenhof sowie Gassen im Norden bietet. Um einen zentralen, aus Holz erbauten Lichthof organisiert, entpuppt sich die einfache äußere Form im Inneren als erstaunlich komplex und räumlich vielfältig.

TOWER HOUSE
SHIM-SUTCLIFFE ARCHITECTS

COUNTRY / LAND	CANADA / KANADA	HOUSE NAME / BEZEICHNUNG DES HAUSES		TOWER HOUSE
LOCATION (CITY/REGION) / LAGE (STADT/REGION)				STRATFORD, ONTARIO
ARCHITECT / ARCHITEKT		SHIM-SUTCLIFFE ARCHITECTS	YEAR OF COMPLETION / BAUJAHR	2001
PHOTOGRAPHER / FOTOGRAF		JAMES DOW	SQUARE FEET / QUADRAT METER	1800 / 167
CITY AND COUNTRY ARCHITECT / STADT UND LAND ARCHITEKT				TORONTO, CANADA
WEBSITE ARCHITECT / HOMEPAGE ARCHITEKT				WWW.SHIM-SUTCLIFFE.COM

ISLAND HOUSE
SHIM-SUTCLIFFE
ARCHITECTS

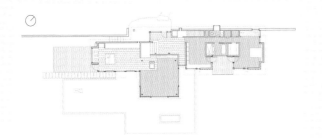

This summer home both engages the existing landscape and creates its own landscape. Its simple plan spatially interlocks two linear flat-roofed rectangular zones around a cube-like living room space. From the entry the living room seems to be an island in the large reflecting pool from which the view extends across a meadow to the river beyond.

Dieses Sommerhaus setzt sich mit der Umgebung auseinander und schafft zugleich eine eigenständige Landschaft. Der einfache Grundriss besteht aus zwei linearen Raumbereichen, welche den kubenähnlichen Wohnraum definieren. Vom Eingang aus gesehen erscheint das Wohnzimmer wie eine Insel im anschließenden Teich, der Blick setzt sich anschließend über die Wiese bis zum Fluss fort.

345

COUNTRY / LAND	CANADA / KANADA	HOUSE NAME / BEZEICHNUNG DES HAUSES	ISLAND HOUSE
LOCATION (CITY/REGION) / LAGE (STADT/REGION)			ST. LAWRENCE RIVER, ONTARIO
ARCHITECT / ARCHITEKT	SHIM-SUTCLIFFE ARCHITECTS	YEAR OF COMPLETION / BAUJAHR	2001
PHOTOGRAPHER / FOTOGRAF	JAMES DOW	SQUARE FEET / QUADRAT METER	2000 / 186
CITY AND COUNTRY ARCHITECT / STADT UND LAND ARCHITEKT			TORONTO, CANADA
WEBSITE ARCHITECT / HOMEPAGE ARCHITEKT			WWW.SHIM-SUTCLIFFE.COM

The new suburban houses being built nearby to replace 1960's ranch homes are constructed of brick facing and fake stone and seem to be the new ideal suburban dream house for countless people. But these homes are the antithesis of their modernist predecessors. This residence stands in defiant contrast to this context. Materially rich, dark, and abstract, it creates a clear threshold to the world within, to the site it creates and to the ravine edge over which it looks. The L-shaped house frames a reconfigured landscape created around shaped, tree covered mounds and a sweeping meadow. Imbedding itself into the centre of the house, the reflecting pool and swimming pool beyond form the intermediary between building and landscape, weaving reflected light, motion and sound into the heart of the home.

Die neuen Vorstadthäuser in der Umgebung, die anstelle abgerissener Häuser aus den 60er Jahren gebaut werden, sind mit Klinkerriemen und Kunststein verkleidet, um den vermeintlichen Geschmack der neuen Bewohner zu entsprechen. Sie stellen somit die Antithese zu den Vorgängerbauten der Moderne dar. Dieses Haus stellt sich bewusst gegen diese Entwicklung. Als abstrakt gehaltene Form stellt es einen klar formulierten Übergang dar zwischen Innen- und Außenwelt, zur Umgebung, und zur Schlucht, die es überblickt. Den Fokus im Inneren bildet der Teich bzw. das Schwimmbecken, das eine Verbindung zwischen Landschaft und Bauwerk herstellt indem es Licht, Naturklang bzw. Bewegung in das Hausinnere führt.

WEATHERING STEEL HOUSE
SHIM-SUTCLIFFE ARCHITECTS

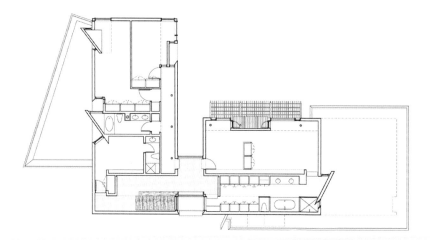

+1

348

From the street this house is seemingly much more opaque than adjacent buildings, but sculptural cut outs in the elevation offer precise transparent glimpses of the ravine beyond. Upon entering, a circulation space parallel to the front elevation connects garage entry, front entry, basement courtyard and second floor in one continuous slice of vertical and horizontal space. From the entry one catches a glimpse of the ravine treetops beyond before rising up a few steps to the main living level. From here the landscape and the house unfold, with the linear watercourse weaving internal and external space together.

Von der Straße aus gesehen erscheint das Haus verschlossener als die Häuser der Umgebung, doch große Auslassungen in der Baumasse umrahmen präzise Durchblicke auf die Landschaft hinter dem Haus. Beim Betreten des Hauses gelangt man in einen Verteilerraum, der die Eingänge aus der Garage sowie von der Straße, dem tiefer gelegenen Hof und dem Obergeschoss vertikal und horizontal miteinander verbindet. Stufen führen hinauf ins Wohnzimmer, von dem aus das Haus und die Landschaft sich entfalten.

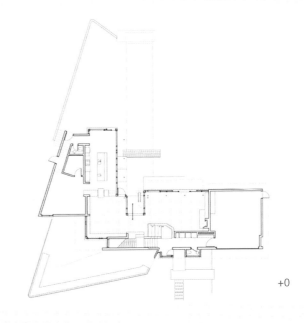

+0

COUNTRY / LAND	CANADA / KANADA	HOUSE NAME / BEZEICHNUNG DES HAUSES	WEATHERING STEEL HOUSE
LOCATION (CITY/REGION) / LAGE (STADT/REGION)			TORONTO, ONTARIO
ARCHITECT / ARCHITEKT	SHIM-SUTCLIFFE ARCHITECTS	YEAR OF COMPLETION / BAUJAHR	2001
PHOTOGRAPHER / FOTOGRAF	JAMES DOW, MICHAEL AWAD	SQUARE FEET / QUADRAT METER	5000 / 465
CITY AND COUNTRY ARCHITECT / STADT UND LAND ARCHITEKT			TORONTO, CANADA
WEBSITE ARCHITECT / HOMEPAGE ARCHITEKT			WWW.SHIM-SUTCLIFFE.COM

This house was conceived to formulate an architectural transition between the steep adjacent hillside and the beach. A steel bridge accesses the entrance and the two-level living room space that creates a portal for a dramatic view through the house to the sea. A private suite with sleeping areas is located on the upper level. The beachside level contains media, home office, and guest spaces.

Zwischen einem steilen Uferhang und dem Strand bildet dieses Haus gewissermaßen die architektonische Verbindung. Eine Stahlbrücke führt zum Eingang und der zweigeschossigen Wohnhalle, die den Blick durch das Haus hindurch wie ein Portal rahmt. Eine Privatsuite mit Schlafbereich befindet sich auf der obersten Etage; das direkt am Strand gelegene Sockelgeschoss nimmt Räume für Medien, Büros und Gäste auf.

SEOLA BEACH HOUSE
EGGLESTON FARKAS ARCHITECTS

351

COUNTRY / LAND	USA	HOUSE NAME / BEZEICHNUNG DES HAUSES	SEOLA BEACH HOUSE
LOCATION (CITY/REGION) / LAGE (STADT/REGION)			BURIEN, WASHINGTON / PACIFIC COAST
ARCHITECT / ARCHITEKT	EGGLESTON FARKAS ARCHITECTS	YEAR OF COMPLETION / BAUJAHR	2005
PHOTOGRAPHER / FOTOGRAF	JIM VAN GUNDY	SQUARE FEET / QUADRAT METER	2432 / 226
CITY AND COUNTRY ARCHITECT / STADT UND LAND ARCHITEKT			SEATTLE, WA, USA
WEBSITE ARCHITECT / HOMEPAGE ARCHITEKT			WWW.EGGFARKARCH.COM

This retreat serves as a base for cross-country skiing and mountain biking. The owners wished to accommodate 6-8 people with a communal area for gathering and dining. The building is aligned with the valley and openings at the ends focus on views that dramatically emphasize the valley's length.

Dieses Refugium dient als Basis für Ausflüge per Langlauf-Ski oder Mountainbike. Es beherbergt 6-8 Personen um einen geräumigen Wohnsaal. Der Baukörper nimmt die Talrichtung auf und öffnet sich an den Enden zu Ausblicken auf die Tallandschaft.

METHOW CABIN
EGGLESTON FARKAS ARCHITECTS

The exterior cedar siding is continued through the living spaces to create a continuum of interior and exterior space. The shed roof echoes the slope of the hills beyond. It creates both a protected entry porch at the low end and a sleeping loft at the high end. The covered entry stair remains snow-free even as snow avalanches off the roof.

Um ein Kontinuum von Innen- und Außenraum zu bewirken, setzt sich das Zedernholz der Fassaden in den Räumen fort. Das Pultdach übernimmt die Neigung des nahen Hügels. Es bildet einen geschützten Eingang am niedrigen Ende und ein Loft mit Schlafplätzen am hohen Ende. So bleibt die überdachte Eingangstreppe auch bei starkem Schneefall schneefrei.

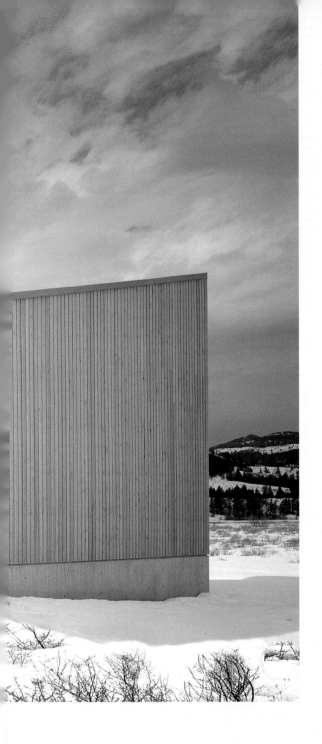

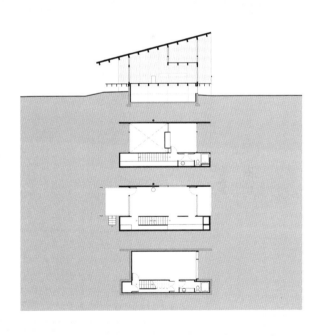

COUNTRY / LAND	USA	HOUSE NAME / BEZEICHNUNG DES HAUSES	METHOW CABIN
LOCATION (CITY/REGION) / LAGE (STADT/REGION)			WINTHROP, WASHINGTON
ARCHITECT / ARCHITEKT	EGGLESTON FARKAS ARCHITECTS	YEAR OF COMPLETION / BAUJAHR	2000
PHOTOGRAPHER / FOTOGRAF	JIM VAN GUNDY	SQUARE FEET / QUADRAT METER	1184 / 110
CITY AND COUNTRY ARCHITECT / STADT UND LAND ARCHITEKT			SEATTLE, WA, USA
WEBSITE ARCHITECT / HOMEPAGE ARCHITEKT			WWW.EGGFARKARCH.COM

EGGLESTON
FARKAS ARCHITECTS

SEATTLE, WASHINGTON
USA

The heart of the early design process is generating a strong concept that addresses all the factors while highlighting the most important ones. By generating a strong concept, the design team creates a critical framework for the entire project. While each project is a unique response to its site and the owner's aspirations, clarity and an economy of means are principles that inform every design.

The work is elemental, not ornamental. It is simple, not in the stylistic sense that "less is more," but rather that nothing has become superfluous and that details have not emerged in conflict with the central design intent. This attention to concept and detail, aspirations and budget, imagination and realities, allows Eggleston Farkas Architects to create work that is "rigorously legible, a modest and elegant expression in an exciting but calm and disciplined new voice."

Photographer: Jim Van Gundy

Die Anfangsaufgabe beim Entwurfsprozess besteht darin, ein starkes Grundkonzept zu entwickeln, das alle wesentlichen Faktoren berücksichtigt und die wichtigsten Elemente betont. Durch die Festlegung eines starken Konzeptes wird schon zu Beginn eines Projektes für einen klaren Rahmen für das gesamte Projekt gesorgt. Obwohl jedes Projekt mit Rücksicht auf die Wünsche und Bedürfnisse der Bauherrschaft bzw. auf die Eigenschaften de Standortes entsteht, sind Klarheit und Einfachheit die Prinzipien, die jeden Entwurf prägen.

Die Arbeiten sind einfach – nicht im Sinne von „weniger ist mehr" – sondern im Weglassen von Überflüssigem und im Vermeiden von Details, die im Konflikt mit dem zentralen Entwurfsgedanken stehen. Diese sorgsame Auseinandersetzung mit Konzept und Detail, Budget, Imagination und den Rahmenbedingungen erlaubt es den Architekten, Arbeiten zu schaffen, die „rigoros lesbar und zugleich zurückhaltender Ausdruck einer ruhigen und disziplinierten neuen Handschrift" sind.

This summerhouse will become a retirement house for a couple and their extended family. The site slopes steeply down to the rocky beach and is forested with mature firs. The simple program was augmented by concerns that natural light be used in contrast to the dark forest. To do this, a thin continuous skylight at the roof peak catches the sun from early morning until late afternoon. Views east to the coast and mountains were maximized. In response to the owner's desire to be able to "use" the site, outdoor porches were added. A glazed roll-up garage door opens the workroom to the site.

Dieses Sommerhaus ist so konzipiert, dass es zukünftig zum Hauptwohnsitz eines Paares und dessen Großfamilie umfunktioniert werden kann. Das Grundstück fällt steil zum felsigen Strand ab und ist mit alten Tannen bewaldet. Der übersichtliche Baukörper wurde durch Maßnahmen zum Einfangen des Sonnenlichtes im dunklen Wald gegliedert – ein Oberlicht in der Dachspitze sorgt ganztägig für Helligkeit im Inneren. Ausblicke nach Osten zur Küste und zu den Bergen werden betont. Auf Wunsch des Klienten wurden überdachte Veranden im Freien vorgesehen. Ein verglastes Rolltor erlaubt es, das Arbeitszimmer zum Wald hin zu öffnen.

+1

SAUNDERS CABIN
THE MILLER /
HULL PARTNERSHIP

COUNTRY / LAND	USA	HOUSE NAME / BEZEICHNUNG DES HAUSES	SAUNDERS CABIN
LOCATION (CITY/REGION) / LAGE (STADT/REGION)			GUEMES ISLAND, WASHINGTON / PACIFIC COAST
ARCHITECT / ARCHITEKT		THE MILLER/HULL PARTNERSHIP	YEAR OF COMPLETION / BAUJAHR 2001
PHOTOGRAPHER / FOTOGRAF		JOHN DIMAIO	SQUARE FEET / QUADRAT METER 1345 / 125
CITY AND COUNTRY ARCHITECT / STADT UND LAND ARCHITEKT			SEATTLE, WA, USA
WEBSITE ARCHITECT / HOMEPAGE ARCHITEKT			WWW.MILLERHULL.COM

The site's natural beauty led to a design that blurs the distinction between indoor and outdoor space. The house is arranged along a central corridor formed by the various parts. Each of these elements is sheathed in natural materials that reflect the setting. These materials - granite, cedar and stucco - run from the exterior to the interior to reinforce the inside/outside concept.

Die Schönheit des Bauplatzes inspirierte den Architekten dazu, die Grenzen zwischen Innen und Außen verschmelzen zu lassen. Das Haus gruppiert sich um einen zentralen, durch die pavillonartigen Bauteile definierten Gang. Die Bauteile sind innen wie außen in natürlichen Materialien – Granit, Zedernholz und Putz – ausgeführt in Fortsetzung des Innen/Außen-Konzepts,

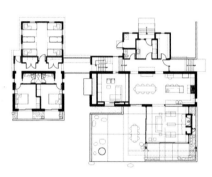

RAINBOW ROCK RESIDENCE
<u>TOM LENCHEK</u>

COUNTRY / LAND	USA	HOUSE NAME / BEZEICHNUNG DES HAUSES	RAINBOW ROCK RESIDENCE
LOCATION (CITY/REGION) / LAGE (STADT/REGION)			LOPEZ ISLAND, WASHINGTON
ARCHITECT / ARCHITEKT	TOM LENCHEK	YEAR OF COMPLETION / BAUJAHR	2004
PHOTOGRAPHER / FOTOGRAF	STEVE KEATING	SQUARE FEET / QUADRAT METER	5272 / 490
CITY AND COUNTRY ARCHITECT / STADT UND LAND ARCHITEKT			SEATTLE, WA, USA
WEBSITE ARCHITECT / HOMEPAGE ARCHITEKT			WWW.BALANCEASSOCIATES.COM

WINTERGREEN CABIN
TOM LENCHEK

This cabin is built into a steep hillside overlooking a stream with a view to the mountains. It anchors into the hill with a concrete base that contains the garage. The upper floor houses the living spaces. The living / dining / kitchen spaces are arrayed along the south side of the cabin with large windows walls on three sides.

Dieses Waldhaus mit Ausblick auf die Berge fügt sich in einen Steilhang oberhalb eines Baches ein. Ein Sockelgeschoss aus Beton verankert das Bauwerk im Berg. Das Obergeschoss beinhaltet die Wohnräume, wobei sich der Wohn-, Eß-, Kochbereich mit großen Fensterfronten entlang der Südfront entwickelt.

COUNTRY / LAND	USA	HOUSE NAME / BEZEICHNUNG DES HAUSES	WINTERGREEN CABIN
LOCATION (CITY/REGION) / LAGE (STADT/REGION)			METHOW VALLEY, WASHINGTON
ARCHITECT / ARCHITEKT	TOM LENCHEK	YEAR OF COMPLETION / BAUJAHR	2005
PHOTOGRAPHER / FOTOGRAF	STEVE KEATING	SQUARE FEET / QUADRAT METER	1613 / 150
CITY AND COUNTRY ARCHITECT / STADT UND LAND ARCHITEKT			SEATTLE, WA, USA
WEBSITE ARCHITECT / HOMEPAGE ARCHITEKT			WWW.BALANCEASSOCIATES.COM

The evocative qualities of wood and stone were explored here to effectively embed the home into the larger order of nature. The structural framework that rises above the granite plinth was constructed in wood columns and roof beams and clad with wood shingles. Wood surfaces are also the formative element inside where they are combined with white wall surfaces to create a light, open ambience.

Die evokativen Kräfte von Holz und Stein werden hier mit dem Ziel zusammengeführt, das Haus in die größere Ordnung der Natur harmonisch einzubetten. Über dem Sockel aus Granit baute man die tragenden Stützen und Dachträger aus Holz auf, die Wandflächen wurden anschließend mit Holzschindeln verschalt. Auch im Inneren ist Holz das prägende Material. Hier wird es mit weißen Wandflächen kombiniert, um eine helle, offene Qualität zu erzeugen.

SEMIAHMOO RESIDENCE
FINNE ARCHITECTS , NILS C. FINNE

COUNTRY / LAND	USA	HOUSE NAME / BEZEICHNUNG DES HAUSES	SEMIAHMOO RESIDENCE
LOCATION (CITY/REGION) / LAGE (STADT/REGION)			SEMIAHMOO, WASHINGTON / PACIFIC COAST
ARCHITECT / ARCHITEKT	FINNE ARCHITECTS, NILS C. FINNE, AIA	YEAR OF COMPLETION / BAUJAHR	2001
PHOTOGRAPHER / FOTOGRAF	ART GRICE	SQUARE FEET / QUADRAT METER	6671 / 620
CITY AND COUNTRY ARCHITECT / STADT UND LAND ARCHITEKT			SEATTLE, WA, USA
WEBSITE ARCHITECT / HOMEPAGE ARCHITEKT			WWW.FINNE.COM

To lessen the impact of the home on the natural setting the architect opted for compacting its mass and elevating it on stilts that allow the ground plane to continue unimpeded underneath the structure. A steel skeleton frame was foreseen to reduce building costs and limit the foundations to four points upon from which the building extends upwards. This strategy has the added advantage that the spaces of the home are elevated one-two levels above the ground plane and therefore enjoy gracious views out over the adjacent meadows to the mountains beyond.

Um die unberührte Natur des Standorts möglichst nicht zu beeinträchtigen, schuf der Architekt eine kompakte Baumasse und hob diese auf Stelzen an, damit das Erdreich sich ungehindert unter dem Bauwerk erstrecken kann. Zudem sah er ein Kosten sparendes Stahlskelett als Fachwerkkonstruktion vor, das die Lasten auf die vier Fundamente des Baus konzentriert. Diese Strategie hat den zusätzlichen Vorzug, dass die angehobenen Nutzebenen großzügige Ausblicke auf die umliegenden Wiesen und Bergen erhalten.

DELTA SHELTER
TOM KUNDIG, OLSON SUNDBERG KUNDIG ALLEN ARCHITECTS

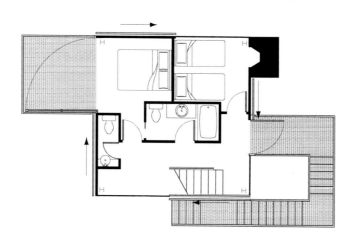

+1

366

Since the shelter is uninhabited much of the year, sliding steel wall panels via which all window surfaces can be completely closed were planned. These are operated by steel wheel cranks inside that give the interiors a factory-like rough sense that reminds one of nearby lumber mills and the history of the American West. This sense is complemented by elegant modern detailing with exposed plywood wall and ceiling sheathing and exposed steel girders throughout the interiors.

Da das Haus über lange Zeiträume nicht bewohnt wird, entwickelte der Architekt verschiebbare Stahlpanelle, mit deren Hilfe die Glasflächen komplett verschlossen werden können. Bedient werden sie über metallene Heberäder im Inneren, die hier ein fabrikähnliches Ambiente schaffen, das an die Holzfabriken der Umgebung und die Geschichte des amerikanischen Westens erinnert. Diese Qualität wird durch im Inneren verwendete Materialien wie die Sperrholzverkleidung der Wände und Decken sowie die sichtbaren Stahlträger der Wand und Dachkonstruktion unterstrichen.

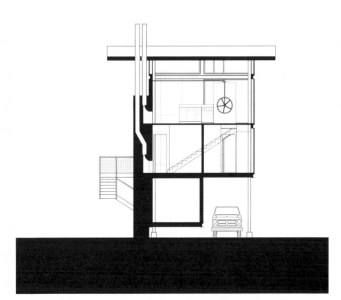

COUNTRY / LAND	USA	HOUSE NAME / BEZEICHNUNG DES HAUSES	DELTA SHELTER
LOCATION (CITY/REGION) / LAGE (STADT/REGION)			WINTHROP, WASHINGTON
ARCHITECT / ARCHITEKT	OLSON SUNDBERG KUNDIG ALLEN ARCHITECTS	YEAR OF COMPLETION / BAUJAHR	2005
PHOTOGRAPHER / FOTOGRAF	TIM BIES & BENJAMIN BENSCHNEIDER	SQUARE FEET / QUADRAT METER	1000 / 93
CITY AND COUNTRY ARCHITECT / STADT UND LAND ARCHITEKT			SEATTLE, WA, USA
WEBSITE ARCHITECT / HOMEPAGE ARCHITEKT			WWW.OLSONSUNDBERG.COM

THE BRAIN
<u>TOM KUNDIG</u>

The Brain is a laboratory where the client, a filmmaker, can work out ideas. Physically, that neighbourhood birthplace of invention, the garage, provides the conceptual model. The form is essentially a cast-in-place concrete box. A steel mezzanine is inserted into the box along the north wall. All interior structures are made of raw, hot-rolled steel sheets.

Das Haus, „The Brain" („das Gehirn") genannt, dient als Ort des Rückzuges für einen Filmemacher, der hier neue Projekte entwickelt. Gestalterisches Vorbild war der Prototyp einer Garage als Sinnbild eines Ortes der Erfindung. Die Bauform ist begrenzt auf eine einfache Kiste aus Sichtbeton. Eine Galerie aus Stahl wurde entlang der nördlichen Wand eingezogen. Sämtliche Einbauten wurden aus unbehandelten Stahltafeln errichtet.

COUNTRY / LAND	USA	HOUSE NAME / BEZEICHNUNG DES HAUSES	THE BRAIN
LOCATION (CITY/REGION) / LAGE (STADT/REGION)			SEATTLE, WASHINGTON
ARCHITECT / ARCHITEKT	TOM KUNDIG	YEAR OF COMPLETION / BAUJAHR	2001
PHOTOGRAPHER / FOTOGRAF	BENSCHNEIDER, PROZZO, DARLEY, BIES, WILD	SQUARE FEET / QUADRAT METER	1340 / 125
CITY AND COUNTRY ARCHITECT / STADT UND LAND ARCHITEKT			SEATTLE, WA, USA
WEBSITE ARCHITECT / HOMEPAGE ARCHITEKT			WWW.OLSONSUNDBERG.COM

This home, conceived as a simple shelter in nature, celebrates the untouched wilderness on the other side of the lake. A large glazed window element can be pivoted upward to create an opening across the entire width of the living room space that frames a portal view of the mountain silhouette.

Dieses Haus, als einfache Hütte in der Natur gedacht, zelebriert die unberührte Wildnis auf der anderen Seite des Sees. Ein großes Glasportal, das sich nach oben kippen lässt, schafft eine Öffnung über der ganzen Breite des Wohnsaals. Dessen Portalöffnung rahmt den Blick auf die Bergsilhouette.

CHICKEN POINT CABIN
OLSON SUNDBERG KUNDIG ALLEN ARCHITECTS

Following the example set by the simple cabins nearby, industrially fabricated materials were utilized: concrete block masonry was used for the walls, the living room floor is made of exposed concrete, basic steel profiles were used for window frames and roof beams, and a segment of steel pipe was transformed into an open fireplace.

Dem Vorbild einfacher Behausungen der Gegend folgend wurden industriell gefertigte Materialien verwendet: die Wände sind aus Betonsteinen gemauert, der Boden aus Sichtbeton, einfache Stahlprofile wurden als Fensterrahmen und Deckenträger eingebaut und ein Stahlrohrsegment wurde in einen offenen Kamin umgewandelt.

COUNTRY / LAND	USA	HOUSE NAME / BEZEICHNUNG DES HAUSES	CHICKEN POINT CABIN
LOCATION (CITY/REGION) / LAGE (STADT/REGION)			IDAHO / LAKE XXX
ARCHITECT / ARCHITEKT	OLSON SUNDBERG KUNDIG ALLEN ARCHITECTS	YEAR OF COMPLETION / BAUJAHR	2002
PHOTOGRAPHER / FOTOGRAF	BENJAMIN BENSCHNEIDER	SQUARE FEET / QUADRAT METER	1291 / 120
CITY AND COUNTRY ARCHITECT / STADT UND LAND ARCHITEKT			SEATTLE, WA, USA
WEBSITE ARCHITECT / HOMEPAGE ARCHITEKT			WWW.OLSONSUNDBERG.COM

Nestled on the crest of a hillside at a former sheep ranch that is now home to commissioned sculptures by Richard Serra, Bruce Nauman, Martin Puryear and others, the bipartite residence for visiting artists is enclosed by two seemingly parallel concrete walls that cut through the hill. The stepped floor creates a constantly shifting section. This shifting of horizontal and vertical planes allows the house itself to be experienced as a sculpture.

Gelegen auf einem Hügel auf dem Grundstück einer ehemaligen Schafweide, auf der heute Skulpturen von Richard Serra, Bruce Naumann und Martin Puryear stehen, wird diese zweiteilige Residenz für Gastkünstler von zwei scheinbar parallelen Betonmauern eingefasst. Die abgestufte Bodenebene lässt eine Verschiebung der horizontalen und vertikalen Ebenen entstehen, so dass der Bau selbst als Skulptur wahrgenommen wird.

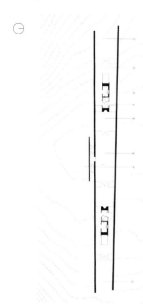

VISITNG ARTISTS HOUSE
JIM JENNINGS ARCHITECTURE

COUNTRY / LAND	USA	HOUSE NAME / BEZEICHNUNG DES HAUSES	VISITING ARTISTS HOUSE
LOCATION (CITY/REGION) / LAGE (STADT/REGION)			t, CALIFORNIA
ARCHITECT / ARCHITEKT		JIM JENNINGS ARCHITECTURE	YEAR OF COMPLETION / BAUJAHR 2003
PHOTOGRAPHER / FOTOGRAF		TIM GRIFFITH	SQUARE FEET / QUADRAT METER 1700 / 156
CITY AND COUNTRY ARCHITECT / STADT UND LAND ARCHITEKT			SAN FRANCISCO, CA, USA
WEBSITE ARCHITECT / HOMEPAGE ARCHITEKT			WWW.JIMJENNINGSARCHITECTURE.COM

SOMA HOUSE
JIM JENNINGS ARCHITECTURE

The residence is situated in a former industrial area of San Francisco's SOMA (South of Market) district. A strong but elegant Cor-ten steel wall stands up to the harshness of the street while hinting at a more refined world inside. The main house with two bedroom suites, a living space and an office can be separated by sliding partitions. Between the guesthouse, garage and the main house an interior courtyard provides a rare element of serenity in the gritty urban setting.

Gelegen in einem ehemaligen Gewerbegebiet, schafft die „Cor-ten" Stahlverkleidung einen Gegenpol zur rauen Straße. Dieser Kontrast lässt bereits die gestalterische Perfektion im Inneren erahnen. Das zwei Schlafzimmer, Wohnzimmer und Büro beinhaltende Haupthaus lässt sich über große Schiebewände abtrennen. Ein Innenhof, gelegen zwischen Gasthaus, Garage und Haupthaus, schafft einen seltenen Ort der Ruhe inmitten der unwirtlichen Umgebung.

375

COUNTRY / LAND	USA	HOUSE NAME / BEZEICHNUNG DES HAUSES	SOMA HOUSE
LOCATION (CITY/REGION) / LAGE (STADT/REGION)			SAN FRANCISCO, CALIFORNIA
ARCHITECT / ARCHITEKT	JIM JENNINGS ARCHITECTURE	YEAR OF COMPLETION / BAUJAHR	2002
PHOTOGRAPHER / FOTOGRAF	SHARON RISEDORPH	SQUARE FEET / QUADRAT METER	4500 / 418
CITY AND COUNTRY ARCHITECT / STADT UND LAND ARCHITEKT			SAN FRANCISCO, CA, USA
WEBSITE ARCHITECT / HOMEPAGE ARCHITEKT			WWW.JIMJENNINGSARCHITECTURE.COM

This home was built to replace and commemorate a beloved 1950's house by Willliam Wurster that was severely damaged in a fire. Accommodation of new earthquake and tsunami guidelines led the architects to raise the structure on pier-like piles. These were reinforced with exposed steel X-bracing as earthquake protection.

Anstelle eines niedergebrannten Gebäudes von William Wurster aus den 50er Jahren wurde das neue Haus in Anlehnung an das beliebte Original erbaut. Nunmehr galt es, neuen Richtlinien zum Schutz gegen Erdbeben und Tsunami zu entsprechen. Das Haus wurde angehoben, um die Holzpfeiler des Fundaments mit Stahlprofilen X-förmig zu verstärken und um eine freie Unterspülung im Falle eines Tsunamis zu ermöglichen.

STINSON BEACH HOUSE
TURNBULL GRIFFIN HAESLOOP
ARCHITECTS

Flooding caused by a tsunami can flow unimpeded under the house. The rooms are organized in spatial ribbons. The living/ dining space forms the core of the composition. Diversely varied spaces with direct connection to the dunes - a sheltered terrace with an exterior fireplace, a broad stair with steps for sitting, and a covered solar veranda - were foreseen.

Die Zimmer sind in Raumbändern organisiert; der Wohn-Essbereich bildet hierbei den Kern. Zum Meer hin befinden sich Räume mit direktem Außenbezug: eine geschützte Freiterrasse mit Kamin, Sitzstufen und eine Sonnenveranda.

COUNTRY / LAND	USA	HOUSE NAME / BEZEICHNUNG DES HAUSES	STINSON BEACH HOUSE
LOCATION (CITY/REGION) / LAGE (STADT/REGION)			CALIFORNIA / PACIFIC COAST
ARCHITECT / ARCHITEKT	TURNBULL GRIFFIN HAESLOOP ARCHITECTS	YEAR OF COMPLETION / BAUJAHR	2004
PHOTOGRAPHER / FOTOGRAF	MATTHEW MILLMAN, PROCTOR JONES JR.	SQUARE FEET / QUADRAT METER	1991 / 185
CITY AND COUNTRY ARCHITECT / STADT UND LAND ARCHITEKT			BERKELEY, CA, USA
WEBSITE ARCHITECT / HOMEPAGE ARCHITEKT			WWW.TGHARCHS.COM

VISTA DUNES RESIDENCE
VS. DESIGN

The design of this full time desert residence is based in the modern heritage of the region. A number of practical issues synonymous with desert living were balanced with this rich architectural environment. Orientation, passive solar strategies, and the extension of the interior space to the outdoors are reflected throughout project. The scale of space and the manipulation of natural light were also critical to the design process. Additionally, the use of renewable products and natural, low maintenance materials give the project both a contemporary and warm feel.

Der Entwurf dieses ganzjährig bewohnten Hauses in der Wüste basiert auf der reichen Tradition der Moderne in dieser Gegend. Praktische Erwägungen, die sich aus der Lage in der Wüste ergeben – richtige Orientierung, Solarnutzung und die Erweiterung der Innenräume in die Landschaft hinein – fanden ebenfalls Berücksichtigung. Zudem wurden nachhaltige bzw. natürliche Materialien, die wenig Pflege bedürfen, verwendet, um dem Bau ein zeitgemäßes, warmes Ambiente zu verleihen.

+0

The site stretches out from east to west in the shadows of the San Jacinto Mountains. Both the main house and guest quarters open up to these westward views, exposing the interior spaces to the natural landscape. The challenge was to provide a sense of protection from the sometimes harsh elements encountered in this arid environment. As a result, several pocket courtyards with different orientations and exposures ensure a comfortable outdoor experience, while allowing the inside to share the expansive landscaping. The pool was oriented to allow the prevailing breezes to produce a cooling effect for the main patio and living space.

Das Grundstück erstreckt sich von Osten nach Westen im Schatten des San Jacinto Gebirges. Sowohl das Haupthaus als auch der Gastbereich öffnen sich zu diesem Ausblick hin und zur umliegenden Landschaft. Die Herausforderung bestand darin, Schutz vor den Auswirkungen des trockenen Klimas zu gewähren. So entstand eine Vielzahl innen liegender Höfe und damit sozusagen Innenräume im Freien. Die Orientierung des Schwimmbeckens führt kühlende Brisen in das angrenzende Hausinnere.

COUNTRY / LAND	USA	HOUSE NAME / BEZEICHNUNG DES HAUSES		VISTA DUNES RESIDENCE
LOCATION (CITY/REGION) / LAGE (STADT/REGION)				v, CALIFORNIA
ARCHITECT / ARCHITEKT		VS. DESIGN	YEAR OF COMPLETION / BAUJAHR	2002
PHOTOGRAPHER / FOTOGRAF		BENNY CHAN, FOTOWORKS	SQUARE FEET / QUADRAT METER	5000 / 465
CITY AND COUNTRY ARCHITECT / STADT UND LAND ARCHITEKT				LOS ANGELES, CA, USA
WEBSITE ARCHITECT / HOMEPAGE ARCHITEKT				WWW.VERSUSDESIGN.NET

As a flexible compound for family gatherings and overnight guests the key requirements here were to maximize volume, light, and privacy on a narrow urban lot, and employ sustainable methods and sensitivity to scale and context. Built of raw, honest materials appropriate to the grittiness of Venice, the home dissolves the barriers between indoors and out, creating multi-use spaces that fully exploit the benign climate.

Als flexiblen Rahmen für Familientreffs und Übernachtungsgäste galt es hier, großzügige, Licht durchflutete und private Räume auf einem engen Grundstück zu schaffen und dabei nachhaltige Baumethoden in Einklang mit Ort und Maßstäblichkeit zu bringen. Erbaut aus rohen, ‚ehrlichen' Materialien, welche den Geist von Venice ideal entsprechen, löst das Haus die Grenzen zwischen Innen und Außen auf, um multifunktionale Räume zu schaffen, welche die Vorzüge des angenehmen Klimas optimal ausnutzen.

+1

700 PALMS RESIDENCE
STEVEN EHRLICH ARCHITECTS

385

COUNTRY / LAND	USA	HOUSE NAME / BEZEICHNUNG DES HAUSES	700 PALMS RESIDENCE
LOCATION (CITY/REGION) / LAGE (STADT/REGION)			VENICE, CALIFORNIA
ARCHITECT / ARCHITEKT	STEVEN EHRLICH ARCHITECTS	YEAR OF COMPLETION / BAUJAHR	2004
PHOTOGRAPHER / FOTOGRAF	ERHARD PFEIFFER	SQUARE FEET / QUADRAT METER	4200 / 390
CITY AND COUNTRY ARCHITECT / STADT UND LAND ARCHITEKT			CULVER CITY, CA, USA
WEBSITE ARCHITECT / HOMEPAGE ARCHITEKT			WWW.S-EHRLICH.COM

This home orients away from the streets for privacy and serenity. The home's principle function, other than the primary residence of a couple with grown children, is to create a gallery for the work of Kharlene Boxenbaum. To do this, the design maximizes large wall expanses bathed in ambient light to create an ideal environment for showcasing art.

Konsequent orientiert sich dieses Haus weg von der Strasse. Zusätzlich zur Funktion als Haus eines Paars mit erwachsenen Kindern dient der Bau als Galerie für das Werk von Kharlene Boxenbaum. So wurden große, mit natürlichem Licht durchflutete Wandflächen geschaffen, welche sich ideal zur Präsentation der Kunst eignen.

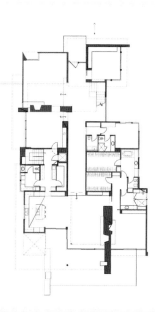

BOXENBAUM RESIDENCE
STEVEN EHRLICH ARCHITECTS

COUNTRY / LAND	USA	HOUSE NAME / BEZEICHNUNG DES HAUSES	BOXENBAUM RESIDENCE
LOCATION (CITY/REGION) / LAGE (STADT/REGION)			BEVERLY HILLS, CALIFORNIA
ARCHITECT / ARCHITEKT	STEVEN EHRLICH ARCHITECTS	YEAR OF COMPLETION / BAUJAHR	2005
PHOTOGRAPHER / FOTOGRAF	JUERGEN NOGAI	SQUARE FEET / QUADRAT METER	8000 / 744
CITY AND COUNTRY ARCHITECT / STADT UND LAND ARCHITEKT			CULVER CITY, CA, USA
WEBSITE ARCHITECT / HOMEPAGE ARCHITEKT			WWW.S-EHRLICH.COM

REDELCO HOUSE
PUGH + SCARPA

The challenge here was alter an unfinished building designed in the 90's to accommodate new building codes and a changed philosophy on architecture after a seven year building pause. The answer was to remove almost all of the interior walls and create a pavilion-like structure that captures extraordinary panoramic views of the San Fernando Valley and Hollywood Hills via tall sliding glass doors that allow the interior and exterior to merge.

Die Herausforderung dieses Projekts bestand darin, ein unfertiges, in den 90er Jahren entworfenes Bauwerk nach einer siebenjährigen Pause in ein Haus umzuwandeln, das dem heutigen Baurecht und der Architekturphilosophie der Gegenwart entspricht. Sämtliche Innenwände wurden entfernt und so entstand ein Neubau, der durch hohe Glastüren großartige Ausblicke auf das San Fernando Tal, sowie auf die Hügel von Hollywood bietet.

COUNTRY / LAND	USA	HOUSE NAME / BEZEICHNUNG DES HAUSES	REDELCO HOUSE
LOCATION (CITY/REGION) / LAGE (STADT/REGION)			STUDIO CITY, CALIFORNIA
ARCHITECT / ARCHITEKT	PUGH + SCARPA	YEAR OF COMPLETION / BAUJAHR	2004
PHOTOGRAPHER / FOTOGRAF	MARVIN RAND	SQUARE FEET / QUADRAT METER	4700 / 437
CITY AND COUNTRY ARCHITECT / STADT UND LAND ARCHITEKT			SANTA MONICA, CA, USA
WEBSITE ARCHITECT / HOMEPAGE ARCHITEKT			WWW.PUGH-SCARPA.COM

+1

Inspired by Paul Rudolph's Umbrella House of 1953, the Solar Umbrella provides a contemporary reinvention of the solar canopy - a strategy that provides thermal protection in climates with intense exposures. A bold display of solar panels wrapping around the south elevation and roof becomes the defining formal expression of the residence. Conceived as a solar canopy, these panels protect the body of the building from thermal heat gain by screening large portions of the structure from direct exposure to the intense southern California sun. Rather than deflecting sunlight, this solar skin provides the residence with 100% of its electricity.

Inspiriert durch Paul Rudolphs ‚Umbrella House' von 1953 bietet dieses Projekt eine Neuinterpretation dieses Konzepts als eine Strategie für Thermalschutz in extrem besonnten Klimazonen. Konsequent um die Südseite und das Dach gewickelte Sonnenkollektoren sind das prägende Gestaltungselement. Als Solarschirm konzipiert, schützen diese Paneele den eigentlichen Hauskörper darunter vor der direkten Bestrahlung durch die südkalifornische Sonne. Anstatt das Sonnenlicht abzuweisen wird es in Strom umgewandelt, der 100% des Strombedarfes abdeckt.

SOLAR UMBRELLA
PUGH + SCARPA

COUNTRY / LAND	USA	HOUSE NAME / BEZEICHNUNG DES HAUSES	SOLAR UMBRELLA
LOCATION (CITY/REGION) / LAGE (STADT/REGION)			VENICE, CALIFORNIA
ARCHITECT / ARCHITEKT		PUGH + SCARPA YEAR OF COMPLETION / BAUJAHR	2005
PHOTOGRAPHER / FOTOGRAF		MARVIN RAND SQUARE FEET / QUADRAT METER	1205 / 112
CITY AND COUNTRY ARCHITECT / STADT UND LAND ARCHITEKT			SANTA MONICA, CA, USA
WEBSITE ARCHITECT / HOMEPAGE ARCHITEKT			WWW.PUGH-SCARPA.COM

This house was designed under challenging conditions generated by the modern problem of building on a hillside. While the site for the house offers panoramic views the irregularly shaped lot is situated on an uneven, downhill slope. With the canonical Eames House nearby, the house provocatively continues the Case Study House tradition of experimentation and reinvention of Los Angeles lifestyles.

Dieses Haus entstand als Antwort auf die Herausforderung, Hangbebauungen an ökologisch sensiblen Standorten zu realisieren. Obwohl das Grundstück sich zu atemberaubenden Ausblicken öffnet, weist es zugleich eine unregelmäßige Geometrie und einen unebenen, steilen Hang auf. Zudem liegt das legendäre Haus der Gebrüder Eames in unmittelbarer Nähe, so dass hier eine besondere Verantwortung entstand, die südkalifornische Tradition der Moderne neu zu interpretieren.

HILL HOUSE
JOHNSTON MARKLEE & ASSOCIATES

Within the building enclosure, individual programmatic components are assembled to fit into the fixed envelope, much like a contortionist compressing the mass of their body into unique configurations. By eroding all non-structural walls and partitions, the program flows effortlessly between three levels stacked within the exterior skin. An upper semi-private loft space and a more secluded lower bedroom suite sandwich the central public living and dining area.

Innerhalb des Hausvolumens wurden die einzelnen Funktionen gekonnt in die vorgegebene, verzehrte Hülle hineingepasst. Der weitgehende Verzicht auf nicht tragende Wände erlaubt es, die Räume ungezwungen zwischen den drei Wohnebenen fließen zu lassen. Der zentrale Wohnbereich wird oben und unten von einer Galerieebene bzw. von dem abgeschiedenen Schlafzimmer darunter gefasst.

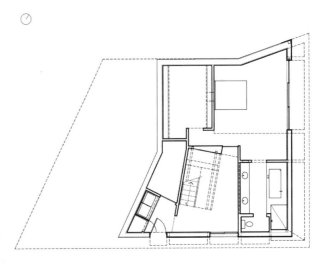

+0

COUNTRY / LAND	USA	HOUSE NAME / BEZEICHNUNG DES HAUSES	HILL HOUSE
LOCATION (CITY/REGION) / LAGE (STADT/REGION)			PACIFIC PALISADES, CALIFORNIA
ARCHITECT / ARCHITEKT	JOHNSTON MARKLEE & ASSOCIATES	YEAR OF COMPLETION / BAUJAHR	2004
PHOTOGRAPHER / FOTOGRAF	ERIC STAUDENMAIER	SQUARE FEET / QUADRAT METER	3600 / 335
CITY AND COUNTRY ARCHITECT / STADT UND LAND ARCHITEKT			LOS ANGELES, CA, USA
WEBSITE ARCHITECT / HOMEPAGE ARCHITEKT			WWW.JOHNSTONMARKLEE.COM

JOHNSTON MARKLEE & ASSOCIATES

LOS ANGELES, CALIFORNIA USA

Johnston Marklee Associates brings a progressive approach to the design of contemporary buildings and interiors. Since its founding in 1998 by Sharon Johnston and Mark Lee, the firm has interrogated the complex interrelationship between design and building technology to produce an impressive catalogue of original architectural solutions.

Recognized for their ability to engage challenging site and structural conditions, the firm has proved equally adept at tailoring solutions to individual clients as to the specific demands of the environment and immediate context. Distilling inherent complexity into coherent concepts, Johnston Marklee deploys volume, light, materials to marshal the exigencies of contemporary building into singular works of architecture.

Photographer: Johnston Marklee Associates

Johnston Marklee Associates bringen eine fortschrittliche Arbeitsweise bei der Erstellung von Entwürfen für zeitgenössische Bauten und Innenräume ein. Seit der Gründung durch Sharon Johnston und Mark Lee 1998 hat sich die Firma mit der komplexen Beziehung zwischen Design und Bautechnologie auseinandergesetzt, um einen beeindruckenden Katalog origineller Architekturlösungen zusammen zu stellen.

Angesehen aufgrund ihrer Fähigkeit, herausfordernde Bauplätze und statische Problemstellungen kreativ zu meistern, haben sie ebenfalls bewiesen, dass sie nicht nur auf Nutzerwünsche, sondern auch auf spezifische Erfordernisse der Umgebung und des Naturraumes effektiv eingehen können. Johnston Marklee setzen Volumen, Licht und Material ein, um inmitten der haltlosen Hektik unserer Zeit einmalige Architekturwerke zu schaffen.

JAI HOUSE
LORCAN O'HERLIHY
ARCHITECTS

The main level of this house runs parallel to a busy road and creates a buffer between it and the garden. It contains the living, dining, kitchen spaces, two bedrooms, and a yoga studio and stretches to extend out to views of the adjacent canyon. The swimming pool and the deck extend the living room outside and continue the garden inside to intertwine interior and exterior spaces. The upper level houses the master bedroom that is shifted at a 90 degree angle to the lower level in order to open onto the views of the nearby mountains.

Die Hauptebene dieses Hauses erstreckt sich parallel zu einer stark befahrenen Strasse und schafft einen Puffer zum Garten. Diese Ebene beherbergt Wohn-, Eß-, Koch- und Schlafbereiche und öffnet sich an einem Ende zu Ausblicken auf einen Canyon. Das Schwimmbecken und die Terrasse setzen das Wohnzimmer im Freien fort und verbinden so den Garten mit dem Innenraum. Das große Schlafzimmer im Obergeschoss wurde um 90 Grad zum Erdgeschoss gedreht, um einen umrahmten Ausblick auf die Berge zu ermöglichen.

COUNTRY / LAND	USA	HOUSE NAME / BEZEICHNUNG DES HAUSES	JAI HOUSE
LOCATION (CITY/REGION) / LAGE (STADT/REGION)			CALABASAS, CALIFORNIA
ARCHITECT / ARCHITEKT	LORCAN O'HERLIHY ARCHITECTS	YEAR OF COMPLETION / BAUJAHR	2004
PHOTOGRAPHER / FOTOGRAF	COOLIDGE, JOHAL, WESCHLER	SQUARE FEET / QUADRAT METER	xxx
CITY AND COUNTRY ARCHITECT / STADT UND LAND ARCHITEKT			CULVER CITY, CA, USA
WEBSITE ARCHITECT / HOMEPAGE ARCHITEKT			WWW.LOHARCHITECTS.COM

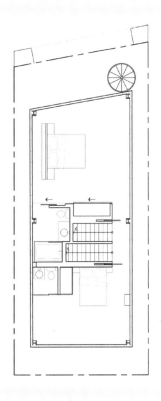

The tight urban parcel led the architect to vertically stack the required uses. An earthquake-proof steel frame structure allows the exterior wall surfaces made of glass and fiber-cement panels to be hung independently from the primary structural grid. The resultant architecture statement is thus defined more by the rhythm of the façade surfaces than by the box-like spatial volume of the house itself. This makes for the creation of especially unique, dynamic interior spaces.

Die beengte städtische Lage veranlasste den Architekten, die Nutzungen vertikal zu stapeln. Die erdbebensichere Stahlrahmenkonstruktion ermöglicht es, die vorgehängten Fassadenelemente aus Glas und Faserzementplatten frei und unabhängig vom Konstruktionsraster zu verteilen. Es entsteht hierdurch eine Architektur, die sich mehr durch die Oberfläche als durch das räumliche Volumen definiert. Dennoch entstehen im Inneren spannungsvolle Räume.

VERTICAL HOUSE
LORCAN O'HERLIHY ARCHITECTS

COUNTRY / LAND	USA	HOUSE NAME / BEZEICHNUNG DES HAUSES	VERTICAL HOUSE
LOCATION (CITY/REGION) / LAGE (STADT/REGION)			VENICE BEACH, CALIFORNIA / PACIFIC COAST
ARCHITECT / ARCHITEKT		LORCAN O'HERLIHY ARCHITECTS	YEAR OF COMPLETION / BAUJAHR 2003
PHOTOGRAPHER / FOTOGRAF		MICHAEL WECHSLER PHOTOGRAPHY	SQUARE FEET / QUADRAT METER 2421 / 225
CITY AND COUNTRY ARCHITECT / STADT UND LAND ARCHITEKT			LOS ANGELES, CA, USA
WEBSITE ARCHITECT / HOMEPAGE ARCHITEKT			WWW.LOHARCHITECTS.COM

The current real estate boom in the Los Angeles region has led to the development of sites that were previously considered too steep or remote to be built upon. The steep hillside site of this home inspired the architect to develop a creative solution. All of the various functions were compacted into one level and stretched out along the elongated building mass that hovers above the ground plane on columns.

Der gegenwärtige Immobilienboom in Los Angeles hat zu der Entwicklung von schwer erschließbaren Grundstücken geführt, die bisher für nicht bebaubar gehalten wurden. Der steile Hang dieses Grundstuckes inspirierte den Architekten zu einer besonders kreativen Lösung. Sämtliche Funktionen des Hauses wurden in einer kompakten, lang gestreckten Geschoßebene zusammengefasst, die über das Geländeniveau auf Stützen angehoben wurde.

HEUSCH RESIDENCE
HEUSCH INC.

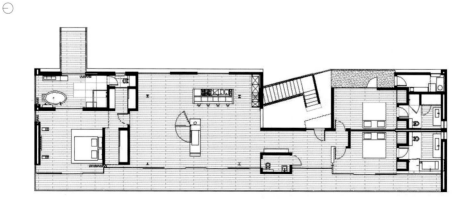

+0

The house is accessed from the lower, poolside level where car parking is also located. Moving underneath the hovering mass that also creates a protected, shaded exterior space, one rises to the entrance on the main level. The central living / kitchen zone displays an open plan that makes the space seem large and generous. Each of the three bedrooms has its own bathroom node and all of the main spaces orient out to the forest view via sliding glass window walls.

Das Haus wird von der unteren Ebene erschlossen, wo sich Pool und Parkplätze befinden. Von diesem geschützten, verschatteten Außenraum aus führt eine Treppe zum Hauptgeschoss hinauf. Der zentrale Wohn- / Kochbereich weist einen offenen Grundriss auf, der ihn großzügig wirken lässt. Jedes der drei Schlafzimmer verfügt über ein dazugehöriges Badezimmer. Die Haupträume öffnen sich über verschiebbare Glaswandelemente zum Ausblick auf den kalifornischen Wald.

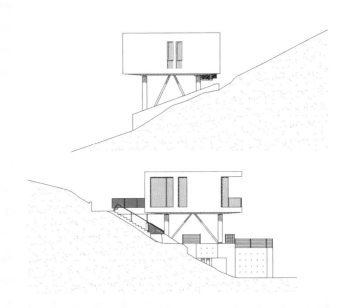

COUNTRY / LAND	USA	HOUSE NAME / BEZEICHNUNG DES HAUSES	HEUSCH RESIDENCE

LOCATION (CITY/REGION) / LAGE (STADT/REGION)   BEVERLY HILLS, CALIFORNIA

ARCHITECT / ARCHITEKT   HEUSCH INC.   YEAR OF COMPLETION / BAUJAHR   2005

PHOTOGRAPHER / FOTOGRAF   FREDERICO ZIGNANI / KEIJI SAITO   SQUARE FEET / QUADRAT METER   3200 / 297

CITY AND COUNTRY ARCHITECT / STADT UND LAND ARCHITEKT   LOS ANGELES, CA, USA

WEBSITE ARCHITECT / HOMEPAGE ARCHITEKT   WWW.HEUSCH.COM

MUSSEL SHOALS HOUSE
<u>DESIGN ARC</u>

The location on the Pacific Coast Highway led the architects to orient the house away from the road toward a protected entrance courtyard and the Pacific Ocean. In response to the direct exposure to weather and the elements on the beachside site the exterior shell of the residence was designed in robust exposed concrete.

Die Lage am stark befahrenen Pacific Coast Highway ließ die Architekten das Haus konsequent zum abgeschirmten Eingangsvorhof und zum Meer hin orientieren. Als Antwort auf die dem Wetter und den Elementen ausgesetzte direkte Meereslage entschied man sich, die Außenhülle des Hauses in robustem Sichtbeton zu erbauen.

This minimalist vocabulary was also implemented inside, where the aesthetic reduction creates a pleasant ambience of healing. Inside, far removed from colourful, hectic Southern California outside, the light-filled, sheltered realm offers both visual and audible tranquility.

Dieses minimalistische Vokabular wird auch im Inneren angewendet, wo die Reduktion der Mittel ein wohltuendes, beruhigendes Ambiente erzeugt. Inmitten der bunten Betriebsamkeit und Hektik Südkaliforniens lebt man hier geborgen in einem behaglichen Reich der visuellen und akustischen Ruhe.

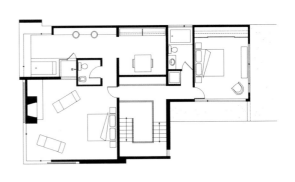

COUNTRY / LAND	USA	HOUSE NAME / BEZEICHNUNG DES HAUSES	MUSSEL SHOALS HOUSE
LOCATION (CITY/REGION) / LAGE (STADT/REGION)			VENTURA, CALIFORNIA / PACIFIC COAST
ARCHITECT / ARCHITEKT	DESIGN ARC	YEAR OF COMPLETION / BAUJAHR	2005
PHOTOGRAPHER / FOTOGRAF	FOTOWORKS BENNY CHAN	SQUARE FEET / QUADRAT METER	3013 / 280
CITY AND COUNTRY ARCHITECT / STADT UND LAND ARCHITEKT			LOS ANGELES, CA, USA
WEBSITE ARCHITECT / HOMEPAGE ARCHITEKT			WWW.DESIGNARC.NET

Per the client's objectives, this home captures exterior space as living space, and harnesses the panoramic views of the valley below. Separate living pods along a central spine allow different activities and interactions to occur simultaneously without mutual disruption. Each living pod is outfitted with its own version of an indoor-outdoor courtyard space, and each connected independently to the central spine of the house.

Auf Wunsch der Bauherrschaft definieren die Baukörper dieses Hauses Außenräume als Wohnraum. Die Panorama-Ausblicke auf das darunter liegende Tal wurden in das Wohnkonzept besonders einbezogen. Die Funktionen sind zu eigenen Raumzonen zusammengefasst, welche entlang der zentralen Achse angeordnet und jeweils mit einem dazugehörigen Außenraum versehen wurden.

BROSMITH RESIDENCE
STUDIO PALI FEKETE ARCHITECTS

Pods are designed around the master suite, the children's' quarters, offices, and caretakers quarters. Entering into the common living areas, one is met with breathtaking vistas of the San Fernando Valley climaxing on the main patio, where a glass-like swimming pool disappears entrancingly over the crisp clean horizon of the site's northern edge.

Der Hauptschlafbereich, die Zone der Kinderzimmer, ein Bürobereich und der Hausmeistertrakt bilden Einheiten, die sich entlang des Rückgrats erstrecken. Beim Betreten des Hauptwohnbereiches öffnen sich atemberaubende Ausblicke auf das San Fernando Tal. Die Komposition findet ihren Höhepunkt im großen Innenhof, wo ein glasähnlicher Pool bis an den Horizont der nördlichen Grundstücksgrenze gezogen wurde.

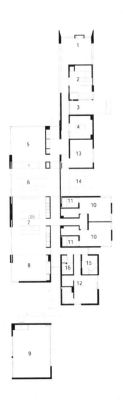

+0

COUNTRY / LAND	USA	HOUSE NAME / BEZEICHNUNG DES HAUSES		BROSMITH RESIDENCE
LOCATION (CITY/REGION) / LAGE (STADT/REGION)				BEVERLY HILLS, CALIFORNIA
ARCHITECT / ARCHITEKT		STUDIO PALI FEKETE ARCHITECTS	YEAR OF COMPLETION / BAUJAHR	2004
PHOTOGRAPHER / FOTOGRAF		JOHN EDWARD LINDEN	SQUARE FEET / QUADRAT METER	5000 / 460
CITY AND COUNTRY ARCHITECT / STADT UND LAND ARCHITEKT				CULVER CITY, CA, USA
WEBSITE ARCHITECT / HOMEPAGE ARCHITEKT				WWW.SPFA.COM

Perched on a steep, nearly 45-degree grade, the structure forms a four-level, multi-faceted viewing station for the Los Angeles basin. The residence features a crisp concrete plinth base of two levels, housing parking garages and a host of recreational amenities. A screening room, gymnasium, wine cellar, and disco lounge (complete with mirrored ball, DJ station and bar) complete the first level interior.

Gelegen auf einem 45 Grad Steilhang, dienen die vier Geschosse des Hauses als vielfältige Plattform, die sich zu Ausblicken auf die Weite der Los Angeles-Ebene darunter öffnen. Die unteren zwei Geschosse, die Garagen und informelle Wohnbereiche beherbergen, wurden aus Beton errichtet. Die Funktionen des Hauses umfassen u.a. einen Filmvorführraum, einen Fitnessbereich, einen Weinkeller sowie Diskothek mit Diskokugel, DJ Pult und Tresen.

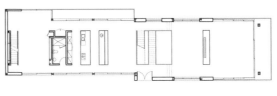

+2

HOUSE ON BLUE JAY WAY
STUDIO PALI FEKETE ARCHITECTS

COUNTRY / LAND	USA	HOUSE NAME / BEZEICHNUNG DES HAUSES		HOUSE ON BLUE JAY WAY
LOCATION (CITY/REGION) / LAGE (STADT/REGION)				WEST HOLLYWOOD, CALIFORNIA
ARCHITECT / ARCHITEKT		STUDIO PALI FEKETE ARCHITECTS	YEAR OF COMPLETION / BAUJAHR	2005
PHOTOGRAPHER / FOTOGRAF		JOHN EDWARD LINDEN	SQUARE FEET / QUADRAT METER	9250 / 860
CITY AND COUNTRY ARCHITECT / STADT UND LAND ARCHITEKT				CULVER CITY, CA, USA
WEBSITE ARCHITECT / HOMEPAGE ARCHITEKT				WWW.SPFA.COM

The transitional entry courtyard introduces the primary design element of this home on Malibu's Pacific Coast Highway - the seamless union between interior and exterior spaces, with crisp linear architecture, ambulating plan, and visual access throughout. The interior design palette of natural woods and limestone, white walls and fabrics, frosted and clear plate-glass creates a crisp and airy environment to appreciate the Pacific Ocean setting.

Der Eingangsvorhof bildet einen Übergang zu diesem Haus am Pacific Coast Highway und verdeutlicht das zentrale Gestaltungsprinzip – die scheinbare Einheit von Innen- und Außenräumen, linearer Architektur und Offenheit. Die verwendeten Materialen - Kalksandstein, Holz, weiße Wände und Stoffe ergänzt durch matte und klare Glasflächen - erzeugen eine luftige Leichtigkeit.

MALIBU BEACH HOUSE
SHUBIN +
DONALDSON ARCHITECTS

COUNTRY / LAND	USA	HOUSE NAME / BEZEICHNUNG DES HAUSES	MALIBU BEACH HOUSE
LOCATION (CITY/REGION) / LAGE (STADT/REGION)			MALIBU, CALIFORNIA / PACIFIC COAST
ARCHITECT / ARCHITEKT	SHUBIN + DONALDSON ARCHITECTS	YEAR OF COMPLETION / BAUJAHR	2002
PHOTOGRAPHER / FOTOGRAF	TOM BONNER	SQUARE FEET / QUADRAT METER	2798 / 260
CITY AND COUNTRY ARCHITECT / STADT UND LAND ARCHITEKT			CULVER CITY, CA , USA
WEBSITE ARCHITECT / HOMEPAGE ARCHITEKT			WWW.SHUBINANDDONALDSON.COM

416

This house was created like a phoenix rising from the ashes of a former house that burned down here. To reduce the risk of renewed catastrophe the new home was designed as a rectilinear volume and tiled with ceramic plating. This clear expression of its resistance to fire, poor weather, withering winds, floods, and earthquakes make it a powerful architectural statement that stands in marked contrast to the natural surroundings. Both interior and exterior spaces orient toward the west, the coastal hill landscape, and the sea beyond. The slim floor plan is especially conducive to natural ventilation.

Gelegen auf Küstenhügeln, die periodisch von verheerenden Buschbränden heimgesucht werden, entstand der Bau wie Phönix aus der Asche eines niedergebrannten Vorgängerhauses. Um der Gefahr einer erneuten Katastrophe vorzubeugen, wurde ein schlichter, mit Keramikplatten verkleideter Baukörper entwickelt. Somit steht das Haus als Ausdruck seiner Widerstandfähigkeit gegen Brände, Wetter, Wind und Überflutungen bewusst im klaren Kontrast zur Umgebung. Die Räume sind nach Westen zum Meer und zur Hügellandschaft ausgerichtet. Der schlanke Grundriss erlaubt eine optimale Querlüftung durch die oft vorhandenen Meereswinde.

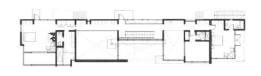

FEINSTEIN RESIDENCE
KANNER ARCHITECTS

COUNTRY / LAND	USA	HOUSE NAME / BEZEICHNUNG DES HAUSES	FEINSTEIN RESIDENCE
LOCATION (CITY/REGION) / LAGE (STADT/REGION)			MALIBU, CALIFORNIA / PACIFIC COAST
ARCHITECT / ARCHITEKT	KANNER ARCHITECTS	YEAR OF COMPLETION / BAUJAHR	2003
PHOTOGRAPHER / FOTOGRAF	JOHN LINDEN	SQUARE FEET / QUADRAT METER	4304 / 400
CITY AND COUNTRY ARCHITECT / STADT UND LAND ARCHITEKT			LOS ANGELES, CA, USA
WEBSITE ARCHITECT / HOMEPAGE ARCHITEKT			WWW.KANNERARCH.COM

Limited to a site the size of a tennis court, the architect created a two-story home that takes advantage of the bright light and cool ocean breezes. The glass-clad main wing fills the north side of the lot and a wide patio extends to the south off of the lower level. Sliding glass doors disappear – marrying indoor and outdoor - and facilitate cross-ventilating sea breezes.

Begrenzt auf Grundstück, das die Größe eines Tennisplatzes aufweist, schuf der Architekt dennoch ein zweigeschossiges Zuhause, welches das klare Licht und die kühlen Meeresbrisen berücksichtigt. Der gläserne Hauptflügel nimmt die Nordseite des Grundstückes ein, davor erstreckt sich die breite Terrasse. Gläserne Schiebetüren verschwinden, um Außen- und Innenräume ineinander übergehen zu lassen und die Querlüftung durch Meeresbrisen zu erleichtern.

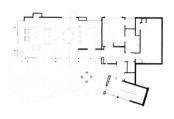

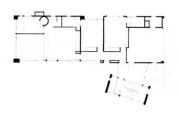

511 HOUSE
KANNER ARCHITECTS

COUNTRY / LAND	USA	HOUSE NAME / BEZEICHNUNG DES HAUSES		511 HOUSE
LOCATION (CITY/REGION) / LAGE (STADT/REGION)				PACIFIC PALISADES, CALIFORNIA
ARCHITECT / ARCHITEKT		KANNER ARCHITECTS	YEAR OF COMPLETION / BAUJAHR	2001
PHOTOGRAPHER / FOTOGRAF		JOHN EDWARD LINDEN	SQUARE FEET / QUADRAT METER	3500 / 325
CITY AND COUNTRY ARCHITECT / STADT UND LAND ARCHITEKT				SANTA MONICA, CA, USA
WEBSITE ARCHITECT / HOMEPAGE ARCHITEKT				WWW.KANNERARCH.COM

CANYON VIEW
KANNER ARCHITECTS

Located on a lush hillside behind a main residence, this small structure was designed to be a psychologist's office and future guesthouse. Though it is just steps away from the main home it feels like a protected sanctuary. The highly articulated form is composed of a series of angled cedar wall planes. Each plan angle responds to room function, view corridors, light quality and programmatic flexibility.

Hinter einem bestehenden Haupthaus befindet sich dieses kleine Haus, das als Praxis eines Psychologen und als künftiges Gästehaus dient. Obwohl es nur um wenige Schritte vom Haupthaus entfernt liegt fühlt man sich hier wie in einer anderen, geschützten Welt. Die Komposition besteht aus schräg angeordneten, mit Zedernholz verkleideten Wandscheiben, welche auf die jeweilige Funktion, die Ausblicke und das Licht reagieren.

COUNTRY / LAND	USA	HOUSE NAME / BEZEICHNUNG DES HAUSES	CANYON VIEW
LOCATION (CITY/REGION) / LAGE (STADT/REGION)			BRENTWOOD, CALIFORNIA
ARCHITECT / ARCHITEKT	KANNER ARCHITECTS	YEAR OF COMPLETION / BAUJAHR	2004
PHOTOGRAPHER / FOTOGRAF	JOHN EDWARD LINDEN	SQUARE FEET / QUADRAT METER	1000 93
CITY AND COUNTRY ARCHITECT / STADT UND LAND ARCHITEKT			SANTA MONICA, CA, USA
WEBSITE ARCHITECT / HOMEPAGE ARCHITEKT			WWW.KANNERARCH.COM

Designed to take full advantage of its secluded location, the one-story courtyard home's white plaster exterior forms are complemented by warm mahogany floors, doors and cabinets within. The floor plan establishes a hierarchy of space through varying ceiling heights. A serene interior court serves as the entry to the house.

Das eingeschossige Haus nutzt seine abgelegenen Lage optimal aus. Ein ruhiger Eingangsvorhof bildet den Auftakt der Komposition. Die kubistisch anmutenden äußeren Formen werden im Inneren durch Materialien komplettiert, die Wärme ausstrahlen - wie der Parkettfußboden, die Türen und die Einbauschränke aus Holz.

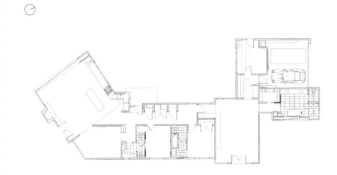

+0

MALIBU HOUSE 4
KANNER ARCHITECTS

COUNTRY / LAND	USA	HOUSE NAME / BEZEICHNUNG DES HAUSES	MALIBU HOUSE 4
LOCATION (CITY/REGION) / LAGE (STADT/REGION)			SANTA MONICA, CALIFORNIA
ARCHITECT / ARCHITEKT		KANNER ARCHITECTS YEAR OF COMPLETION / BAUJAHR	x
PHOTOGRAPHER / FOTOGRAF		JOHN EDWARD LINDEN SQUARE FEET / QUADRAT METER	3200 / 297
CITY AND COUNTRY ARCHITECT / STADT UND LAND ARCHITEKT			SANTA MONICA, CA, USA
WEBSITE ARCHITECT / HOMEPAGE ARCHITEKT			x

This is an infill project, in which the single-family house is built on a vacant lot, abandoned for many years, and situated in between multiple-housing structures. The house was set back from the site boundaries to allow more breathing room for the neighbouring properties, and save ocean views for them. Energy costs are reduced by both the extensive glazing and a skylight in the middle core that induces abundant sunlight inside and cross ventilation via ocean breezes.

Dieses Projekt entstand als Nachverdichtungsmaßnahme auf einem seit langem ungenutzten Grundstück zwischen Mehrfamilienhäusern. Das Haus wurde von der Grundstücksgrenze zurückgesetzt, um die Meeresausblicke der Nachbarparzellen nicht zu blockieren. Energiekosten werden reduziert sowohl durch die Verglasung als auch durch ein Oberlicht im Kern des Grundrisses, das Tageslicht in das Hausinnere führt.

URBAN BEACH HOUSE
LEE + MUNDWILER ARCHITECTS

COUNTRY / LAND	USA	HOUSE NAME / BEZEICHNUNG DES HAUSES — URBAN BEACH HOUSE
LOCATION (CITY/REGION) / LAGE (STADT/REGION)		SANTA MONICA, CALIFORNIA
ARCHITECT / ARCHITEKT	LEE + MUNDWILER ARCHITECTS	YEAR OF COMPLETION / BAUJAHR — 2006
PHOTOGRAPHER / FOTOGRAF	JUERGEN NOGAI	SQUARE FEET / QUADRAT METER — 2500 / 232
CITY AND COUNTRY ARCHITECT / STADT UND LAND ARCHITEKT		SANTA MONICA, CA, USA
WEBSITE ARCHITECT / HOMEPAGE ARCHITEKT		WWW.IM-ARCH.COM

This is an infill project tightly built in a densely populated neighbourhood that consists of typical thin stucco houses hastily built after World War II for families of returning soldiers and workers. Along a busy thoroughfare, familiar typology – a traditional pitched roof, a view window to street, and a chimney - is introduced to provoke an inner childhood yearning for the archetypical "home". The linear approach from the street leads to the point of arrival, a courtyard situated at the middle core of the house.

Dieses Nachverdichtungsprojekt entstand in einer dicht bebauten Wohnsiedlung, die nach dem zweiten Weltkrieg für die aus dem Krieg heimkehrenden Soldaten und Arbeiter gebaut wurde. Bei dem an einer Hauptverkehrsstrasse gelegenen Gebäude setzten die Architekten urtypische Elemente wie das Steildach, den Blick zur Straße und einen Kamin ein, um ein archetypisches „Zuhause" zu kreieren. Der gerade Zugangsweg führt zum Ankunftspunkt: ein Hof inmitten des Hauses.

THE COCONUT HOUSE
LEE + MUNDWILER ARCHITECTS

Through subtracting volumes from the building mass, light, air, and nature penetrate deeply inside to create a sense of spaciousness that allows the small house to seem large and generous. Hues of white illuminate the inner core of the dwelling, flirting with light coming through the skylight and the louver of the courtyard. The façade of dark fibre core panels with natural wood veneer emulates the tough shell of a "coconut". This maintenance-free façade was built without petroleum products, such as paints and sealers, to last for many years.

Licht, Luft und die Natur werden in das Haus geführt, indem der einfache Baukörper gezielt ausgehöhlt wird. So entsteht Großzügigkeit auf kleinstem Raum. Ein subtiles Spektrum von Weißtönen im Inneren kontrastiert mit der dunklen Fassade aus Holzpanellen, die wie die Schale einer Kokosnuss das Haus nach außen schützt. Die wartungsarme Fassade wurde unter Verzicht auf konventionelle Farben und Lacke ausgeführt.

+0

+1

COUNTRY / LAND	USA	HOUSE NAME / BEZEICHNUNG DES HAUSES	THE COCONUT HOUSE
LOCATION (CITY/REGION) / LAGE (STADT/REGION)			LOS ANGELES, CALIFORNIA
ARCHITECT / ARCHITEKT	LEE + MUNDWILER ARCHITECTS	YEAR OF COMPLETION / BAUJAHR	2005
PHOTOGRAPHER / FOTOGRAF	JUERGEN NOGAI / JULIUS SHULMAN	SQUARE FEET / QUADRAT METER	1800 / 167
CITY AND COUNTRY ARCHITECT / STADT UND LAND ARCHITEKT			SANTA MONICA, CA, USA
WEBSITE ARCHITECT / HOMEPAGE ARCHITEKT			WWW.IM-ARCH.COM

The architects strove here to create light-filled interior spaces with views to the garden. Interior walls were eliminated to generate flowing spaces. The walls literally bend and project the spaces out from the centre of the house to enhance the flow of light and view. The floor plan employs torsion, perspective distortions, folded surfaces, spatial slippage and obliquity to transcend the rationalizing grid of Cartesian modernism.

Die Architekten strebten die Schaffung von mit Licht gefüllten Innenräumen an, welche über Ausblicke in den Garten verfügen. Auf Innenwände wurde weitgehend verzichtet, um fließende Räume entstehen zu lassen. Der Grundriss arbeitet mit Torsion, perspektivischen Verzerrungen, räumlichen Verschiebungen und gefalteten Ebenen, um die Bindungen eines strengen Rasters aufzulösen.

+0

BERGER RESIDENCE
ABRAMSON TEIGER ARCHITECTS

429

COUNTRY / LAND	USA	HOUSE NAME / BEZEICHNUNG DES HAUSES BERGER RESIDENCE
LOCATION (CITY/REGION) / LAGE (STADT/REGION)		LOS ANGELES, CALIFORNIA
ARCHITECT / ARCHITEKT	ABRAMSON TEIGER ARCHITECTS	YEAR OF COMPLETION / BAUJAHR 2004
PHOTOGRAPHER / FOTOGRAF	KEVIN SMITH	SQUARE FEET / QUADRAT METER 4500 / 418
CITY AND COUNTRY ARCHITECT / STADT UND LAND ARCHITEKT		CULVER CITY, CA, USA
WEBSITE ARCHITECT / HOMEPAGE ARCHITEKT		WWW.ABRAMSONTEIGER.COM

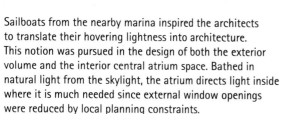

Sailboats from the nearby marina inspired the architects
to translate their hovering lightness into architecture.
This notion was pursued in the design of both the exterior
volume and the interior central atrium space. Bathed in
natural light from the skylight, the atrium directs light inside
where it is much needed since external window openings
were reduced by local planning constraints.

Segelboote vom nah gelegenen Marina inspirierten
die Architekten, ihre schwebende Leichtigkeit baulich
umzusetzen. Dieser Einfall wurde sowohl bei der Ausformung
des Baukörpers als auch im zentralen Atrium konsequent
umgesetzt. Das zentrale Atrium führt Licht in die Tiefe
des Hauses, denn Öffnungen nach außen wurden durch
planungsrechtliche Vorschriften begrenzt.

KNIGHT RESIDENCE
ABRAMSON TEIGER
ARCHITECTS

COUNTRY / LAND	USA	HOUSE NAME / BEZEICHNUNG DES HAUSES	KNIGHT RESIDENCE
LOCATION (CITY/REGION) / LAGE (STADT/REGION)			NEWPORT BEACH, CALIFORNIA / PACIFIC COAST
ARCHITECT / ARCHITEKT	ABRAMSON TEIGER ARCHITECTS	YEAR OF COMPLETION / BAUJAHR	2001
PHOTOGRAPHER / FOTOGRAF	BILL TIMMERMAN	SQUARE FEET / QUADRAT METER	4196 / 390
CITY AND COUNTRY ARCHITECT / STADT UND LAND ARCHITEKT			CULVER CITY, CA, USA
WEBSITE ARCHITECT / HOMEPAGE ARCHITEKT			WWW.ABRAMSONTEIGER.COM

ELK RUN RESIDENCE
ABRAMSON TEIGER
ARCHITECTS

Composed of four distinct wings, this house is unified by sweeping sculptural copper roofs. The main living space is a rectilinear barn-shaped building with soaring vaulted open truss ceilings. The guest wing and an art studio were foreseen as separate wings, each with its own individual architectural expression.

Dieses aus vier Flügeln bestehende Haus wird durch das verbindende Element der fließenden Kupferdächer zu einer Einheit zusammengeführt. Der Hauptwohnbereich erhielt ein scheunenartiges Dach, während der Gästetrakt und ein Atelier als architektonisch eigenständige Flügel errichtet wurden.

431

COUNTRY / LAND	USA	HOUSE NAME / BEZEICHNUNG DES HAUSES	ELK RUN RESIDENCE
LOCATION (CITY/REGION) / LAGE (STADT/REGION)			TELLURIDE, COLORADO
ARCHITECT / ARCHITEKT	ABRAMSON TEIGER ARCHITECTS	YEAR OF COMPLETION / BAUJAHR	2000
PHOTOGRAPHER / FOTOGRAF	JOHN LINDEN	SQUARE FEET / QUADRAT METER	6500 / 604
CITY AND COUNTRY ARCHITECT / STADT UND LAND ARCHITEKT			CULVER CITY, CA, USA
WEBSITE ARCHITECT / HOMEPAGE ARCHITEKT			WWW.ABRAMSONTEIGER.COM

This vacation home / guest house complex is located on a large ranch that has a few select home sites, with the balance of the land set aside as common grazing land and open space. The site is a spectacular plateau with stands of aspen and distant mountain views. The project is comprised of three small separate buildings - the main house, guest house, and the garage. The clients wished a solution that would feel part of the American west, take full advantage of the site, and withstand the tough winter conditions.

Dieser aus einem Ferienhaus und einem Gasthaus bestehende Komplex liegt im Gebiet einer großen Gebirgsranch, die jedoch noch weitgehend aus Weiden und offener Landschaft besteht. Das Projekt besteht aus drei kleinen Bauten – Haupthaus, Gasthaus und Garage. Die Bauherrschaft wünschte eine Lösung, die der spezifischen Lage im amerikanischen Westen entspricht, das Potential des Grundstücks voll ausschöpft und den harschen Wetterbedingungen standhält.

PRIVATE RESIDENCE
TURNBULL GRIFFIN
HAESLOOP ARCHITECTS

434

In the main house, two white-washed cubes define the interior space; one cube contains the pantry, the other a staircase to the second-floor and master bedroom. The roof structure extends well beyond the house itself to create a protected outdoor room with fireplace. The houses intrude on the natural setting as little as possible. They are barely visible in the aspen grove at the edge of the large meadow. The two-bedroom guest house recedes into the background between the house and the garage.

Zwei weiße Kuben, die einen Hauswirtschaftsraum bzw. eine Treppe enthalten, definieren den zentralen Raum des Haupthauses. Das Dach wurde weit nach vorne gezogen, um einen geschützten Freiraum mit offenem Kamin zu bilden. Die Häuser nehmen sich gegenüber der Landschaft zurück und verschwinden optisch am Rande einer großen Gebirgsweide. Das Gasthaus tritt in den Hintergrund zwischen Haupthaus und Garage.

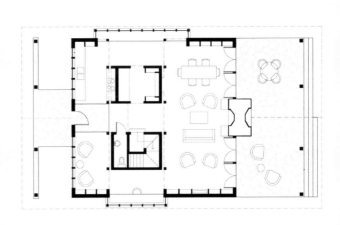

+0

COUNTRY / LAND	USA	HOUSE NAME / BEZEICHNUNG DES HAUSES	PRIVATE RESIDENCE
LOCATION (CITY/REGION) / LAGE (STADT/REGION)			JACKSON COUNTY, COLORADO
ARCHITECT / ARCHITEKT	TURNBULL GRIFFIN HAESLOOP ARCHITECTS	YEAR OF COMPLETION / BAUJAHR	2004
PHOTOGRAPHER / FOTOGRAF	DAVID WAKELY	SQUARE FEET / QUADRAT METER	2058 / 191
CITY AND COUNTRY ARCHITECT / STADT UND LAND ARCHITEKT			BERKELEY, CA, USA
WEBSITE ARCHITECT / HOMEPAGE ARCHITEKT			WWW.TGHARCHS.COM

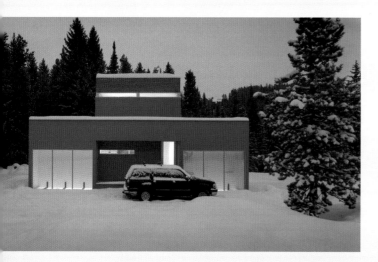

HILLER RESIDENCE
MICHAEL P. JOHNSON
DESIGN STUDIOS

The existing 1950's residence on site was relocated elsewhere, leaving the architects with existing basement walls upon which the new structure was designed. The two storey solution elevates the living, dining, and kitchen on the upper level to "fly" above the dense evergreen forest. The lower level contains bedrooms and the main entry and a painting studio naturally lit by skylight wells was foreseen in the basement.

Ein bestehendes Haus aus den 1950er Jahren wurde abgetragen und an einen anderen Ort versetzt. Dennoch entwarfen die Architekten das neue Haus so, dass die bestehenden Kellerwände erhalten werden konnten. Die zweigeschossige Anordnung sieht den Hauptwohnbereich mit Ausblicken auf den Wald im Obergeschoss vor. Das untere Geschoss beherbergt Schlafzimmer und den Eingangsbereich; ein über Oberlichter belichtetes Atelier befindet sich im Keller.

COUNTRY / LAND	USA HOUSE NAME / BEZEICHNUNG DES HAUSES	HILLER RESIDENCE
LOCATION (CITY/REGION) / LAGE (STADT/REGION)		WINTER PARK, COLORADO
ARCHITECT / ARCHITEKT	MICHAEL P. JOHNSON DESIGN STUDIOS YEAR OF COMPLETION / BAUJAHR	2005
PHOTOGRAPHER / FOTOGRAF	BILL TIMMERMAN SQUARE FEET / QUADRAT METER	2400 / 223
CITY AND COUNTRY ARCHITECT / STADT UND LAND ARCHITEKT		CAVE CREEK, ARIZONA
WEBSITE ARCHITECT / HOMEPAGE ARCHITEKT		WWW.MPJSTUDIO.COM

Two demands formed the design solution: the client request
for a residence on a single level and the City of Phoenix Zoning
Department regulations that stipulated the retention of the
boulder strewn slopes. The house was articulated into two levels,
a lower level with garages and the entrance that is connected to
the upper entrance level via an elevator. This allows the upper
structure to hover above the ground plane, and achieves 100%
protection of the desert landscape here.

Zwei Prämissen dienten als Ausgangsbasis des Entwurfes:
der Wunsch der Bauherrschaft nach einer Unterbringung
der Hauptfunktionen des Hauses auf einer Ebene und
planungsrechtliche Bindungen, welche den Erhalt der felsigen
Hanglandschaft festschrieben. Das Haus wurde in zwei Bereiche
unterteilt. Von der unteren Eingangsebene führt ein Aufzug
zum darüber schwebenden Haupthaus hinauf. Somit berührt
dieses die Topographie nicht, was den umfassenden Schutz der
Wüstenlandschaft ermöglichte.

+0

YODER-DOORNBOS RESIDENCE
MICHAEL P. JOHNSON
DESIGN STUDIOS

COUNTRY / LAND	USA	HOUSE NAME / BEZEICHNUNG DES HAUSES	YODER-DOORNBOS RESIDENCE
LOCATION (CITY/REGION) / LAGE (STADT/REGION)			PHEONIX, ARIZONA
ARCHITECT / ARCHITEKT	MICHAEL P. JOHNSON DESIGN STUDIOS	YEAR OF COMPLETION / BAUJAHR	1999
PHOTOGRAPHER / FOTOGRAF	BILL TIMMERMAN	SQUARE FEET / QUADRAT METER	5000 / 465
CITY AND COUNTRY ARCHITECT / STADT UND LAND ARCHITEKT			CAVE CREEK, ARIZONA
WEBSITE ARCHITECT / HOMEPAGE ARCHITEKT			WWW.MPJSTUDIO.COM

This home is sited within a late 50's era neighbourhood where the urban grid of Phoenix is overtaken by the organic land forms of the North Phoenix mountain preserve. Located at the end of two dead-end streets, the residence is positioned upon the upward slope of a double lot facing the mountain preserve to the north and the city centre to the south. The two-story lower level design studio descends down into the earth and the single story residence above the studio is accessed solely by an external stair. To access the residence, the visitor ascends an exterior steel staircase to an upper level balcony before entering the common room (sitting, dining, and kitchen).

Das Grundstück befindet sich im Übergangsbereich zwischen dem Raster des Straßennetzes von Phoenix und den organischen Formen des nah gelegenen Naturreservats. Am Ende zweier Sackgassen gelegen, liegt der Bau im oberen Teil eines Hanggrundstückes und verfügt somit auf Ausblicke auf die Stadt und die Berge. Ein zweigeschossiges Atelier wurde in den Hang eingebettet; darüber befindet sich die Wohnebene, die über eine stählerne Außentreppe erschlossen wird.

XEROS RESIDENCE
BLANK STUDIO, INC

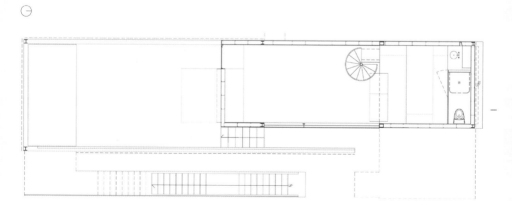

+1

The path continues through a central gallery towards the cantilevered master suite / media room. This space is completely glazed on the north façade to enjoy the mountain preserve views. The primary building material is exposed steel (as structure, cladding, and shading) that is allowed to weather naturally and meld with the colour of the surrounding hills. The house turns an opaque face towards the intense western afternoon sun and the more exposed faces to the south and east are shielded by an external layer of woven metal shade mesh.

Am oberen Balkon angekommen, betritt der Besucher den Wohn-, Eß- und Kochbereich. Der Weg setzt sich über eine innere Halle zur weit auskragenden Schlafzimmersuite fort. Die Nordwand dieses Bereichs wurde komplett verglast, um den freien Ausblick auf die Berge zu ermöglichen. Stahl bildet das Hauptmaterial des Hauses, das bewusst der Witterung ausgesetzt ist - auch um die Farbigkeit der umliegenden Hügel aufzunehmen. Das Haus verschließt sich gegen die harsche Westsonne und öffnet sich nach Süden und Osten mit Glasfronten, die durch Streckmetallschleier verschattet sind.

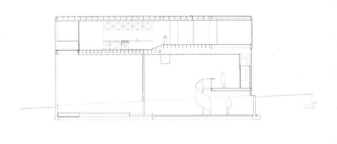

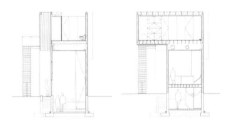

COUNTRY / LAND	USA	HOUSE NAME / BEZEICHNUNG DES HAUSES	XEROS RESIDENCE
LOCATION (CITY/REGION) / LAGE (STADT/REGION)			PHOENIX, ARIZONA
ARCHITECT / ARCHITEKT		BLANK STUDIO, INC YEAR OF COMPLETION / BAUJAHR	2005
PHOTOGRAPHER / FOTOGRAF		BILL TIMMERMAN SQUARE FEET / QUADRAT METER	2200 / 204
CITY AND COUNTRY ARCHITECT / STADT UND LAND ARCHITEKT			PHOENIX, AZ, USA
WEBSITE ARCHITECT / HOMEPAGE ARCHITEKT			WWW.BLANCKSPACES.NET

BLANK STUDIO, INC

PHOENIX, ARIZONA
USA

Blank Studio was created to honor the capacity for architecture to challenge, inspire and elevate design awareness in an environment that is directed toward increasingly simplistic and synthetic solutions. The design process centers upon investigation and synthesis, the experiential use of space, and the engagement of the senses. Within this inclusive method of design, Blank Studio endeavors through its work to transcend meaninglessness

and create that which is a testimony to the potential of the designed environment. In addition to realized projects, Blank Studio actively participates in the theoretical realm as well, through teaching and by taking part in various local and international design competitions. As an emerging concern in our natural and built environments today, explorations into sustainable technology and practices inform much of the current work of Blank Studio.

Blank Studio wurde gegründet mit dem Ziel, Architektur als ein Instrument einzusetzen, das herausfordern und inspirieren kann – gerade in einer Umwelt, die zunehmend durch vereinfachende Lösungen bestimmt wird. Der Entwurfsprozess von Blank Studio wird durch Erforschung und Synthese, die direkte Wahrnehmung von Raum und die Anregung der Sinne bestimmt. So bemüht man sich, Beliebigkeit zu überwinden und das Potential einer sorgsam gestalteten Umwelt zu erkunden.

Zusätzlich zu gebauten Werken entwickelt Blank Studio auch theoretische Ansätze, die durch Lehrtätigkeit an Architekturfakultäten und Teilnahme an internationalen Architekturwettbewerben differenziert und erprobt werden. Zunehmend bestimmt die Auseinandersetzung mit nachhaltigen Entwurfsansätzen die gegenwärtige Arbeit im Büro von Blank Studio.

TEXAS TWISTER
BUILDINGSTUDIO

This country home is used as a second house for weekday visits and weekend stays. The main structure, oriented on an east-west axis, sits between hardwoods and an open meadow. The entrance is situated adjacent to a stand of live oak that shades the entry from the afternoon sun. The roofs are supported by a post-and-beam system that allows them to float above the main body of the building. This creates a ribbon of clerestory windows that extends to provide an abundance of natural light inside.

Dieses Landhaus dient als Zweithaus für Besuche unter der Woche und längere Aufenthalte am Wochenende. Orientiert entlang einer Ost-West Achse, liegt das Haupthaus zwischen einem Wald und einer offenen Weide. Der Eingang befindet sich neben einem Baumhain, der diesen vor der Nachmittagssonne verschattet. Die Dächer werden durch schlanke Stützen getragen und scheinen über dem Haus zu schweben. Somit entsteht ein Oberlichtstreifen, der optimal Licht in das Hausinnere führt.

COUNTRY / LAND	USA HOUSE NAME / BEZEICHNUNG DES HAUSES	TEXAS TWISTER
LOCATION (CITY/REGION) / LAGE (STADT/REGION)		ELLIS COUNTY, TEXAS
ARCHITECT / ARCHITEKT	BUILDINGSTUDIO YEAR OF COMPLETION / BAUJAHR	2003
PHOTOGRAPHER / FOTOGRAF	TIMOTHY HURSLEY SQUARE FEET / QUADRAT METER	4500 / 418
CITY AND COUNTRY ARCHITECT / STADT UND LAND ARCHITEKT		MEMPHIS, TN, USA
WEBSITE ARCHITECT / HOMEPAGE ARCHITEKT		WWW.BUILDINGSTUDIO.NET

An existing barn was gutted and refurbished to create a gathering space that is used as an auxiliary space for the nearby main house. The main structural beams and columns were retained and foreseen with a new shell of metal sheeting and translucent polycarbonate façade panels. This project provides a striking example of the potentials inherent in the conversion of agricultural buildings into new residential structures.

Eine bestehende Scheune wurde bis auf den Rohbau zurückgebaut, um neue Gemeinschaftsräume für das sich in der Nähe befindende Haupthaus zu schaffen. Die Haupttrageelemente wie Stützen und Balken wurden erhalten und mit einer neuen Außenschale aus Metalltafeln und durchschimmernden Polykarbonatpanellen versehen. Dieses Projekt dokumentiert die großen Potentiale, welche die Umnutzung ehemaliger Agrarbauten in neue Wohnnutzungen bietet.

WILLOUGHBY BARN
EL DORADO INC

COUNTRY / LAND	USA	HOUSE NAME / BEZEICHNUNG DES HAUSES	WILLOUGHBY BARN
LOCATION (CITY/REGION) / LAGE (STADT/REGION)			WESTON, MISSOURI
ARCHITECT / ARCHITEKT		EL DORADO INC YEAR OF COMPLETION / BAUJAHR	2002
PHOTOGRAPHER / FOTOGRAF		MIKE SINCLAIR SQUARE FEET / QUADRAT METER	2440 / 227
CITY AND COUNTRY ARCHITECT / STADT UND LAND ARCHITEKT			KANSAS CITY, MO, USA
WEBSITE ARCHITECT / HOMEPAGE ARCHITEKT			WWW.ELDORADOARCHITECTS.COM

The main living level on the ground floor is clad in black panels and stretches to create a plinth upon which the white bedroom cubes of the upper level were skilfully placed. The palette of colours is continued inside, where the grey floors and white ceiling panels are complemented with wooden ceiling beams and wooden frames.

Die Hauptwohnräume im Erdgeschoss sind in einem schwarz verkleideten Sockel untergebracht, über den die weißen Schlafzimmerkuben angeordnet wurden. Die Farbpalette setzt sich im Inneren fort: graue Böden und weiße Deckenpanelle werden durch die Holzbalken der Decke und der Fensterrahmen komplettiert.

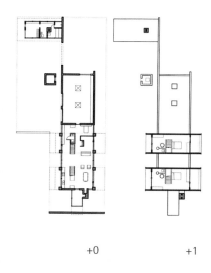

+0   +1

STREETER HOUSE
SALMELA ARCHITECT

COUNTRY / LAND	USA HOUSE NAME / BEZEICHNUNG DES HAUSES	STREETER HOUSE
LOCATION (CITY/REGION) / LAGE (STADT/REGION)		DEEPHAVEN, MINNESOTA
ARCHITECT / ARCHITEKT	SALMELA ARCHITECT YEAR OF COMPLETION / BAUJAHR	2004
PHOTOGRAPHER / FOTOGRAF	PETER BASTIANELLI-KERZE SQUARE FEET / QUADRAT METER	3000 / 279
CITY AND COUNTRY ARCHITECT / STADT UND LAND ARCHITEKT		DULUTH, MN, USA
WEBSITE ARCHITECT / HOMEPAGE ARCHITEKT		WWW.SALMELAARCHITECT.COM

PFANNER HOUSE
ZOKA ZOLA

The urban site led the architects to compact the building mass into a clear cube form. The succinct compactness of the exterior gives way to generous multiple-story interior spaces. In contrast to the earthy solidity of the warm brick used outside, the white walls inside create abstract spatial planes that define the relaxed contemporary interiors.

Die urbane Lage veranlasste die Architekten, die Baumasse in eine kubenähnliche Form zusammen zu fassen. Die Kompaktheit im Äußeren relativiert sich in den großzügigen mehrgeschossigen Innenräumen. Im Kontrast zu erdigen Solidität der Klinkerfassaden schaffen die weißen Wände im Inneren abstrakte Raumebenen, welche entspannte zeitgenössische Wohninterieurs definieren.

451

COUNTRY / LAND	USA	HOUSE NAME / BEZEICHNUNG DES HAUSES	PFANNER HOUSE
LOCATION (CITY/REGION) / LAGE (STADT/REGION)			CHICAGO, ILLINOIS
ARCHITECT / ARCHITEKT		ZOKA ZOLA YEAR OF COMPLETION / BAUJAHR	2002
PHOTOGRAPHER / FOTOGRAF		DOUG FOGELSON SQUARE FEET / QUADRAT METER	3000 / 279
CITY AND COUNTRY ARCHITECT / STADT UND LAND ARCHITEKT			CHICAGO, IL, USA
WEBSITE ARCHITECT / HOMEPAGE ARCHITEKT			WWW.ZOKAZOLA.COM

The L-shaped floor plan creates an entrance driveway / forecourt for this home that is placed at the back edge of the plot. The transparent middle section of the plan contains the entrance and the living room whereas the bedroom and garage spaces on the ends of the house are foreseen with solid stone-clad walls.

Der L-förmige Grundriss definiert einen repräsentativen Vorhof für dieses im hinteren Teil des Grundstücks angeordnete Haus. Der transparente Mittelteil beherbergt den Eingang und das Wohnzimmer. Die Schlafzimmer bzw. Garagenbereiche an den Hausenden sind hingegen eher verschlossen und mit hellem Naturstein verkleidet.

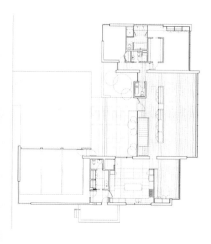

+0

KAPLAN HOUSE
<u>JOHN RONAN ARCHITECT</u>

COUNTRY / LAND	USA	HOUSE NAME / BEZEICHNUNG DES HAUSES	KAPLAN HOUSE
LOCATION (CITY/REGION) / LAGE (STADT/REGION)			NORTHBROOK, ILLINOIS
ARCHITECT / ARCHITEKT	JOHN RONAN ARCHITECT	YEAR OF COMPLETION / BAUJAHR	2001
PHOTOGRAPHER / FOTOGRAF	STEVE HALL, HEDRICH-BLESSING	SQUARE FEET / QUADRAT METER	5400 / 502
CITY AND COUNTRY ARCHITECT / STADT UND LAND ARCHITEKT			CHICAGO, IL, USA
WEBSITE ARCHITECT / HOMEPAGE ARCHITEKT			WWW.JRARCH.COM

COACH HOUSE
JOHN RONAN ARCHITECT

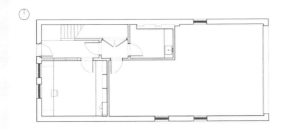

This urban house was erected within the existing brick walls of a former coach house. The brick walls were retained, refurbished and left exposed, both on the exteriors and the interiors. The roughness of the old brick walls is augmented by austere, crisp wooden insertions – the kitchen cabinets and parquet flooring - inside.

Dieses städtische Haus wurde innerhalb der Wände eines bestehenden Kutscherhauses errichtet. Die Klinkerwände wurden erhalten, instand gesetzt und sichtbar belassen, sowohl außen als auch innen. Die Schroffheit der alten Wandflächen wird durch die schlichte Glätte der neuen hölzernen Einbauten – Küchenschränke und Parkettböden – komplettiert.

453

COUNTRY / LAND	USA	HOUSE NAME / BEZEICHNUNG DES HAUSES	COACH HOUSE
LOCATION (CITY/REGION) / LAGE (STADT/REGION)			CHICAGO, ILLINOIS
ARCHITECT / ARCHITEKT	JOHN RONAN ARCHITECT	YEAR OF COMPLETION / BAUJAHR	2000
PHOTOGRAPHER / FOTOGRAF	NATHAN KIRKMAN	SQUARE FEET / QUADRAT METER	2000 / 186
CITY AND COUNTRY ARCHITECT / STADT UND LAND ARCHITEKT			CHICAGO, IL, USA
WEBSITE ARCHITECT / HOMEPAGE ARCHITEKT			WWW.JRARCH.COM

PERRY-BURLING HOUSE
JOHN RONAN ARCHITECT

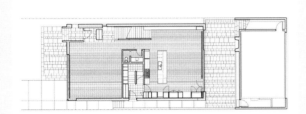

A narrow slot site with adjacent fire walls on both sides generated a three-storey floor plan that stretches back into the depths of the site. The garage at the back of the lot creates a protected urban patio court with an outdoor fireplace onto which the living room orients. Bedrooms and auxiliary functions are located on the two upper levels.

Die schmale Form der Grundstücksparzelle mit geschlossenen Brandwänden zu beiden Seiten führte zu einer 3-geschossigen Grundrisslösung. Eine Garage am hinteren Grundstücksrand definiert einen privaten Hof mit Außenkamin, zu dem sich das Wohnzimmer orientiert. Schlaf- und Nebenräume befinden sich in den beiden oberen Etagen.

COUNTRY / LAND	USA	HOUSE NAME / BEZEICHNUNG DES HAUSES	PERRY-BURLING HOUSE
LOCATION (CITY/REGION) / LAGE (STADT/REGION)			CHICAGO, ILLINOIS
ARCHITECT / ARCHITEKT		JOHN RONAN ARCHITECT YEAR OF COMPLETION / BAUJAHR	2005
PHOTOGRAPHER / FOTOGRAF		STEVE HALL, HEDRICH-BLESSING SQUARE FEET / QUADRAT METER	7200 / 670
CITY AND COUNTRY ARCHITECT / STADT UND LAND ARCHITEKT			CHICAGO, IL, USA
WEBSITE ARCHITECT / HOMEPAGE ARCHITEKT			WWW.JRARCH.COM

The client brief for Prairie House was simply titled "land, sky and seasons" and demanded among other things, a sense of space, of the farmland, and of the prairie. The house was therefore designed as a simple box clad in a zinc galvanized metal skin, akin to many agricultural buildings nearby, such as neighbouring silos. Seen from a distance, it appears as a stoic structure in the landscape, an object of utility that only reveals its purpose when one comes near it.

Das Programm des Bauherrn ließe sich in den Begriffen „Boden, Himmel und Jahreszeiten" zusammenfassen. Hiernach galt es insbesondere, das Haus räumlich sensibel in die Agrarlandschaft und in die Prärie einzupassen. Deshalb wurde die einfache Hausform, versehen mit einer Außenhülle aus verzinktem Metall, als Ableitung der Formensprache der umliegenden Agrarbauten und Getreidesilos entwickelt. Von weitem gesehen erscheint der Bau als eine stoische Figur in der Landschaft, wie ein Nutzbau dessen eigentliche Funktion als Wohnhaus nur aus der Nähe ersichtlich wird.

FIELD HOUSE
WENDELL BURNETTE ARCHITECT

The apparent simplicity of this home is articulated by specific moments of experience. These encompass notions of the house as a tuneable instrument - to connect to - and - be responsible to - the environment and range from compression release, to intimate conversations by the warmth of fire, to a morning coffee in the sun, to a gallery of "the art and books of a lifetime", and to a silo ladder that ascends to a secret roof-top observatory.

Die scheinbare Einfachheit des Baues bildet den Rahmen für spezifische Erlebnismomente. Das Haus wurde daher wie ein Musikinstrument aufgefasst, das sich „stimmen" lässt, um intime Gespräche am Kamin, den Kaffee in der Morgensonne, eine Galerie der „Bücher und Kunstobjektes eines Lebens" und eine siloähnliche Leiter zum „geheimen" Dachobservatorium zu ermöglichen.

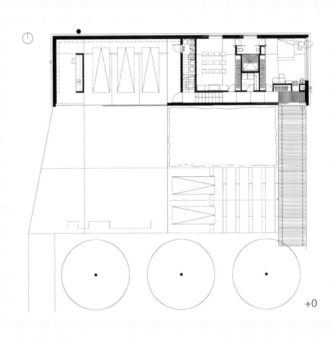

COUNTRY / LAND	USA	HOUSE NAME / BEZEICHNUNG DES HAUSES	FIELD HOUSE
LOCATION (CITY/REGION) / LAGE (STADT/REGION)			ELLINGTON, WISCONSIN
ARCHITECT / ARCHITEKT	WENDELL BURNETTE ARCHITECT	YEAR OF COMPLETION / BAUJAHR	2004
PHOTOGRAPHER / FOTOGRAF	BILL TIMMERMAN	SQUARE FEET / QUADRAT METER	5000 / 460
CITY AND COUNTRY ARCHITECT / STADT UND LAND ARCHITEKT			PHOENIX, AZ, USA
WEBSITE ARCHITECT / HOMEPAGE ARCHITEKT			WWW.WENDELLBURNETTEARCHITECTS.COM

BROOKLYN HOUSE
PHILIPPE BAUMANN

Originally a one-story brick carriage house, this 120-year-old building has served many purposes. The new second floor contains a steel-framed loft space that is offset from the neighbouring building to let light in below. To admit as much natural light as possible many new openings were made: in the party wall which abuts the neighbouring houses; in the front façade - where a full-width clerestory admits afternoon light - and in the living room ceiling with its long skylight.

Ursprünglich als ein eingeschossiges Kutscherhaus erbaut, hat dieser Bau im Laufe seiner 120 jährigen Geschichte viele Nutzungen erfahren. Das neue Obergeschoss, das in Stahlskelettbauweise errichtet wurde, beinhaltet ein großzügiges Loft. Um Licht in die Räume zu führen wurden viele neue Öffnungen – z.b. in der Wand zu den Nachbarhäusern, in der Straßenfassade und in der Decke über dem Wohnzimmer, wo ein langes Oberlicht eingebaut wurde, geschaffen.

COUNTRY / LAND	USA	HOUSE NAME / BEZEICHNUNG DES HAUSES	BROOKLYN HOUSE
LOCATION (CITY/REGION) / LAGE (STADT/REGION)			BROOKLYN, NEW YORK
ARCHITECT / ARCHITEKT	PHILIPPE BAUMANN	YEAR OF COMPLETION / BAUJAHR	2005
PHOTOGRAPHER / FOTOGRAF	ALFONSO PAREDES	SQUARE FEET / QUADRAT METER	6500 / 620
CITY AND COUNTRY ARCHITECT / STADT UND LAND ARCHITEKT			NEW YORK, NY, USA
WEBSITE ARCHITECT / HOMEPAGE ARCHITEKT			WWW.BAUMANNARCHITECTURE.COM

The linear plan of this vacation house enhances lake views while the low roof profile and stained green exterior cedar siding meld into the surrounding forest. All major rooms have a view of the lake. The living room, dining room and kitchen flow into each other to create a seamless living space. Adjacent to the living room, the master bedroom opens onto a deck with views through the forest to a secluded cove.

Der lineare Grundriss dieses Ferienhauses betont die Ausblicke auf den See, während sich das geduckte Dachprofil und die grün gebeizten Holzfassaden sensibel in den Wald einfügen. Die Haupträume sind sämtlich mit Seeblick angelegt. Die Wohn-, Ess- und Kochbereiche werden zu einem locker miteinander verbundenen Raumgefüge zusammengeführt. Das Elternschlafzimmer daneben öffnet sich zu einer Terrasse mit Wald- und Seeblick.

SHELVING ROCK HOUSE
BOHLIN CYWINSKI JACKSON

COUNTRY / LAND	USA	HOUSE NAME / BEZEICHNUNG DES HAUSES	SHELVING ROCK HOUSE
LOCATION (CITY/REGION) / LAGE (STADT/REGION)			NEW YORK STATE / LAKE XXX
ARCHITECT / ARCHITEKT		BOHLIN CYWINSKI JACKSON	YEAR OF COMPLETION / BAUJAHR 2004
PHOTOGRAPHER / FOTOGRAF		NIC LEHOUX SQUARE FEET / QUADRAT METER	4304 / 400
CITY AND COUNTRY ARCHITECT / STADT UND LAND ARCHITEKT			WILKES-BARRE, PE, USA
WEBSITE ARCHITECT / HOMEPAGE ARCHITEKT			WWW.BCJ.COM

POINT HOUSE
BOHLIN CYWINSKI JACKSON

The pristine site called for a sensitive intervention that respects the natural setting and the rugged climate with its seasonal extremes. The house stretches from a rock ledge to a wetland of cattails. A linear wall plane with a rusted, weathering steel skin slices through the site. The living spaces to the south extend onto a house-long wood deck.

Die unberührte Landschaft und die extremen Klimabedingungen stellten für dieses Projekt eine große Herausforderung dar. Der Bau erstreckt sich zwischen einem Felsrücken und einem Feuchtbiotop. Die Funktionsbereiche wurden entlang einer das Grundstück durchschneidenden Wandscheibe angeordnet. Mit Holz eingeschalte Badezimmer sind nach Norden, die Wohnbereiche nach Süden zur hauslangen Holzterrasse orientiert.

COUNTRY / LAND	USA	HOUSE NAME / BEZEICHNUNG DES HAUSES	POINT HOUSE
LOCATION (CITY/REGION) / LAGE (STADT/REGION)			RURAL MONTANA
ARCHITECT / ARCHITEKT	BOHLIN CYWINSKI JACKSON	YEAR OF COMPLETION / BAUJAHR	2002
PHOTOGRAPHER / FOTOGRAF	NIC LEHOUX	SQUARE FEET / QUADRAT METER	1900 / 175
CITY AND COUNTRY ARCHITECT / STADT UND LAND ARCHITEKT			SEATTLE, WA, USA
WEBSITE ARCHITECT / HOMEPAGE ARCHITEKT			WWW.BCJ.COM

This design was developed with careful consideration of site conditions, daily living needs, and an understanding of individual lifestyles. By utilizing prefabricated building technology, the home is superior to site-built homes both in the quality and efficiency of building, as well as in the cost and speed of construction. The result is a more affordable and better-designed home that is environmentally friendly with less material waste.

Der Entwurf dieses Hauses entstand unter besonderer Berücksichtigung des Standorts und der Bedürfnisse der Nutzer. Der Einsatz vorgefertigter Bauelemente gewährleistete gegenüber konventionell erbauten Häusern ein Resultat, das bessere Qualität, niedrigere Kosten und eine schnellere Umsetzung sowie einen nachhaltigeren Umgang mit Baumaterialien aufweist.

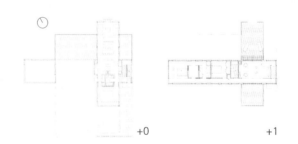

+0   +1

THE DWELL HOME
RESOLUTION: 4
ARCHITECTURE

COUNTRY / LAND	USA	HOUSE NAME / BEZEICHNUNG DES HAUSES	THE DWELL HOME
LOCATION (CITY/REGION) / LAGE (STADT/REGION)			PITTSBORO, NEW YORK STATE
ARCHITECT / ARCHITEKT	RESOLUTION: 4 ARCHITECTURE	YEAR OF COMPLETION / BAUJAHR	2004
PHOTOGRAPHER / FOTOGRAF	ROGER DAVIES	SQUARE FEET / QUADRAT METER	2042 / 190
CITY AND COUNTRY ARCHITECT / STADT UND LAND ARCHITEKT			NEW YORK, NY, USA
WEBSITE ARCHITECT / HOMEPAGE ARCHITEKT			WWW.RE4A.COM

The three-level design creates a solid 'wall' behind a palm forecourt toward the busy road and opens with large glazed walls toward the sea. The ground floor contains the entry, internal reflecting pools, the garage, exercise room, and swimming pool.

Das dreigeschossige Haus formt eine solide Wand zu dem mit Palmen bepflanzten Vorplatz und öffnet sich über großzügige Glasfronten zur Meerseite hin. Das Erdgeschoss beherbergt neben dem Eingangsbereich reflektierende Becken, die Garage, den Fitness Raum und den Pool. Dieser wurde an die Südseite des Hauses gerückt, um so die günstige Besonnung optimal auszunutzen.

OCEAN BOULEVARD HOUSE
GUY PETERSON / OFA, INC.

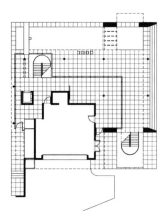

The pool is located on the south side of the structure for full sun and designed into the 'base' of the house. On the first level, the living, dining and kitchen areas look out over a large covered terrace to the Gulf of Mexico. The master bedroom and owner's study are on the top floor and have private terraces that enjoy panoramic views.

Wohn-, Eß- und Kochbereiche liegen im 1. OG mit Ausblick auf den Golf von Mexiko. Das große Schlafzimmer und die Bibliothek wurden in der obersten Etage untergebracht, Sie verfügen über private Terrassen und Panoramaausblicke.

COUNTRY / LAND	USA	HOUSE NAME / BEZEICHNUNG DES HAUSES	OCEAN BOULEVARD HOUSE
LOCATION (CITY/REGION) / LAGE (STADT/REGION)			LONGBOAT KEY, FLORIDA / ATLANTIC COAST
ARCHITECT / ARCHITEKT	GUY PETERSON/OFA, INC.	YEAR OF COMPLETION / BAUJAHR	2003
PHOTOGRAPHER / FOTOGRAF	STEVEN BROOKE STUDIOS	SQUARE FEET / QUADRAT METER	4842 / 450
CITY AND COUNTRY ARCHITECT / STADT UND LAND ARCHITEKT			SARASOTA, FL, USA
WEBSITE ARCHITECT / HOMEPAGE ARCHITEKT			WWW.GUYPETERSON.COM

The clear, L-shaped plan contains public functions in one wing and private functions in the other. The major functions all orient toward a central courtyard with a swimming pool and entertainment space. The roof floats over the courtyard on both interior legs of the "L" to provide covered exterior space. The "minimalist" interior of the design is reduced to the simplest of materials: exposed block, concrete floor and plywood interior walls and volumes.

Die Schenkel dieses klaren, L-förmigen Grundrisses beherbergen jeweils öffentliche, bzw. private Funktionen. Die Haupträume orientieren sich zum zentralen Innenhof mit dem Schwimmbecken. Das Dach kragt zum Hof weit aus, um vor der Sonne geschützte Außenbereiche zu definieren. Bei den „minimalistisch" gehaltenen Interieurs wurde die Materialienpalette auf einfache Baustoffe wie sichtbares Betonmauerwerk, Estrichböden und Sperrholzwände reduziert.

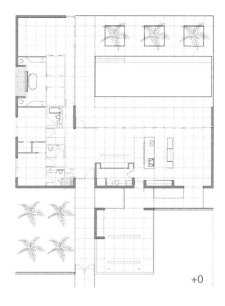

+0

HAWTHORNE STREET HOUSE
GUY PETERSON / OFA, INC.

COUNTRY / LAND	USA	HOUSE NAME / BEZEICHNUNG DES HAUSES	HAWTHORNE STREET HOUSE
LOCATION (CITY/REGION) / LAGE (STADT/REGION)			SARASOTA, FLORIDA
ARCHITECT / ARCHITEKT		GUY PETERSON YEAR OF COMPLETION / BAUJAHR	2005
PHOTOGRAPHER / FOTOGRAF		STEVEN BROOKE SQUARE FEET / QUADRAT METER	2500 / 232
CITY AND COUNTRY ARCHITECT / STADT UND LAND ARCHITEKT			SARASOTA, FL, USA
WEBSITE ARCHITECT / HOMEPAGE ARCHITEKT			WWW.GUYPETERSON.COM

SANDERLING BEACH HOUSE
GUY PETERSON / OFA, INC.

The guiding principle of this design was the creation of a temple-like concrete framework that forms a superstructure within which cube volumes containing the living functions were skilfully placed. The cube volumes are interconnected by interior bridges and multi-level atrium spaces. The vibrant colours utilized were derived from the underside of a seashell found on the nearby beach.

Leitgedanke dieses Entwurfs war die Schaffung eines tempelähnlichen Betonrahmenwerkes. Die verschiedenen Funktionen des Hauses werden als Kuben in dieses Rahmenwerk eingefügt, deren Farben von einer in der Nähe gefundenen Muschel abgeleitet wurden. Die Wohnkuben werden im Inneren über Brücken und durch mehrgeschossige Wohnhallen miteinander verbunden.

473

COUNTRY / LAND	USA	HOUSE NAME / BEZEICHNUNG DES HAUSES	SANDERLING BEACH HOUSE
LOCATION (CITY/REGION) / LAGE (STADT/REGION)			FLORIDA / ATLANTIC COAST
ARCHITECT / ARCHITEKT	GUY PETERSON/OFA, INC.	YEAR OF COMPLETION / BAUJAHR	2000
PHOTOGRAPHER / FOTOGRAF	STEVEN BROOKE STUDIOS	SQUARE FEET / QUADRAT METER	7532 / 700
CITY AND COUNTRY ARCHITECT / STADT UND LAND ARCHITEKT			SARASOTA, USA
WEBSITE ARCHITECT / HOMEPAGE ARCHITEKT			WWW.GUYPETERSON.COM

PR34 HOUSE
ROJKIND ARQUITECTOS

This home was built as a remodel / addition of an existing 1960's house. The existing house was gutted to create bigger and better areas. Then, a new independent house for the client's daughter, a ballet dancer, was designed. From the entrance at the garage level the two wings of the house can be accessed independently. A spiral staircase leads up two flights from here to the new addition. Resembling a ballet dance composed of two bodies in motion, the looping sensual forms were inspired by the client.

Dieses Haus entstand als Um- bzw. Anbau eines bestehenden Hauses aus den 1960er Jahren, das zunächst komplett ausgehöhlt wurde, um größere Räume zu schaffen. Danach entstand ein zweites, autarkes Haus für die Tochter des Bauherrn, eine Ballet-Tänzerin. Vom Eingang auf der Garagenebene aus werden die beiden Flügel des Hauses separat erschlossen. Eine Wendeltreppe führt über zwei Stockwerke zum neuen Anbau. Einem Ballett ähnelnd wurden die fließenden Bauformen als zwei sich scheinbar in Bewegung befindliche Körper konzipiert.

476

The house it is organized on a split-level floor plan. The upper level contains the kitchen, dining and living areas and the lower level houses a TV room and the master bedroom. The roof of the existing house with its skylights was utilized as the new terrace. Remnants of the chipped lava rocks used for the main walls of the house were used to surface the terrace, and the new skylights were foreseen as acrylic domes that can also be used as outdoor seating.

Die Wohnebenen sind halbversetzt angeordnet. Die obere Ebene nimmt den Wohnbereich auf, während sich Fernsehzimmer und Schlafzimmer auf der unteren Ebene befinden. Das Dach des bestehenden Hauses wurde zur nun Terrasse des Neubaus. Lavasteinreste aus dem Hausbau wurden als Terrassenbelag verwendet und die neuen Oberlichter aus Acryl dienen zusätzlich als Sitzmöglichkeiten auf der Terrasse.

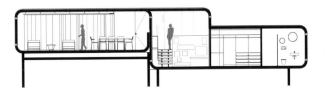

COUNTRY / LAND	MEXICO	HOUSE NAME / BEZEICHNUNG DES HAUSES	PR34 HOUSE
LOCATION (CITY/REGION) / LAGE (STADT/REGION)			MEXICO CITY
ARCHITECT / ARCHITEKT		ROJKIND ARQUITECTOS YEAR OF COMPLETION / BAUJAHR	2003
PHOTOGRAPHER / FOTOGRAF		JAIME NAVARRO SQUARE FEET / QUADRAT METER	1453 / 135
CITY AND COUNTRY ARCHITECT / STADT UND LAND ARCHITEKT			MEXICO DF
WEBSITE ARCHITECT / HOMEPAGE ARCHITEKT			WWW.ROJKINDARQUITECTOS.COM

This house resulted through consideration of the topography, the views, the orientations, and the program provided by the client. The topography allowed arraying the house functions on three levels. The orientation coincided with the topography of the site, but a concrete portal was foreseen as a shading device. The clients program generated an L shaped plan that separates the different functions appropriately.

Der Entwurf entstand unter Berücksichtigung der Topographie, der Ausblicke, der Sonnenorientierung und des Programms der Bauherrschaft. Die Lage des Grundstücks erlaubte die Anordnung der Funktionen auf drei Ebenen. Als Reaktion auf die Sonnenorientierung entstand ein Portal aus Beton als Verschattungselement. Um dem Raumprogramm zu entsprechen, wurden die Funktionen des Hauses auf zwei Schenkel eines L-förmigen Grundrisses verteilt.

F2 HOUSE
ROJKIND ARQUITECTOS

COUNTRY / LAND	MEXICO	HOUSE NAME / BEZEICHNUNG DES HAUSES	F2 HOUSE
LOCATION (CITY/REGION) / LAGE (STADT/REGION)			MEXICO CITY
ARCHITECT / ARCHITEKT		ROJKIND ARQUITECTOS YEAR OF COMPLETION / BAUJAHR	2001
PHOTOGRAPHER / FOTOGRAF		UNDINE PROHL SQUARE FEET / QUADRAT METER	6940 / 645
CITY AND COUNTRY ARCHITECT / STADT UND LAND ARCHITEKT			MEXICO DF
WEBSITE ARCHITECT / HOMEPAGE ARCHITEKT			WWW.ROJKINDARQUITECTOS.COM

A two level, steel-frame glass volume contains the main spaces of this house. The living room, dining room and kitchen are located on the upper level and extend out to the wide terrace that is cantilevered out over the steep hillside. The closed north façade shields from the cold dominant winds. The south, east and west façades open graciously to the adjacent forest.

Eine zweigeschossige Glashalle in Stahlrahmenbauweise beherbergt die Haupträume dieses Hauses. Wohn-, Eß- und Kochbereiche liegen im obersten Geschoss und setzen sich auf der breiten, über dem Hang auskragenden Terrasse im Freien fort. Die verschlossene Nordfassade schützt das Haus vor den harschen Nordwinden. Die Süd-, Ost- und Westfassaden öffnen sich großzügig zum Ausblick auf den Wald hin.

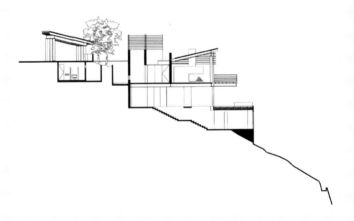

CASA EN BOSQUES DE SANTA FE
GRUPO LBC ARQ

COUNTRY / LAND	MEXICO	HOUSE NAME / BEZEICHNUNG DES HAUSES	CASA EN BOSQUES DE SANTA FE
LOCATION (CITY/REGION) / LAGE (STADT/REGION)			BOSQUES DE SANTA FE
ARCHITECT / ARCHITEKT	LÓPEZ BAZ, CALLEJA, SANCHEZ & QUIROZ	YEAR OF COMPLETION / BAUJAHR	2003
PHOTOGRAPHER / FOTOGRAF	HECTOR VELASCO FACIO	SQUARE FEET / QUADRAT METER	6456 / 600
CITY AND COUNTRY ARCHITECT / STADT UND LAND ARCHITEKT			MEXICO DF
WEBSITE ARCHITECT / HOMEPAGE ARCHITEKT			XXX

CASA EN LOMAS DE CHAPULTEPEC
GRUPO LBC ARQ

+0

The functions of this house are arrayed into five individual buildings that are interconnected by a double-height entrance foyer. This allows for an ideal separation of the various uses that are then appropriately articulated in an abstract architectural language as villa-like pavilions. Wood slats were mounted on the garden wall and below the glass roof of the entrance foyer to give protection from the harsh sun and introduce a friendly natural material into the interiors.

Die Raumbereiche dieses Projekts wurden auf fünf Einzelbauten verteilt, welche über das zentrale, zweigeschossige Foyer miteinander verknüpft sind. Dies erlaubt eine ideale Trennung der Nutzungsbereiche in villenähnliche Pavillons, die in einer abstrakten Architektursprache ausgearbeitet wurden. Holzlatten wurden hinter der Fassade und unter der Glasdecke des Foyers als Sonnenschutzelemente montiert und verleihen dem Hallenraum ein freundliches, natürliches Ambiente.

483

COUNTRY / LAND	MEXICO	HOUSE NAME / BEZEICHNUNG DES HAUSES	CASA EN LOMAS DE CHAPULTEPEC
LOCATION (CITY/REGION) / LAGE (STADT/REGION)			BOSQUES DE LAS LOMAS, MEXICO CITY
ARCHITECT / ARCHITEKT	CALLEJA, KALACH & LOPEZ BAZ	YEAR OF COMPLETION / BAUJAHR	2003
PHOTOGRAPHER / FOTOGRAF	HECTOR VELASCO FACIO	SQUARE FEET / QUADRAT METER	10760 / 1000
CITY AND COUNTRY ARCHITECT / STADT UND LAND ARCHITEKT			MEXICO DF
WEBSITE ARCHITECT / HOMEPAGE ARCHITEKT			XXX

The site generated an L-shaped floor plan that opens toward pools and gardens and is closed toward the neighbouring houses. A massive middle wall separates the living/dining rooms from the entrance hall, kitchen and bedrooms. This allows the exterior garden spaces to seamlessly extend into the interior, a dramatic effect that is heightened by the completely glazed walls here. Elegant metal louvers filter the harsh sunlight and reduce the need for energy-consuming air conditioning.

Die Parzellenform führte zu einem L-förmigen Grundriss, der sich zu Wasserbecken und Gärten hin öffnet und zur Nachbarbebauung hin schließt. Eine massive Innenwand trennt Wohn- und Essbereich von der Eingangshalle, der Küche und den Schlafzimmern. Dies verstärkt den Eindruck der Verschmelzung zwischen dem Wohn- und Essbereich und den Gärten, was zusätzlich durch die Komplettverglasung der Gartenfassade unterstrichen wird.

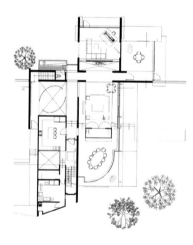

+0

CASA EN ACUEDUCTO RIO ESCONDIDO
GRUPO LBC ARQ

COUNTRY / LAND	MEXICO	HOUSE NAME / BEZEICHNUNG DES HAUSES	CASA RIO ESCONDIDO
LOCATION (CITY/REGION) / LAGE (STADT/REGION)			ACUEDUCTO RIO ESCONDIDO, MEXICO CITY
ARCHITECT / ARCHITEKT	LÓPEZ BAZ, CALLEJA & HERNÁNDEZ	YEAR OF COMPLETION / BAUJAHR	2003
PHOTOGRAPHER / FOTOGRAF	HECTOR VELASCO FACIO	SQUARE FEET / QUADRAT METER	8608 / 800
CITY AND COUNTRY ARCHITECT / STADT UND LAND ARCHITEKT			MEXICO DF
WEBSITE ARCHITECT / HOMEPAGE ARCHITEKT			XXX

RICHARDSON RESIDENCE
DIAMOND AND SCHMITT ARCHITECTS

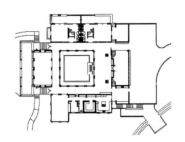

+0

This home focuses internally toward a central courtyard with a spacious pool. The architecture was developed with reference to both Roman atrium houses and to local building traditions in the Caribbean region. The courtyard arcade underscores the Roman atrium house predecessor and the vaulted living room space creates a tent-like quality reminiscent of colonial houses nearby.

Dieses Haus orientiert sich nach innen zu einem zentralen Hof mit großzugigem Schwimmbecken hin. Die Architektur wurde unter Bezug auf römische Atriumhäuser, aber auch auf lokale Bautraditionen der Karibik entwickelt. Die Hofarkade unterstreicht die Referenz an Atriumhäuser, während das Holzdach des Wohnzimmers an die Kolonialarchitektur der Häuser in der Umgebung erinnert.

485

COUNTRY / LAND	WEST INDIES, WEST INDIEN	HOUSE NAME / BEZEICHNUNG DES HAUSES	RICHARDSON RESIDENCE
LOCATION (CITY/REGION) / LAGE (STADT/REGION)			MUSTIQUE, GRENADINES
ARCHITECT / ARCHITEKT	DIAMOND AND SCHMITT ARCHITECTS	YEAR OF COMPLETION / BAUJAHR	2003
PHOTOGRAPHER / FOTOGRAF	MASSIMO LISTRI	SQUARE FEET / QUADRAT METER	11480 / 1067
CITY AND COUNTRY ARCHITECT / STADT UND LAND ARCHITEKT			TORONTO, CANADA
WEBSITE ARCHITECT / HOMEPAGE ARCHITEKT			WWW.DSAI.CA

Aldeia da Serra House - Barueri, Brasil - SPBR Arquitetos- Photographer Nelson Kon

SOUTH AMERICA / SÜD AMERIKA

490   494–498

500

502

504–538, 560   550–556

540

544

561, 562   569, 570

564

568

563

BEACH HOUSE IN LAS ARENAS
<u>JAVIER ARTADI</u>

The hot summers on the Peruvian coast confronted the architect with a difficult design challenge. To create a sun-protected outdoor space he extended the white cubist shell of the main house mass to enclose an indoor-outdoor space. By simply extending the house volume and leaving out all glazing in this portion of the home a striking merge of interior and exterior spaces was achieved.

Das unbarmherzige Sommerklima dieser Küstenregion Perus konfrontierte den Architekten mit einer schwierigen Herausforderung. Um einen vor der Sonne geschützten Bereich zu schaffen verlängerte er die kubische weiße Schale des Baukörpers ins Freie. Durch diese einfache Geste und den konsequenten Verzicht auf Verglasung ist eine eindrucksvolle Synthese von Innen- und Außenräumen entstanden.

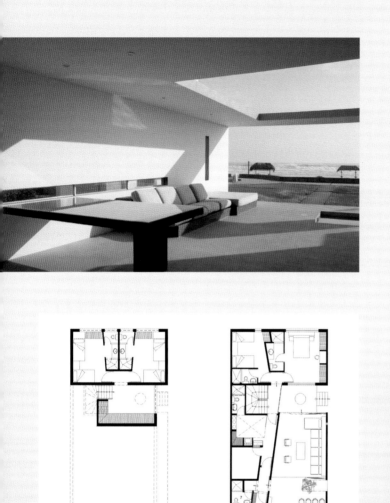

The living-dining room is defined as a sheltered outdoor space and as an integral part of building composition. To emphasize the special function of this wing it cantilevers out from the recessed plinth to hover above the ground plane. A rectangular opening frames the view out to the ocean and back into the interior. This courageous design strikes up an innovative dialogue that forms a striking contrast to the natural surroundings and at the same time allows architecture and nature to dramatically merge.

Um die besondere Funktion dieses Traktes zu betonen kragt über dem zurück springenden Sockel aus und scheint über dem Boden zu schweben. Das rechteckige Fassadenportal rahmt den Blick aufs nah gelegene Meer. Dieser mutige Entwurf lebt vom Kontrast mit der Natur und stellt zugleich eine nahtlose Verbindung zwischen Architektur und Naturraum her.

COUNTRY / LAND	PERU	HOUSE NAME / BEZEICHNUNG DES HAUSES	BEACH HOUSE IN LAS ARENAS
LOCATION (CITY/REGION) / LAGE (STADT/REGION)			LIMA
ARCHITECT / ARCHITEKT	JAVIER ARTADI	YEAR OF COMPLETION / BAUJAHR	2004
PHOTOGRAPHER / FOTOGRAF	ALEX KORNHUBER	SQUARE FEET / QUADRAT METER	2561 / 238
CITY AND COUNTRY ARCHITECT / STADT UND LAND ARCHITEKT			LIMA, PERU
WEBSITE ARCHITECT / HOMEPAGE ARCHITEKT			WWW.JAVIERARTADI.COM

This house was conceived as a mass from which openings were "excavated", resulting in a merging of interior and exterior spaces. An entrance patio leads into the intimate space of the house towards the ocean and a large terrace with its long pool. The roof of the living/dining space hovers like a beach umbrella. Borders between the living/dining space and the terrace are erased by frameless glass sliding panels.

Dieses Haus wurde als solide Masse konzipiert, aus der Stücke „gehauen" wurden. Der Eingangsvorhof führt Richtung Meer in das Hausinnere und zur großen Terrasse mit dem lang gestrecktem Pool. Das Dach des Wohn-Essbereichs schwebt darüber wie ein Strandschirm. Die Grenzen zwischen Wohn-Essbereich und Terrasse sind dank der großen rahmenlosen Glasschiebeelemente fließend.

CASA EQUIS
BARCLAY & CROUSSE ARCHITECTURE

An open staircase follows the topography and leads to the bedroom level beneath the terrace. The children's bedrooms are accessed by a pergola covered by the terrace deck. The parents' bedroom under the pool is reached at the end of the staircase.

Eine offene Freitreppe folgt der Topografie und führt Hang abwärts zur Schlafzone unter der Terrasse. Hier werden die Kinderzimmer über eine Pergola unter der Terrasse erschlossen. Das Elternzimmer unter dem Pool wird am Ende der Treppe erreicht.

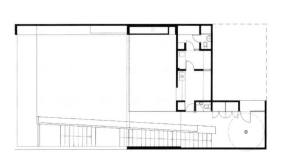

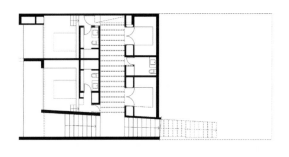

COUNTRY / LAND	PERU	HOUSE NAME / BEZEICHNUNG DES HAUSES	CASA EQUIS
LOCATION (CITY/REGION) / LAGE (STADT/REGION)			CAÑETE / PACIFIC COAST
ARCHITECT / ARCHITEKT	BARCLAY & CROUSSE ARCHITECTURE	YEAR OF COMPLETION / BAUJAHR	2003
PHOTOGRAPHER / FOTOGRAF	JEAN PIERRE CROUSSE	SQUARE FEET / QUADRAT METER	1872 / 174
CITY AND COUNTRY ARCHITECT / STADT UND LAND ARCHITEKT			PARIS, FRANCE
WEBSITE ARCHITECT / HOMEPAGE ARCHITEKT			WWW.BARCLAYCROUSSE.COM

498

A creative design was conceived to integrate this home into the steep slope. An exterior stair leads down the side of the house. The entrance is located on the first landing that accesses the bedroom level. The living room was deployed on the lower, poolside level. It interconnects to the bedroom level above via a high, two-story spatial volume. Vibrant colours were employed to heighten the plasticity of the cube-like volumes that weather under the relentless sun of the Peruvian coast. The main house glows in a clear red, beige was used on the walls that border to neighbouring plots, and a white tower creates a vertical focus.

Das Haus ist auf kreative Weise in die Hanglage eingepasst. Eine seitliche Treppe im Freien führt vom Eingangshof am Hang herunter. Auf dem ersten Zwischenpodest betritt man die Ebene der Schlafzimmer, ein Geschoss tiefer liegt der zweigeschossige Wohnraum auf der Poolebene. Leuchtende Farben werden eingesetzt, um die plastische Qualität der Baukörper unter der gleißenden Sonne der peruanischen Küste zu überhöhen. Das Haupthaus leuchtet in klarem Rot, beigefarbene Wandscheiben grenzen das Grundstück ab, und ein weißer Bügel wird als vertikale Dominante betont.

M-HOUSE

BARCLAY & CROUSSE
ARCHITECTURE

COUNTRY / LAND	PERU	HOUSE NAME / BEZEICHNUNG DES HAUSES	M-HOUSE
LOCATION (CITY/REGION) / LAGE (STADT/REGION)			CAÑETE / PACIFIC COAST
ARCHITECT / ARCHITEKT	BARCLAY & CROUSSE ARCHITECTURE	YEAR OF COMPLETION / BAUJAHR	1999
PHOTOGRAPHER / FOTOGRAF	JEAN PIERRE CROUSSE	SQUARE FEET / QUADRAT METER	1679 / 156
CITY AND COUNTRY ARCHITECT / STADT UND LAND ARCHITEKT			PARIS, FRANCE
WEBSITE ARCHITECT / HOMEPAGE ARCHITEKT			WWW.BARCLAYCROUSSE.COM

To avoid infringing on the exposed, lagoon natural setting with clumsy building masses the architect opted for embedding this three-story home in the natural slope. This allows it to integrate into the horizon as a seemingly one-story mass on the entrance side. But the steep, wing-like roof forms rise to contain an additional level with a complete bedroom wing. The kitchen is located on the lower, beachside level. Here, covered exterior spaces with direct access to pool and beach serve as spaces for relaxation in the cooling shade under the house.

Um die exponierte Lage an einer abgelegenen Lagune nicht durch störende Baumassen zu beeinträchtigen, wurde der dreigeschossige Bau in das Gelände eingepasst. Von der Eingangsseite aus betrachtet wirkt das Haus eingeschossig, die flügelähnlichen Dachformen beherbergen jedoch auch ein komplettes Schlafgeschoss. Ein weiterer Schlafraum und ein großes Wohnzimmer sind auf der Eingangsebene untergebracht. Die Küche befindet sich auf der unteren Ebene auf Strandniveau. Hier werden Raumbereiche im Freien in den kühlen Schatten unter dem Haus gebildet, die zum erholsamen Aufenthalt direkt am Pool einladen.

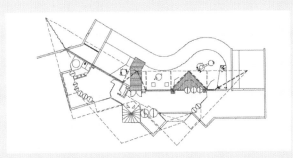

CASA IN LAGOA DE URUAÚ

GERSON
CASTELO BRANCO

COUNTRY / LAND	BRAZIL / BRASILIEN	HOUSE NAME / BEZEICHNUNG DES HAUSES	CASA IN LAGOA DE URUAÚ
LOCATION (CITY/REGION) / LAGE (STADT/REGION)			LAGOA DE URUAÚ, CEARÁ
ARCHITECT / ARCHITEKT	GERSON CASTELO BRANCO	YEAR OF COMPLETION / BAUJAHR	1999
PHOTOGRAPHER / FOTOGRAF	TADEU LUBAMBO	SQUARE FEET / QUADRAT METER	10222 / 950
CITY AND COUNTRY ARCHITECT / STADT UND LAND ARCHITEKT			FORTALEZA, BRASIL
WEBSITE ARCHITECT / HOMEPAGE ARCHITEKT			WWW.GERSONCASTELOBRANCO.COM.BR

Reinterpretation of local traditions and response to climate formed the points of departure for this design. The exposed structural framework constructed in planed tree trunks carries the roof of woven palm fronds. An informal sequence of interconnected spaces is defined under the protective roof with its wide eaves. The living spaces on the ground floor flow into each other and continue out to the exterior veranda and terraces.

Die Weiterentwicklung lokaler Bautraditionen und Berücksichtigung klimatischer Bedingungen boten zwei Anhaltspunkte bei diesem Entwurf einer Wohnoase. Ein sichtbares Trageskelett aus behobelten Baumstämmen nimmt die dicht verflochtenen Palmenblätter des Daches auf. Unter dem Schutz des weit ausladenden Daches entwickeln sich diverse Wohnzonen, die im Erdgeschoss ineinander fließen und sich unter der Veranda und auf der Terrasse im Freien fortsetzen.

ARRIAL D' AJUDA
FABRIZIO CECCARELLI

COUNTRY / LAND	BRAZIL / BRASILIEN	HOUSE NAME / BEZEICHNUNG DES HAUSES		ARRIAL D' AJUDA
LOCATION (CITY/REGION) / LAGE (STADT/REGION)				BAHIA / ATLANTIC COAST
ARCHITECT / ARCHITEKT		FABRIZIO CECCARELLI	YEAR OF COMPLETION / BAUJAHR	2002
PHOTOGRAPHER / FOTOGRAF		OTTO WEISSER	SQUARE FEET / QUADRAT METER	5918 / 550
CITY AND COUNTRY ARCHITECT / STADT UND LAND ARCHITEKT				RIO DE JANIERO, BRASIL
WEBSITE ARCHITECT / HOMEPAGE ARCHITEKT				xxx

CASA GUAECÁ BEACH
<u>MARIO BISELLI</u>

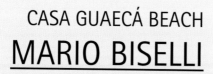

The site lies in the midst of the Serra do Mar coast range and the lush Mata Atlântica rain forest. The central living hall is the focus of the composition. It is enclosed on three sides and opens out via a glazed two-story window to a view of the nearby Atlantic Ocean. The upper floor houses four bedrooms and a TV room. Living and kitchen areas are located on the ground floor. The south and east perimeters are formed by terraces, verandas, and the elongated pool. Both on the interior and exterior, white surfaces are played off natural wooden surfaces to form an airy sense of generosity.

Das Grundstück liegt inmitten des Serra do Mar Küstengebirges und des Mata Atlântica Regenwaldes. Eine zentrale Wohnhalle bildet den Fokus der Komposition. Diese wird an drei Seiten räumlich gefasst und öffnet sich über einer zweigeschossigen Glasfront zum Blick auf den nahen Atlantik. Das OG beherbergt vier Schlafzimmer und ein TV-Zimmer. Wohn- und Kochzonen befinden sich im EG. Nach Süden und Osten setzen Terrassen, Veranden und der lange Pool die Architektur im Freien fort. Sowohl innen als auch außen werden weiße Flächen gegen hölzerne Flächen gesetzt, um ein luftiges Ambiente der Großzügigkeit zu erzeugen.

COUNTRY / LAND	BRAZIL / BRASILIEN	HOUSE NAME / BEZEICHNUNG DES HAUSES	CASA GUAECÁ BEACH
LOCATION (CITY/REGION) / LAGE (STADT/REGION)			SÁO SEBASTIÁO / ATLANTIC COAST
ARCHITECT / ARCHITEKT	MARIO BISELLI	YEAR OF COMPLETION / BAUJAHR	2003
PHOTOGRAPHER / FOTOGRAF	NELSON KON	SQUARE FEET / QUADRAT METER	7457 / 693
CITY AND COUNTRY ARCHITECT / STADT UND LAND ARCHITEKT			SÃO PAULO, BRASILIA
WEBSITE ARCHITECT / HOMEPAGE ARCHITEKT			WWW.BKWEB.COM.BR

506

This beachside home is an exercise in simplicity and efficient use of available resources. Constructed by local residents utilizing vernacular techniques, it reinterprets Brazilian building traditions. A framework of wood trusses forms an elegant skeleton supporting the exposed roof tiles. Rising upward toward the southeast elevation, the roof defines a spacious living/dining hall and extends outside to cover the wooden deck. The bedrooms, each with deck access, are enclosed in bright blue walls. A service zone with bathrooms and the open kitchen forms a buffer on the northern street elevation.

Das Konzept dieses Strandhauses beruht auf Einfachheit und schonendem Umgang mit vorhandenen Ressourcen. Erbaut in lokal typischer Bauweise interpretiert das Haus brasilianische Traditionen neu. Rahmen aus Holz bilden ein elegantes Gerippe, auf dem die sichtbaren Dachziegel lagern. Nach Südosten ansteigend definiert das Dach einen geräumigen Wohn-/ Essbereich und setzt sich im Freien über dem Holzdeck fort. Die Schlafzimmer sind von strahlend blauen Wänden umfasst. Der Nutzbereich mit Bädern und der offenen Küche erstreckt sich entlang der Nordseite.

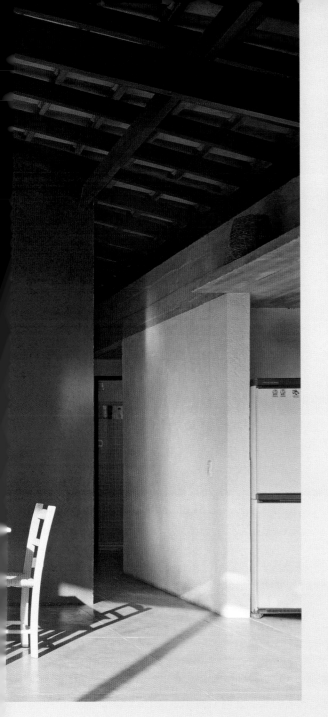

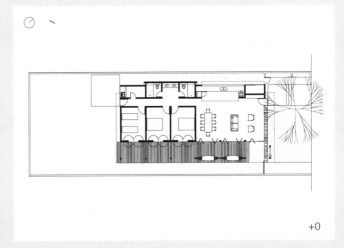

+0

CASA IN PRAIA JUQUEHY
PUNTONI ARQUITETOS

COUNTRY / LAND	BRAZIL / BRASILIEN	HOUSE NAME / BEZEICHNUNG DES HAUSES		CASA IN PRAIA JUQUEHY
LOCATION (CITY/REGION) / LAGE (STADT/REGION)				SÁO SEBASTIÁO / ATLANTIC COAST
ARCHITECT / ARCHITEKT		PUNTONI ARQUITETOS	YEAR OF COMPLETION / BAUJAHR	2001
PHOTOGRAPHER / FOTOGRAF		NELSON KON	SQUARE FEET / QUADRAT METER	1162 / 108
CITY AND COUNTRY ARCHITECT / STADT UND LAND ARCHITEKT				SAO PAULO, BRASIL
WEBSITE ARCHITECT / HOMEPAGE ARCHITEKT				WWW.PUNTONI.ARQ.BR

The architects developed a house form that employs simple means to effectively react to the extreme high levels of humidity and high temperatures that prevail in this region. The floor slab was elevated above site and the roof was raised over the internal volume to allow cooling air currents to flow unimpeded around the building core.

Weitab von der Schwüle der Millionenstadt São Paulo entwickelten die Architekten eine Hausform, die mit einfachen Mitteln konsequent der extrem hohen Luftfeuchtigkeit und den hohen Temperaturen der Region gerecht wird. Die Bodenplatte wurde vom Erdreich gelöst und das Dach wurde angehoben, damit kühlende Luftströme ungehindert zirkulieren können.

CASA IN BARRA DO SAHY
NITSCHE AQUITETOS ASSOCIADOS

Interior hallways were eliminated as continuous decks on both sides of the house serve as terraces and circulation spines. Large sliding glass wall elements can be opened to achieve a seamless merge between indoor and outdoor spaces.

Auf innenliegende Flure wurde verzichtet; durchgehende Decks an beiden Hausseiten fungieren zugleich als Terrasse und Flur im Freien. Große Glasschiebeelemente erlauben das komplette Öffnen der Wohnräume und schaffen einen nahtlosen Übergang zwischen Innen und Außen.

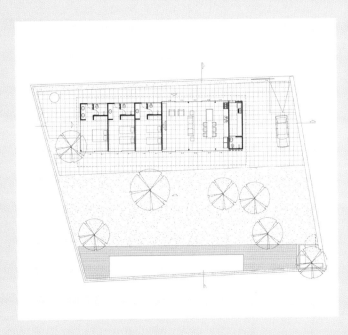

COUNTRY / LAND	BRAZIL / BRASILIEN	HOUSE NAME / BEZEICHNUNG DES HAUSES	CASA IN BARRA DO SAHY
LOCATION (CITY/REGION) / LAGE (STADT/REGION)			BARRA DO SAHY / ATLANTIC COAST
ARCHITECT / ARCHITEKT	NITSCHE AQUITETETOS ASSOCIADOS	YEAR OF COMPLETION / BAUJAHR	2002
PHOTOGRAPHER / FOTOGRAF	NELSON KON	SQUARE FEET / QUADRAT METER	1399 / 130
CITY AND COUNTRY ARCHITECT / STADT UND LAND ARCHITEKT			SÃO PAULO, BRASIL
WEBSITE ARCHITECT / HOMEPAGE ARCHITEKT			xxx

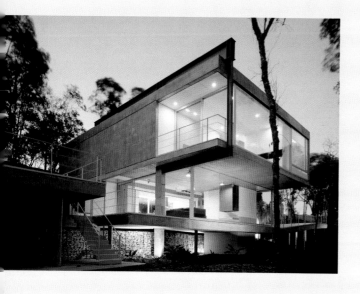

In this new residence in São Paulo the architects creatively explored the potentials that Modernism offers. Whereas famous Brazilian architects such as Oscar Niemeyer created a special brand of South American Modernism firmly rooted in the expressive vocabulary of Le Corbusier's late work, the architects here pursued a more Minimalist approach with clear, rectilinear forms.

Bei diesem neuen Haus in São Paulo erforschten die Architekten die kreativen Potentiale, der modernen Architektur. Weltbekannte brasilianische Architekten wie Oscar Niemeyer entwickelten eine südamerikanische Ausprägung der Moderne, die im expressiven Spätwerk Le Corbusiers begründet liegt. Die Architekten verfolgten hier einen minimalistischen Ansatz mit klaren, rechtwinkeligen Formen.

RESIDÊNCIA MORATO
ANDRADE E MORETTIN

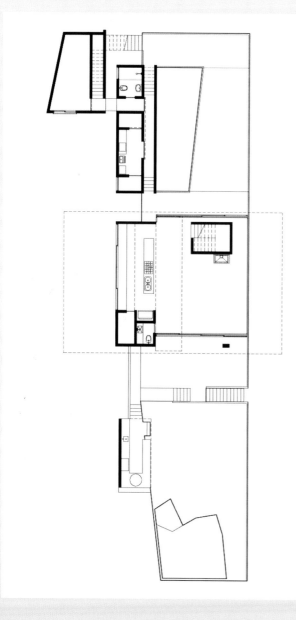

Concrete is the formative material used on the exterior and interior of this home. It was employed not only on wall surfaces but also on floors and ceilings where the in-situ concrete was left exposed. The central wing with the dramatically cantilevered upper level forms the focal point of the composition. Here, the living-dining space opens via a sliding glass wall onto the spacious terrace. Large frameless windows facilitate the direct view into the surrounding jungle landscape.

Sichtbeton wird als das stilprägendes Material im Inneren und Äußeren des Bauwerks eingesetzt. Es fand nicht nur bei Wänden Verwendung, sondern auch bei den Decken und Böden Der zentrale Flügel mit dem dramatisch ausgekragten Obergeschoss bildet den Fokus der Komposition. Der Koch-Essbereich öffnet sich hier über einer gläsernen Schiebewandanlage auf die großzügige Terrasse. Große, rahmenlose Verglasungen eröffnen den ungehinderten Ausblick auf den umliegenden Dschungel.

COUNTRY / LAND	BRAZIL / BRASILIEN	HOUSE NAME / BEZEICHNUNG DES HAUSES	RESIDÊNCIA MORATO
LOCATION (CITY/REGION) / LAGE (STADT/REGION)			SÃO PAULO
ARCHITECT / ARCHITEKT	ANDRADE E MORETTIN	YEAR OF COMPLETION / BAUJAHR	2003
PHOTOGRAPHER / FOTOGRAF	NELSON KON	SQUARE FEET / QUADRAT METER	4304 / 400
CITY AND COUNTRY ARCHITECT / STADT UND LAND ARCHITEKT			SÃO PAULO, BRASIL
WEBSITE ARCHITECT / HOMEPAGE ARCHITEKT			WWW.ANDRADEMORETTIN.COM.BR

Sited to avoid destruction of the natural jungle setting, the basic structure of the house consists of two contrasting building volumes. The main living volume, a hall space built in light wood-frame construction, is enclosed by semi-transparent polycarbonate panels, which alternate with glass to allow dramatic open views out to the nearby lake. The hall espouses open informality due to the undulating light and the high level of connection between inside and out.

Angelegt um den Naturraum des Dschungels nicht zu zerstören, besteht das Haus aus zwei entgegen gesetzten Bauvolumen. Der Wohnsaal, in leichter Holzbauweise erbaut, ist mit halbtransparenten Acrylplatten behängt. Diese wechseln sich mit Glas ab, um Freiblicke zum nahen See zu ermöglichen. Der Wohnsaal wirkt informell dank des changierenden Lichteinfalls und des starken Bezugs zwischen innen und außen.

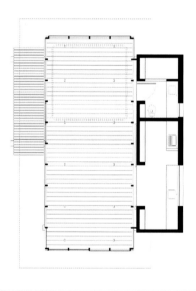

D'ALESSANDRO HOUSE
ANDRADE E MORETTIN

COUNTRY / LAND	BRAZIL / BRASILIEN	HOUSE NAME / BEZEICHNUNG DES HAUSES	D'ALESSANDRO HOUSE
LOCATION (CITY/REGION) / LAGE (STADT/REGION)			SÃO PAULO
ARCHITECT / ARCHITEKT	ANDRADE E MORETTIN	YEAR OF COMPLETION / BAUJAHR	1998
PHOTOGRAPHER / FOTOGRAF	NELSON KON	SQUARE FEET / QUADRAT METER	667 / 62
CITY AND COUNTRY ARCHITECT / STADT UND LAND ARCHITEKT			SÃO PAULO, BRASIL
WEBSITE ARCHITECT / HOMEPAGE ARCHITEKT			WWW.ANDRADEMORETTIN.COM.BR

RESIDÊNCIA R.L
ANDRADE, MORETTIN E NITSCHE

The challenge here was to create an optimised, low-cost home with intense interconnection to the natural surroundings. To minimise the "footprint" the main volume of the home was elevated on point foundations that allowed retention of the thick tree roots present here. By elevating the house above the ground plane, the architects employed passive cooling techniques to reduce energy costs.

Die Herausforderung hier bestand darin, ein kostengünstiges Haus in intensiver Verbindung mit dem umliegenden Naturraum zu realisieren. Um den Eingriff in die Natur zu minimieren wurde der Bau auf Punktfundamenten errichtet, welche den Erhalt der dicken Baumwurzel ermöglichten. Durch Anheben der Baumasse über die Erde setzten die Architekten eine natürliche, kosten sparende Kühltechnik ein.

COUNTRY / LAND	BRAZIL / BRASILIEN	HOUSE NAME / BEZEICHNUNG DES HAUSES		RESIDÊNCIA R.L
LOCATION (CITY/REGION) / LAGE (STADT/REGION)				SÃO SEBASTIÃO
ARCHITECT / ARCHITEKT	ANDRADE, MORETTIN E NITSCHE	YEAR OF COMPLETION / BAUJAHR		2005
PHOTOGRAPHER / FOTOGRAF	JOÃO NITSCHE	SQUARE FEET / QUADRAT METER		624 / 58
CITY AND COUNTRY ARCHITECT / STADT UND LAND ARCHITEKT				SÃO PAULO, BRASIL
WEBSITE ARCHITECT / HOMEPAGE ARCHITEKT				WWW.ANDRADEMORETTIN.COM.BR

ANDRADE E MORETTIN

SÃO PAULO
BRAZIL / BRASILIEN

Andrade (born 1968) and Morettin (born 1969) both studied at the Faculty of Architecture and Urbanism of the University of São Paulo where they graduated in 1991-92. Their work picks up where the legendary Brazilian Modernist Architecture exemplified by Oscar Niemeyer leaves off.

And their architectural oeuvre is not limited to expressive concrete structures or strongly emphasized, poetic sculptural forms. Their work also includes austere wooden homes nestled into the Brazilian jungle that, although simple and inexpensive, create aunique sense of relaxed contemporary living in the very midst of nature.

Photo: Andrade e Morettin

Andrade und Morettin studierten beide am Lehrstuhl für Architektur und Urbanismus an der Universität São Paulo, wo sie ihre Studienabschlüsse 1991-1992 machten. Ihre Arbeit fängt da an, wo die legendäre brasilianische Moderne eines Oscar Niemeyer aufhört.

Ihr Oeuvre ist keineswegs begrenzt auf expressive Betonbauten oder stark betonte, poetisch anmutende Formen. Zu ihren Arbeiten zählen auch einfache Holzhäuser, die sich nahtlos in den brasilianischen Dschungel einfügen und, obwohl sie einfach und kostengünstig sind, eine außergewöhnliche Synthese zwischen Architektur, Bewohner und Naturraum ermöglichen.

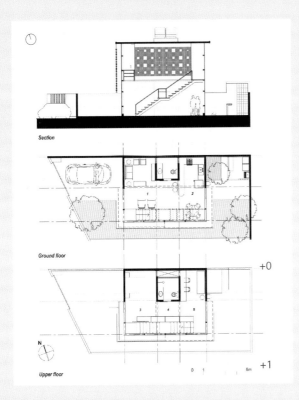

Section

Ground floor

+0

+1

N

Upper floor

0 1   5m

This home is comprised of two contrasting volumes - a transparent, south-facing living hall and a closed spatial zone with bedroom, kitchen and bathrooms to the north. This dichotomy between transparency and enclosure is emphasized, allowing the small spaces to feel much larger than they are. The gallery wall enclosing the private zone upstairs was foreseen with art that creates a link between interior and exterior and imbues the small house with generous ambience. Fixed wooden "brise-soleil" slats mounted on the steel frame provide sun protection and filter warm light into the interior.

Das Haus besteht aus zwei sich ergänzenden Volumen: eine transparente, nach Süden gerichtete Wohnhalle und eine geschützte Raumzone im Norden mit Schlafzimmer, Bädern und Küche. Diese Dichotomie zwischen Transparenz und Geschlossenheit wird betont, um die kleinen Räume größer wirken zu lassen. Die Galeriewand ist zugleich ein Ort der Kunst. Die hier montierte Installation schafft eine Verbindung zwischen Innen und Außen und verleiht dem kleinen Haus Großzügigkeit. Holzlatten vor dem leichten Stahlskelett leisten Sonnenschutz und filtern warmes Licht ins Innere.

VILA MADALENA HOUSE
NAVE ARQUITETOS ASSOCIADOS

521

COUNTRY / LAND	BRAZIL / BRASILIEN	HOUSE NAME / BEZEICHNUNG DES HAUSES	VILA MADALENA HOUSE
LOCATION (CITY/REGION) / LAGE (STADT/REGION)			SAO PAULO
ARCHITECT / ARCHITEKT	NAVE ARQUITETOS ASSOCIADOS	YEAR OF COMPLETION / BAUJAHR	2003
PHOTOGRAPHER / FOTOGRAF	NELSON KON	SQUARE FEET / QUADRAT METER	861 / 80
CITY AND COUNTRY ARCHITECT / STADT UND LAND ARCHITEKT			SAO PAULO, BRASIL
WEBSITE ARCHITECT / HOMEPAGE ARCHITEKT			WWW.NAVE.ARQ.BR

By limiting the materials used to various wooden surfaces that are complemented with white stuccoed wall and ceiling surfaces the architects created a sense of spaciousness on a small floor plan. A free-spanning pergola with wooden latticework marks the entrance from which the combined living-dining space is accessed.

Durch Reduktion der verwendeten Materialien auf Holz und weiße verputzte Wände und Decken schufen die Architekten ein Gefühl der Großzügigkeit – trotz des kleinen zur Verfügung stehenden Platzes. Eine frei spannende Pergola markiert den Eingang, von dem aus das offene Eß- / Wohnzimmer direkt erschlossen wird.

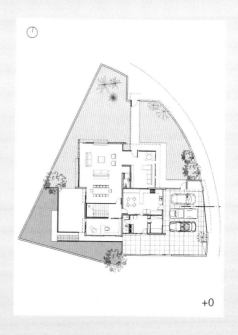

+0

HOUSE AT PACAEMBU
NAVE ARQUITETOS ASSOCIADOS

COUNTRY / LAND	BRAZIL / BRASILIEN	HOUSE NAME / BEZEICHNUNG DES HAUSES	HOUSE AT PACAEMBU
LOCATION (CITY/REGION) / LAGE (STADT/REGION)			PACAEMBU, SÃO PAULO
ARCHITECT / ARCHITEKT		NAVE ARQUITETOS ASSOCIADOS	YEAR OF COMPLETION / BAUJAHR 2006
PHOTOGRAPHER / FOTOGRAF		NELSON KON	SQUARE FEET / QUADRAT METER 4842 / 450
CITY AND COUNTRY ARCHITECT / STADT UND LAND ARCHITEKT			SÃO PAULO, BRASIL
WEBSITE ARCHITECT / HOMEPAGE ARCHITEKT			WWW.NAVE.ARQ.BR

HOUSE AT VILA ZELINA
NAVE ARQUITETOS ASSOCIADOS

+1

+0

The narrow slot of the building site generated a floor plan that is characterised by a chain-like sequence of rooms. To make the ground floor spaces seem larger terrazzo flooring, light colours, and sliding door elements were foreseen. In spite of the tight urban location the home seems spacious, light-filled, and comfortable.

Das lang gestreckte, schmale Grundstück führte zu einem Grundriss, der aus einer kettenartigen Reihung der Räume besteht. Um diese größer erscheinen zu lassen wurde ein durchgehender Terrazzoboden, helle Farben und Schiebewände vorgesehen. Trotz der urbanen Dichte der Lage wirkt das Haus großzügig, hell und wohnlich.

COUNTRY / LAND	BRAZIL / BRASILIEN	HOUSE NAME / BEZEICHNUNG DES HAUSES		HOUSE AT VILA ZELINA
LOCATION (CITY/REGION) / LAGE (STADT/REGION)				VILA SELINA, SÃO PAULO
ARCHITECT / ARCHITEKT		NAVE ARQUITETOS ASSOCIADOS	YEAR OF COMPLETION / BAUJAHR	2005
PHOTOGRAPHER / FOTOGRAF		NELSON KON	SQUARE FEET / QUADRAT METER	2152 / 200
CITY AND COUNTRY ARCHITECT / STADT UND LAND ARCHITEKT				SÃO PAULO, BRASIL
WEBSITE ARCHITECT / HOMEPAGE ARCHITEKT				WWW.NAVE.ARQ.BR

GLASS HOUSE
REINACH MENDONÇA
ARQUITETOS ASSOCIADOS

This home makes a gracious statement on contemporary country living. Rather than resorting to rustic, rough materials the architect opted for a palette of clear Modernist forms and materials that create a well balanced mix of dramatic and small-scaled residential spaces.

Dieses Haus formuliert eine großzügige zeitgenössische Aussage zur Bautypologie des Landhauses. Anstatt auf rustikale, raue Materialien zurück zu greifen entschied sich der Architekt für eine Palette von klaren, modernen Formen und Materialien, welche eine ausgewogene Mischung von dramatischen und kleinmaßstäblichen Räumen definieren.

+0

The L-shaped floor plan is enclosed on two sides by white, cube-like building wings that are intimately scaled and contain auxiliary spaces such as the bedrooms. The main garden-facing facades are completely glazed and two stories high. The recessed covered terrace forms the focal point of the home. Here, the warm climate allows the living room zone to seamlessly merge with the covered outdoor space and the adjacent pool.

Der L-förmige Grundriss ist an zwei Seiten durch weiße, kubenähnliche Baukörper gekennzeichnet, die einen wohnlichen Maßstab ausweisen und Nebenräume wie Schlafzimmer beherbergen. Die betonten Gartenfronten sind komplett verglast und zweigeschossig ausgebildet. Die zurückgesetzte Terrasse bildet den Fokalpunkt des Hauses. Hier verschmelzen Wohnraum und Terrasse zu einer lockeren Wohnzone am Rand des anschließenden Pools.

COUNTRY / LAND	BRAZIL / BRASILIEN	HOUSE NAME / BEZEICHNUNG DES HAUSES	GLASS HOUSE
LOCATION (CITY/REGION) / LAGE (STADT/REGION)			SÃO PAULO
ARCHITECT / ARCHITEKT	REINACH MENDONÇA ARQUITETOS ASSOCIADOS	YEAR OF COMPLETION / BAUJAHR	2004
PHOTOGRAPHER / FOTOGRAF	NELSON KON	SQUARE FEET / QUADRAT METER	4734 / 440
CITY AND COUNTRY ARCHITECT / STADT UND LAND ARCHITEKT			SÃO PAULO, BRASIL
WEBSITE ARCHITECT / HOMEPAGE ARCHITEKT			WWW.RMAA.COM.BR

The architects, newcomers to the Brazilian architectural scene, used this first major residential commission to demonstrate their uncompromising approach to architecture. The main living spaces on the ground floor received extensive window surfaces to create a transparent plinth above which the wood-clad volume of the upper level seems to float.

Die Architekten, Neulinge der Architektenszene Brasils, benutzten diesen ersten größeren Auftrag um ihren kompromisslosen Ansatz zu demonstrieren. Die Hauptwohnbereiche im Frdgeschoss erhielten großflächige Glasfronten, die einen transparenten Sockel für den darüber auskragenden, scheinbar schwebenden Baukörper aus Holz bilden.

+0

ARAÇOIABA HOUSE
FLAVIA CANCIAN E RENATA FURLANETTO

COUNTRY / LAND	BRAZIL / BRASILIEN	HOUSE NAME / BEZEICHNUNG DES HAUSES	ARAÇOIABA HOUSE
LOCATION (CITY/REGION) / LAGE (STADT/REGION)			ARAÇOIABA, SAO PAULO
ARCHITECT / ARCHITEKT	FLAVIA CANCIAN E RENATA FURLANETTO	YEAR OF COMPLETION / BAUJAHR	2004
PHOTOGRAPHER / FOTOGRAF	NELSON KON	SQUARE FEET / QUADRAT METER	4950 / 460
CITY AND COUNTRY ARCHITECT / STADT UND LAND ARCHITEKT			SAO PAULO, BRASIL
WEBSITE ARCHITECT / HOMEPAGE ARCHITEKT			XXX

By reducing forms and materials to their clearly defined Minimalist essence the architects created a poetic reinterpretation of the traditional urban villa. The square floor plan reminds one of classical villas of the Antiquity or Renaissance period, but all historic analogies end there. Sinking the hovering form into the topography allowed a novel entrance sequence: a bridge leads across a ravine-like space to the flat roof from where one descends down into the house.

Durch Reduktion der Formen und Materialien auf ihre Essenz schufen die Architekten eine poetische Interpretation der traditionellen urbanen Villa. Der quadratische Grundriss erinnert an Vorbilder der Antike oder der Renaissance, doch damit erschöpfen sich die historischen Referenzen. Durch Einsenken der schwebenden Bauform in die Topographie ist eine eigenwillige Eingangssituation entstanden: eine Brücke führt über eine schluchtartige Mulde auf das Flachdach von dem aus man in das Haus herunter steigt.

ALDEIA DA SERRA HOUSE
SPBR ARQUITETOS

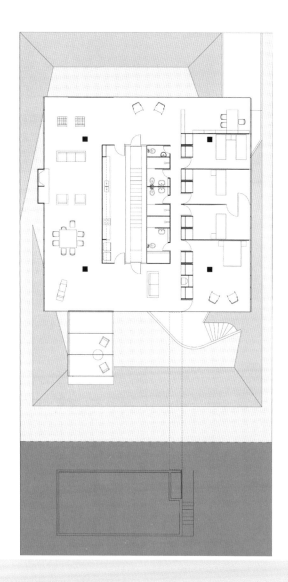

The main living and bedroom spaces are oriented around the central stairwell core where the kitchen and bathrooms are also located. Concrete waffle-slabs were developed for the floor and roof slabs between which fully glazed window fronts were mounted on the entrance and back elevations. Structural bearing loads are carried by four columns that clearly delineate the flowing, open floor plan.

Die Wohn- und Schlafzimmer sind um den zentralen Treppenkern angeordnet, wo sich die Küche und die Badezimmer ebenfalls befinden. Zwischen den Waffeldecken aus Beton sind die voll verglasten Fensterfronten der Eingangs- und Rückfront gehängt. Die Haupttragelasten werden durch vier Stützen aufgenommen, die den offenen, fließenden Grundriss klar akzentuieren.

COUNTRY / LAND	BRAZIL / BRASILIEN	HOUSE NAME / BEZEICHNUNG DES HAUSES	ALDEIA DA SERRA HOUSE
LOCATION (CITY/REGION) / LAGE (STADT/REGION)			BARUERI
ARCHITECT / ARCHITEKT		SPBR ARQUITETOS YEAR OF COMPLETION / BAUJAHR	2002
PHOTOGRAPHER / FOTOGRAF		NELSON KON SQUARE FEET / QUADRAT METER	2755 / 256
CITY AND COUNTRY ARCHITECT / STADT UND LAND ARCHITEKT			SÃO PAULO, BRASIL
WEBSITE ARCHITECT / HOMEPAGE ARCHITEKT			WWW.SPBR.ARQ.BR

HOUSE IN RIBEIRÃO
SPBR ARQUITETOS

This home hovers on a U-shaped, elevated concrete slab completely removed from the ground plane. A second slab forms the flat roof of this uncompromising residential statement. Lighter materials such as transparent and translucent glazing span between the structural slabs to frame diverse panoramas and variegated spatial experiences throughout the house.

Dieses Haus schwebt auf einer U-förmigen Bodenscheibe aus Beton, die komplett vom Erdboden gelöst scheint. Eine zweite Scheibe darüber bildet das Flachdach dieses kompromisslosen Bauwerkes. Leichte Materialien, wie transparente und opake Verglasungsfelder, sind zwischen Boden und Deckenscheibe gehängt, um verschieden Panoramen und räumliche Erlebnisse zu inszenieren.

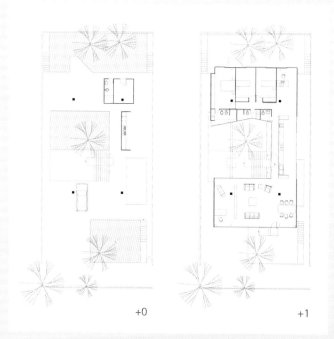

+0　　　　　　　　+1

The U-shaped floor plan is well suited to accommodate the rooms and functions. A stair rises from the central courtyard to access the main entrance door. The bedrooms are located in the northern wing, and the kitchen zone connects this zone with the living-dining space in the southern wing. Use of steel-reinforced structural concrete made it possible to reduce the main load bearing structure to four columns that support the entire structure.

Der U-förmige Grundriss eignet sich gut zur Aufnahme der Räume und Funktionsbereiche. Eine Freitreppe steigt vom zentralen Hof zum Eingang an. Die Schlafzimmer befinden sich im nördlichen Flügel, die Küche erstreckt sich von dort aus zum Wohn-Essbereich im südlichen Flügel. Die Verwendung von Stahlbeton ermöglichte die Reduktion der tragenden Bauteile auf vier Stützen, welche das gesamte Bauwerk alleine tragen.

COUNTRY / LAND	BRAZIL / BRASILIEN	HOUSE NAME / BEZEICHNUNG DES HAUSES		HOUSE IN RIBEIRÃO
LOCATION (CITY/REGION) / LAGE (STADT/REGION)				RIBEIRÃO PRETO
ARCHITECT / ARCHITEKT		SPBR ARQUITETOS	YEAR OF COMPLETION / BAUJAHR	2001
PHOTOGRAPHER / FOTOGRAF		NELSON KON	SQUARE FEET / QUADRAT METER	1937 / 180
CITY AND COUNTRY ARCHITECT / STADT UND LAND ARCHITEKT				SÃO PAULO, BRASIL
WEBSITE ARCHITECT / HOMEPAGE ARCHITEKT				WWW.SPBR.ARQ.BR

CASA FELIX
ANNE MARIE SUMNER

The steep hillside site inspired the architect to organize this home on two levels. She foresaw the large living room with adjoining kitchen on the upper level. A broad window ribbon spanned by a reinforced concrete beam frames the breathtaking view of the terrace and the Atlantic below. The bedrooms on the lower level were deployed in front of the living room wing. Their roof forms the generous terrace. Both terrace and living hall were paved with small-format cobblestones, allowing interior and exterior spaces to flow together and effectively merge house and nature.

Das stark abfallende Gelände inspirierte die Architektin dazu, die Räume auf zwei Ebenen anzuordnen. Den großen Wohnraum mit anschließender Küche hat sie auf der oberen Etage angeordnet. Hier ermöglicht die Stahlbetonkonstruktion die Ausbildung einer stützenfreien Öffnung zur Terrasse mit atemberaubenden Ausblick. Die Schlafräume der unteren Ebene lagern vor dem Wohnraumtrakt, ihr Dach fungiert zugleich als Freiterrasse. Terrasse und Wohnsaal wurden mit Kleinsteinpflaster gepflastert, was die wirkungsvolle Verschmelzung von Freiraum und Interieur verstärkt.

COUNTRY / LAND	BRAZIL / BRASILIEN	HOUSE NAME / BEZEICHNUNG DES HAUSES		CASA FELIX
LOCATION (CITY/REGION) / LAGE (STADT/REGION)			UBATUBA / ATLANTIC COAST	
ARCHITECT / ARCHITEKT	ANNE MARIE SUMNER	YEAR OF COMPLETION / BAUJAHR		1999
PHOTOGRAPHER / FOTOGRAF	NELSON KON	SQUARE FEET / QUADRAT METER		4939 / 459
CITY AND COUNTRY ARCHITECT / STADT UND LAND ARCHITEKT			SÃO PAULO, BRASIL	
WEBSITE ARCHITECT / HOMEPAGE ARCHITEKT				XXX

HOUSE IN CURITIBA
<u>UNA ARQUITETOS</u>

The cubist white mass of this home seems at first glance to be a rather simple box, but the architects employed a range of creative ideas to hone their composition to architectural perfection and create an intricate framework of well-proportioned rooms. The entrance vestibule, marked by a striking blue wall and the vertical fireplace chimney tower, is deeply recessed into the building mass and doubles in use as a covered terrace for the adjacent living room.

Der kubisch-weiße Baukörper dieses Hauses wirkt auf den ersten Blick wie eine einfache Kiste. Doch die Architekten setzten eine ganze Palette kreativer Ideen ein, um innerhalb dieser einfachen Form eine abwechslungsreiche räumliche Komposition zu schaffen. Das Eingangsvestibül, markiert durch eine auffallende blaue Wand und den vertikalen Schornsteinturm, wird tief in den Baukörper eingeschnitten und fungiert zugleich als überdachte Terrasse für den direkt angrenzenden Wohnraum.

542

The main spatial zones were concentrated at both ends of the house to leave ample space for the central stairwell hall that directs natural light into the the middle portion of the building. A steel stair with elegant railing and wooden steps rises from the garage on the subterranean level to the bedrooms on the upper level.

Die Hauptraumzonen wurden an beiden Enden des Hauses zusammengefasst, um den mittleren Teil für die Treppenhalle frei zu halten, die Licht in die Tiefe des Grundrisses führt. Eine Stahltreppe mit filigranen Stahlgeländer und Holzstufen steigt von der unteren Ebene wo sich die Garage befindet bis in die Schlafzimmerebene.

+0

COUNTRY / LAND	BRAZIL / BRASILIEN	HOUSE NAME / BEZEICHNUNG DES HAUSES	HOUSE IN CURITIBA
LOCATION (CITY/REGION) / LAGE (STADT/REGION)			CURITIBA, PARANÁ
ARCHITECT / ARCHITEKT	UNA ARQUITETOS	YEAR OF COMPLETION / BAUJAHR	2004
PHOTOGRAPHER / FOTOGRAF	NELSON KON	SQUARE FEET / QUADRAT METER	3379 / 314
CITY AND COUNTRY ARCHITECT / STADT UND LAND ARCHITEKT			SAO PAULO, BRASIL
WEBSITE ARCHITECT / HOMEPAGE ARCHITEKT			WWW.UNAARQUITETOS.COM

The project was conceived as a built slice on a 3.5 m wide x 40 m long site. A series of unique spaces, such as an 8 m long kitchen counter/outdoor dining table linking the internal courtyard with the living area, emphasize the dramatic narrowness of the site.

Das Haus wurde als gebaute Scheibe aufgefasst, die ein 3,5 x 40 Meter schmales Grundstück füllt. Eine Kette von eigenwilligen Räumen betont die dramatische Enge des Grundstückes ebenso wie die 8 Meter lange Tischscheibe zwischen Innenhof und Wohnbereich.

SLICE HOUSE
PROCTER-RIHL ARCHITECTS

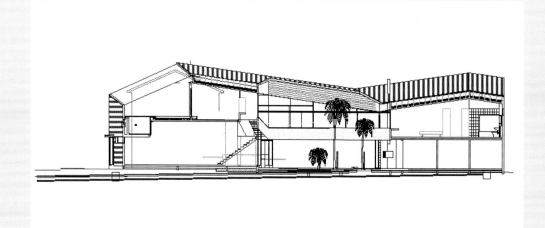

Throughout, understated materials are used to create finely knit spaces, with ceiling height gradually rising as one moves through the house. Natural light is filtered inside through a courtyard, louvers and the glass side of the second floor swimming pool. The dreamlike light achieved during the day through the movement of water and daylight is extended at night with artificial illumination.

Einfache Materialien wurden verwendet, um feingestrickte Raumstrukturen zu schaffen, z. B. indem die Decke graduell ansteigt. Natürliches Licht wird über Lamellen, den kleinen Innenhof, und die verglaste Seite des Schwimmbeckens im 2. OG ins Innere geleitet. Dieses traumähnliche, durch das Wasser gebrochene Licht illuminiert die Räume auch nachts, wenn Strahler das Lichtspiel fortsetzen.

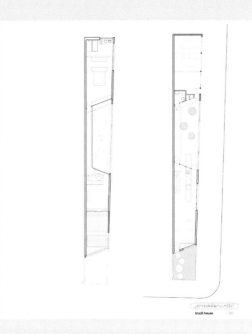

COUNTRY / LAND	BRAZIL / BRASILIEN	HOUSE NAME / BEZEICHNUNG DES HAUSES		SLICE HOUSE
LOCATION (CITY/REGION) / LAGE (STADT/REGION)				PORTO ALEGRE
ARCHITECT / ARCHITEKT	PROCTER-RIHL ARCHITECTS	YEAR OF COMPLETION / BAUJAHR		2004
PHOTOGRAPHER / FOTOGRAF	MARCELO NUNES / SU BARR	SQUARE FEET / QUADRAT METER		1345 / 125
CITY AND COUNTRY ARCHITECT / STADT UND LAND ARCHITEKT				LONDON, UK
WEBSITE ARCHITECT / HOMEPAGE ARCHITEKT				WWW.PROCTER-RIHL.COM

PROCTER-RIHL
ARCHITECTS

LONDON
UNITED KINGDOM

Procter (born 1958) and Rihl (born 1962) have their office in London, but due to the fact that Rihl was born in Brazil, they also work in South America. Their work explores complex geometries and spatial distortion. Observation of other disciplines, such as fine arts, building and computer technology often infiltrate the architectural projects or, as with furniture design, stand as distinct streams of work within their oeuvre.

Procter-Rihl believes computer technology has greatly impacted on the definition of space, specifically in the articulation of surfaces in architecture and landscape design. The ambiguity between surfaces questions the classical modernist notion of vertical and horizontal planes. In the last decade in Europe, there seems to be an emphasis on developing ideas in the digital media. Rather than focusing on virtual spaces, Procter-Rihl prefers to test ideas in real projects regardless of their size or budget.

Photo: Marcelo Nunes

Procter (geboren 1958) und Rihl (geboren 1962) haben ihr Büro in London. Da Rihl aus Brasilien stammt arbeiten sie häufig auch in Südamerika. In ihren Arbeiten erforschen sie komplexe Geometrien und räumliche Verzerrungen. Angeregt durch Impulse aus der Kunst, der Bautechnologie oder der Informatik lassen sie sich zu neuen Lösungen inspirieren, auch beim Möbeldesign. Procter-Rihl sind davon überzeugt, dass Computer-Technologie einen starken Einfluss auf die heutige Schaffung von Räumen genommen hat, insbesondere auf die Ausbildung von Ebenen in der Architektur und der Landschaftsarchitektur. Diese neue Qualität stellt das klassische Verständnis der modernen Architektur von vertikalen und horizontalen Ebenen in Frage. Obwohl bei Procter-Rihl im letzten Jahrzehnt eine gewisse Vorherrschaft von virtueller Architektur festzustellen ist ziehen sie es vor, wirkliche Projekte, egal wie klein oder kostenbegrenzt, zu verwirklichen.

Two building masses were juxtaposed to create a lively residential composition. The higher volume contains the main spaces and extends out toward the hillside slope to enclose protected exterior spaces – a two-story high terrace, a covered living room terrace with exterior fireplace, and a spacious bedroom balcony on the upper level.

Zwei Baukörper wurden schräg zueinender gestellt, um eine abwechslungsreiche Wohnkomposition zu schaffen. Der höhere Baukörper beherbergt die Haupträume und setzt sich in Richtung des Hangs fort um geschützte Räume im Freien zu definieren; eine zweigeschossige Terrasse, eine Wohnzimmerterrasse mit Außenkamin und einen großzügigen Schlafzimmerbalkon.

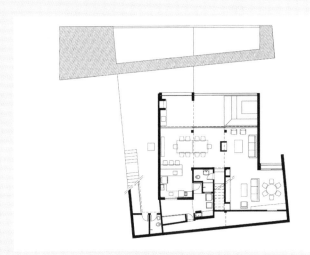

PETROPOLIS HOUSE
JOSE RIPPER KOS

COUNTRY / LAND	BRAZIL / BRASILIEN	HOUSE NAME / BEZEICHNUNG DES HAUSES	PETROPOLIS HOUSE
LOCATION (CITY/REGION) / LAGE (STADT/REGION)			PETROPOLIS
ARCHITECT / ARCHITEKT		JOSE RIPPER KOS YEAR OF COMPLETION / BAUJAHR	2003
PHOTOGRAPHER / FOTOGRAF		NELSON KON SQUARE FEET / QUADRAT METER	2367 / 220
CITY AND COUNTRY ARCHITECT / STADT UND LAND ARCHITEKT			RIO DE JANEIRO, BRASIL
WEBSITE ARCHITECT / HOMEPAGE ARCHITEKT			WWW.PROURB.FAU.UFRJ.BR/JKOS.HTM

552

In departure from strict axes and rectilinear forms the architect created an organic shell for living. The diverse auxiliary spaces such as bedrooms and sanitary facilities are grouped around the central living room node. The curving forms of the exterior reveal themselves as richly variegated interior spaces inside.

In Negation strikter Achsen und rechteckiger Formen schafft der Architekt eine organisch anmutende Schale zum Wohnen. Die diversen Nebenräume wie Schlafzimmer und Sanitärbereich sind um den zentralen Wohnraum gruppiert. Die gekrümmten Formen der äußeren Schale entpuppen sich im Inneren als gekonnt geformte Hüllen zum Wohlfühlen.

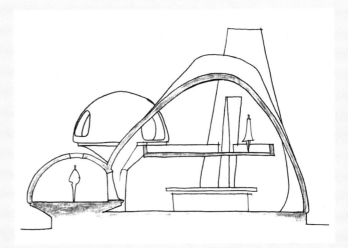

ROUND HOUSE AT MANGUINHOS
<u>NICOLETTI DE FRAGA</u>

COUNTRY / LAND	BRAZIL / BRASILIEN	HOUSE NAME / BEZEICHNUNG DES HAUSES	ROUND HOUSE AT MANGUINHOS
LOCATION (CITY/REGION) / LAGE (STADT/REGION)			SERRA
ARCHITECT / ARCHITEKT	PAULO NICOLETTI DE FRAGA	YEAR OF COMPLETION / BAUJAHR	2004
PHOTOGRAPHER / FOTOGRAF	BRIGIDA SOLÉ	SQUARE FEET / QUADRAT METER	1291 / 120
CITY AND COUNTRY ARCHITECT / STADT UND LAND ARCHITEKT			SERRA, BRASIL
WEBSITE ARCHITECT / HOMEPAGE ARCHITEKT			PLANETA.TERRA.COM.BR/ARTE/ORGANICA

MARCIO KOGAN

SÃO PAULO
BRAZIL / BRASILIEN

These notions, supplied to us by Marcio Kogan, sum up his creative stance on creating architecture in the Southern Brazilian metropolis São Paulo.

1. On Life: What matters is life and not architecture, as was said by Oscar Niemeyer.
2. On Death: "I never think that people die. They just go to department stores." I can not omit this phrase by Andy Warhol.
3. Emotion: The transatlantic crossing of Rex in the movie Amarcord by Federico Fellini.
4. A house: Villa Arpell, of the movie "My Uncle", by Jaques Tati.

5. São Paulo: The frightening city in which we live and a big urban disaster. It is one of the ugliest cities in the world which – thanks to its liveliness - is one of the most attractive.
6. The essential: Humor, for me absolutely fundamental and invariably distant from architecture, which is almost always very serious.
7. Music :Brasilian, without a doubt.
8. Self-criticism: Great torture. I never think a project is good.
9. The Office: Working with people I like is fundamental. Go back to number 1.

Photo: Rui Mendes

Diese uns durch Marcio Korgan zur Verfügung gestellten Gedanken verdeutlichen seinen kreativen Standpunkt zur Architektur in der Millionenstadt São Paulo.

1. Leben: „Wichtig ist Leben, nicht Architektur", wie schon Oscar Niemeyer sagte.

2. Tod: „Ich glaube niemand stirbt, sie gehen lediglich in Kaufhäuser". Dieses Zitat von Andy Warhol darf nicht fehlen.

3. Emotion: die Überquerung des Atlantiks durch Rex in Fellini's Amarcord

4. Ein Haus: Villa Arpel, im Film „Mein Onkel" von Jacques Tati.

5. São Paulo: Eine angst einflössende, hässliche Stadt., die aber durch ihre Lebendigkeit auch eine der attraktivsten Städte ist.

6. Essentiell: Humor. Das ist fundamental für mich und meilenweit entfernt von der Architektur, die meistens Ernsthaftigkeit besitzt.

7. Musik: Brasilianische, ohne Frage.

8. Selbstkritik: Eine wunderbare Tortur. Ich glaube nie, dass ein Projekt gut ist.

9. Das Büro: Mit Leuten zusammenarbeiten, die ich mag. Siehe hierzu auch Pkt. 1.

BR HOUSE
MARCIO KOGAN

Here, the architect actively strives to create a clearly Modernist expression that at the same time emanates warmth and comfort. This is achieved by employing contemporary materials such as concrete and glass to create a bridge-like house form that nestles next to the adjacent slope. At the same time softer materials such as rough-hewn stone and wood in subtle variations are used to ensure that the austere ambience remains lively, welcoming, and elegant.

Der Architekt strebt einen modernen Ausdruck an, der zugleich Wärme und Wohlbefinden ausstrahlt. Dies wird durch den Einsatz zeitgenössischer Materialien wie Beton und Glas erreicht, die zusammen eine brückenartige Bauform bilden, die sich an den benachbarten Hang anschmiegt. Gleichzeitig wurden weichere Naturmaterialien wie Stein und Holz in verschiedenen Variationen verwendet um sicher zu stellen, dass das schlichte Ambiente lebendig, einladend und elegant bleibt.

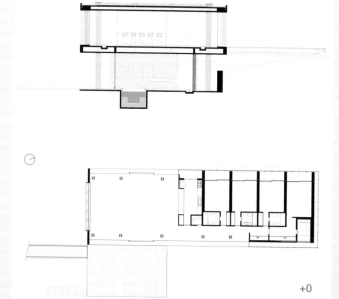

+0

The main living level is accessed from an elevated deck and covers the outdoor spaces on the lower level where the fountain-like pool is located. Upstairs, the living room is foreseen with fully glazed walls whereas the fully glazed kitchen and bedroom windows receive an exterior layer of vertical wooden slats that create a veil-like filter of the landscape view. The use of natural materials allows the building to effectively merge with the surrounding wooded site.

Die über ein Plattform erschlossene Hauptwohnebene erstreckt sich über den Außenräumen darunter, wo sich der brunnenähnliche Pool befindet. Der Wohnraum darüber wurde mit vollflächigen Verglasungen versehen, die Küche und die Schlafzimmer erhielten durchgehende Fensterfronten mit einem Schleier aus vertikal angeordneten Holzlamellen. Die Verwendung von Naturmaterialien gewährleistet eine wirksame Verbidung von Bauwerk und der bewaldeten Lage.

COUNTRY / LAND	BRAZIL / BRASILIEN	HOUSE NAME / BEZEICHNUNG DES HAUSES	BR HOUSE
LOCATION (CITY/REGION) / LAGE (STADT/REGION)			ARARAS, RIO DE JANEIRO
ARCHITECT / ARCHITEKT		MARCIO KOGAN	YEAR OF COMPLETION / BAUJAHR 2004
PHOTOGRAPHER / FOTOGRAF		NELSON KON	SQUARE FEET / QUADRAT METER 7962 / 740
CITY AND COUNTRY ARCHITECT / STADT UND LAND ARCHITEKT			SÃO PAULO, BRASIL
WEBSITE ARCHITECT / HOMEPAGE ARCHITEKT			WWW.MARCIOKOGAN.COM.BR

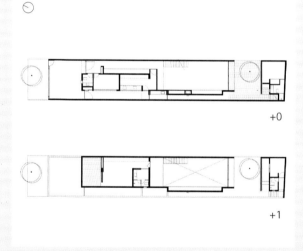

+0

+1

A very tight urban slot site with limited frontage to natural light was filled with this gracious home that seems especially generous and spacious in spite of the extremely narrow floor plan. This sense is heightened by the two-storey living room space that extends out onto the private patio space and the stone wall behind.

Das sehr beengte städtische Grundstück mit wenig Sonnenlicht wurde mit diesem eleganten Haus bebaut, das trotz des äußerst schmalen Grundrisses großzügig wirkt. Diese Wahrnehmung wird in dem zweigeschossigen Wohnraum verstärkt, der sich im Freien im privaten Innenhof mit der abschließenden Natursteinmauer fortsetzt.

HELENA MONTANARINI HOUSE
MARCIO KOGAN

COUNTRY / LAND	BRAZIL / BRASILIEN	HOUSE NAME / BEZEICHNUNG DES HAUSES	HELENA MONTANARINI HOUSE
LOCATION (CITY/REGION) / LAGE (STADT/REGION)			SÃO PAULO
ARCHITECT / ARCHITEKT	MARCIO KOGAN	YEAR OF COMPLETION / BAUJAHR	2005
PHOTOGRAPHER / FOTOGRAF	TUCA REINÉS	SQUARE FEET / QUADRAT METER	2453 / 228
CITY AND COUNTRY ARCHITECT / STADT UND LAND ARCHITEKT			SÃO PAULO, BRASIL
WEBSITE ARCHITECT / HOMEPAGE ARCHITEKT			WWW.MARCIOKOGAN.COM.BR

8 AL CUBO HOUSE
MATHIAS KLOTZ

The L-shaped floor plan was variegated to create interior and exterior spaces with differing qualities. A protected courtyard with storey-high walls serves as the focus for part of the living room. The bedrooms, kitchen, and dining area orient out to the more open, second courtyard where a shade-spending roof extends out to create sheltered terraces.

Der L-förmige Grundriss wurde gekonnt angeordnet um Innen- und Außenräume mit verschiedenen Qualitäten zu schaffen. Ein geschützter Innenhof mit umgebenden Wänden dient als Fokus für einen Teil des Wohnzimmers. Die Schlafzimmer, die Küche sowie der Essplatz orientieren sich zum zweiten, offenen Hof hin wo Schatten spendende Vordächer Terrassen überdachen.

COUNTRY / LAND	CHILE	HOUSE NAME / BEZEICHNUNG DES HAUSES		8 AL CUBO HOUSE
LOCATION (CITY/REGION) / LAGE (STADT/REGION)				MARBELLA
ARCHITECT / ARCHITEKT		MATHIAS KLOTZ	YEAR OF COMPLETION / BAUJAHR	2005
PHOTOGRAPHER / FOTOGRAF		JUAN PURCELL	SQUARE FEET / QUADRAT METER	2690 / 250
CITY AND COUNTRY ARCHITECT / STADT UND LAND ARCHITEKT				SANTIAGO, CHILE
WEBSITE ARCHITECT / HOMEPAGE ARCHITEKT				WWW.MATHIASKLOTZ.COM

A spatial backbone containing the main and auxiliary spaces of this residence stretches across the hillside site above the Pacific Ocean. Three shell-like annexes extend out from this backbone to create a striking seaside front. The special spaces here, such as leisurely living room niche with the custom-built couch enjoy impressive panorama views of the ocean below.

Ein räumliches Rückgrat, das die Haupt- und Nebenräume beherbergt, erstreckt sich quer zum abfallenden Hanggrundstück hoch über dem Pazifik. Davor gelagert wurden drei Muschel-ähnliche Vorbauten angeordnet, um eine beeindruckende Hausfront an der Meersseite zu schaffen. Die besonderen Räume hier, wie das Wohnzimmer mit eingebauter Sitzmöbelgruppe erhalten einen ungehinderten Ausblick auf das Meer darunter.

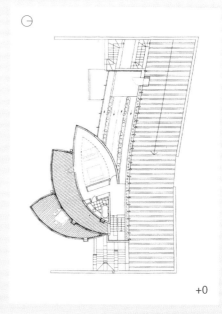

+0

HOUSE IN ZAPALLAR II
ENRIQUE BROWNE

COUNTRY / LAND	CHILE	HOUSE NAME / BEZEICHNUNG DES HAUSES	HOUSE IN ZAPALLAR II
LOCATION (CITY/REGION) / LAGE (STADT/REGION)			ZAPALLAR
ARCHITECT / ARCHITEKT	ENRIQUE BROWNE	YEAR OF COMPLETION / BAUJAHR	2002
PHOTOGRAPHER / FOTOGRAF	GUY WENBORNE, ENRIQUE BROWNE	SQUARE FEET / QUADRAT METER	3637 / 338
CITY AND COUNTRY ARCHITECT / STADT UND LAND ARCHITEKT			SANTIAGO, CHILE
WEBSITE ARCHITECT / HOMEPAGE ARCHITEKT			WWW.EBROWNE.CL

RIVO HOUSE
PEZO VON ELLRICHHAUSEN ARCHITECTS

The simple cube-like form of this home creates a neutral hull for the refined spatial composition the architects developed inside. Stairs here rise to accommodate the steep slope of the hillside site. Exterior surfaces such as the walls and balcony flooring were sheathed in wooden slats that are echoed by the lacquered wood floor planks inside to create an effective merge between interior and exterior spaces.

Die scheinbar einfache, kuben-ähnliche Form dieses Hauses schafft eine Hülle, die eine belebte räumliche Komposition im Inneren umgibt. Die Treppen steigen an, um die Neigung des Hanggrundstückes im Inneren erlebbar zu machen. Außenflächen wie Wände und Balkonböden sind mit Holz verkleidet worden. Dieses Material setzt sich im Inneren bei den lackierten Fußbodenplanken fort.

COUNTRY / LAND	CHILE	HOUSE NAME / BEZEICHNUNG DES HAUSES		RIVO HOUSE
LOCATION (CITY/REGION) / LAGE (STADT/REGION)				VALDIVIA
ARCHITECT / ARCHITEKT	PEZO VON ELLRICHSHAUSEN ARCHITECTS	YEAR OF COMPLETION / BAUJAHR		2005
PHOTOGRAPHER / FOTOGRAF	CRISTOBAL PALMA	SQUARE FEET / QUADRAT METER		1722 / 160
CITY AND COUNTRY ARCHITECT / STADT UND LAND ARCHITEKT				CONCEPCIÓN, CHILE
WEBSITE ARCHITECT / HOMEPAGE ARCHITEKT				WWW.PEZO.CL

The remote, uninhabited location challenged the architects to respond with a unique architectural strategy. To express the remoteness and primitive quality of the site they created an especially raw ambience that reinterprets the stark clarity of the adjacent cliffs in built form. Inside, this rawness is countered by an intricately knit web of interior spaces.

Der entlegene, fast unbewohnte Standort forderte von dem Architektenpaar einen ungewöhnlichen Ansatz. Dem ersten Bauwerk, das in diesem Landstrich je errichtet wurde, verliehen sie einen ausgeprägt rohen Charakter, der die Schroffheit der Felsklippen in Architektur fortsetzt. Dies wird im Inneren durch eine vielfältige Raumkomposition relativiert.

POLI HOUSE
PEZO VON ELLRICHHAUSEN

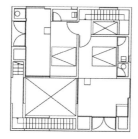

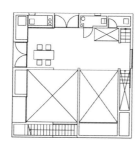

They extend up to skillfully connect the levels and define neutral hull for living, cultural, and exhibit use. Local workers used wood boards to build the concrete forms and poured the hand-mixed concrete layer by layer, largely without the use of conventional construction machinery.

Die Räume erstrecken sich teilweise über mehrere Ebenen und sind als neutrale Hüllen für Wohnen, aber auch für kulturelle Veranstaltungen und Ausstellungen gedacht. Lokal engagierte Arbeiter verschalten den Bau lagenweise mit handgemischtem Beton und vergossen ihn fast ohne Hilfe von Maschinen.

COUNTRY / LAND	CHILE	HOUSE NAME / BEZEICHNUNG DES HAUSES	POLI HOUSE
LOCATION (CITY/REGION) / LAGE (STADT/REGION)			COLIUMO / PACIFIC COAST
ARCHITECT / ARCHITEKT	PEZO VON ELLRICHHAUSEN ARCHITECTS	YEAR OF COMPLETION / BAUJAHR	2005
PHOTOGRAPHER / FOTOGRAF	CRISTOBAL PALMA	SQUARE FEET / QUADRAT METER	1937 / 180
CITY AND COUNTRY ARCHITECT / STADT UND LAND ARCHITEKT			CONCEPCIÓN, CHILE
WEBSITE ARCHITECT / HOMEPAGE ARCHITEKT			WWW.PEZO.CL

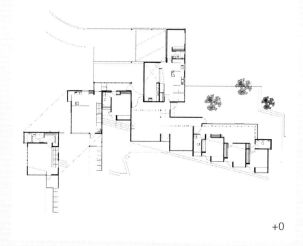

The generously dimensioned building site outside Santiago, Chile allowed arraying the individual spaces of this house to form a village-like house group. The main entrance is accessed via a small plaza-patio that reminds one of village squares in the nearby pueblos. The shed roofs are designed to emphasize the individual rooms and underscore the house's appearance as a small hillside village.

Das großzügig dimensionierte Grundstück erlaubte es, die Einzelräume des Hauses so anzuordnen, dass eine dorfähnliche Hausanlage entsteht. Der Haupteingang wird über einen kleinen Hof erschlossen, der an die Plätze der nah gelegenen Dörfer erinnert. Die unterschiedlich geneigten Pultdächer über den einzelnen Räumen unterstreichen den Dorfcharakter zusätzlich.

+0

CASA LAGO COLICO
CRUZ & BROWNE

COUNTRY / LAND	CHILE	HOUSE NAME / BEZEICHNUNG DES HAUSES		CASA LAGO COLICO
LOCATION (CITY/REGION) / LAGE (STADT/REGION)				LAGO COLICO
ARCHITECT / ARCHITEKT	CRUZ & BROWNE ARQUITECTOS ASOCIADOS	YEAR OF COMPLETION / BAUJAHR		2004
PHOTOGRAPHER / FOTOGRAF	ALBERTO BROWNE C.	SQUARE FEET / QUADRAT METER		3250 / 302
CITY AND COUNTRY ARCHITECT / STADT UND LAND ARCHITEKT				SANTIAGO, CHILE
WEBSITE ARCHITECT / HOMEPAGE ARCHITEKT				WWW.CRUZYBROWNE.CL

CASA B-B
CRUZ & BROWNE

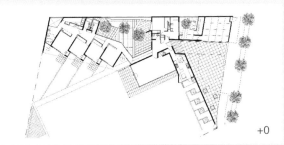

+0

The diverse spaces and wings of this home are also creatively arrayed to create a diverse house ensemble that reminds of a small village. A variety of exterior spaces ranging from a glass-walled patio, a terraced green lawn, to a triangular service courtyard are defined by the diverse building wings. A covered terrace with an exterior fireplace serves as the focal point of the main garden side.

Die Räume dieses Hauses wurden ebenfalls kreativ angeordnet, um ein Ensemble zu schaffen, das an ein kleines Dorf erinnert. Eine Vielfalt an Außenräumen - ein von Glaswänden umgebener Innenhof, die terrassierte Rasenfront und ein dreieckiger Andienungshof - werden durch die Gebäudeflügel definiert. Eine überdachte Terrasse mit Außenkamin dient als Blickfang auf der Hauptgartenseite.

569

COUNTRY / LAND	CHILE	HOUSE NAME / BEZEICHNUNG DES HAUSES	CASA B-B
LOCATION (CITY/REGION) / LAGE (STADT/REGION)			SANTIAGO
ARCHITECT / ARCHITEKT	CRUZ & BROWNE ARQUITECTOS ASOCIADOS	YEAR OF COMPLETION / BAUJAHR	2002
PHOTOGRAPHER / FOTOGRAF	ALBERTO BROWNE C.	SQUARE FEET / QUADRAT METER	2615 / 243
CITY AND COUNTRY ARCHITECT / STADT UND LAND ARCHITEKT			SANTIAGO, CHILE
WEBSITE ARCHITECT / HOMEPAGE ARCHITEKT			WWW.CRUZYBROWNE.CL

The seemingly simple forms of this home are effectively stretched across a hillside site to create a strikingly refined poetic statement on contemporary living in nature. The main house volume, constructed in exposed in-situ concrete, elegantly cantilevers out above the stone retaining wall that runs parallel to the slope. A central stair rises from the main entrance on the lower level to a rooftop terrace via the glazed skylight pavilion.

Die scheinbar einfachen Formen dieses Hauses wurden quer über das Hanggrundstück gestreckt, um eine auffallend raffinierte, poetische Aussage zum Thema Wohnen in der Natur zu formulieren. Der Hauptbaukörper, erbaut in Sichtbeton, kragt elegant aus vor einer parallel zum Hang verlaufenden Stützmauer aus Stein. Die zentrale Treppe steigt vom Haupteingang im Sockelgeschoss an bis zur Dachterrasse mit der verglasten Oberlichtlaterne.

OMNIBUS HOUSE
PEDRO GUBBINS FOXLEY

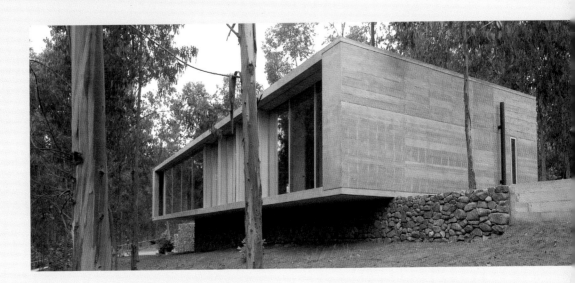

The main elevation is entirely glazed with windows that are modulated with recessed slanted surfaces to assure that the large glass front doesn't become monotonous. The living-dining room can be completely opened via sliding glass wall elements to the adjacent shaded exterior terrace. The bedroom tract contains four bedrooms with views into the forest and two bathrooms. By clearly limiting the materials used on all surfaces including the furniture to concrete, natural stone, and wood a convincing elegance prevails throughout this home.

Die Hauptansicht ist komplett verglast, wobei hier Vor- und Rücksprünge vorgesehen wurden, um die Glasfront effektiv zu gliedern und Monotonie zu vermeiden. Das Wohn-Esszimmer lässt sich über große Schiebetüren aus Glas ganz zum anschließenden Freiraum öffnen. Der Schlafzimmertrakt beinhaltet vier Schlafzimmer mit Ausblick in den Wald sowie zwei Badezimmer. Durch die konsequente Reduktion der für Bauteile und Möbel verwendeten Materialien auf Holz, Naturstein und Beton konnte eine durchgehend überzeugende Eleganz erreicht werden.

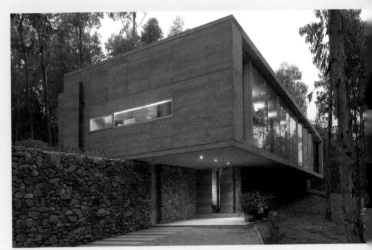

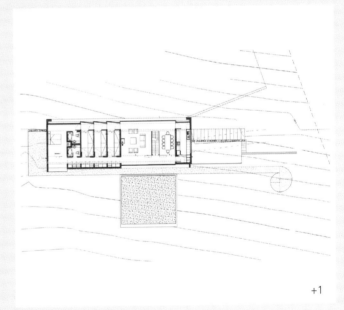

+1

COUNTRY / LAND	CHILE	HOUSE NAME / BEZEICHNUNG DES HAUSES	OMNIBUS HOUSE
LOCATION (CITY/REGION) / LAGE (STADT/REGION)			CACHAGUA
ARCHITECT / ARCHITEKT	PEDRO GUBBINS FOXLEY	YEAR OF COMPLETION / BAUJAHR	2003
PHOTOGRAPHER / FOTOGRAF	MARCOS MENDIZABAL SANGUINETTI	SQUARE FEET / QUADRAT METER	1937 / 180
CITY AND COUNTRY ARCHITECT / STADT UND LAND ARCHITEKT			SANTIAGO, CHILE
WEBSITE ARCHITECT / HOMEPAGE ARCHITEKT			WWW.GUBBINSARQUITECTOS.CL